Dynamics in the French ⌒

The promulgation of the Fifth French Republic Constitution in 1958 marked the end of a complex constitutional history that has since 1789 seen more than twenty constitutions and five Republics. Lasting now for more than fifty years, the Fifth Republic Constitution has proven to be the right settlement for the French people: a consensual text.

However, while offering the appearance of stability, the Fifth French Republic Constitution has often been reconsidered and changed, not least in the year of its fiftieth anniversary, when the Constitution was 'modernised'. These dynamics of the Fifth Republic Constitution are neither a recent matter nor entirely the result of the successive constitutional amendments. Instead, the history of the Constitution has involved the resurgence of repressed archaic elements from the *ancien régime*, while the social, economic and environmental contexts have penetrated not only the text itself but more extensively its spirit and, behind it, the philosophy and our perception of the Republic.

In *Dynamics in the French Constitution*, David Marrani questions the foundations of the French Fifth Republic. In using specific themes, current and traditional debates, contemporary and archaic factors, that have enlightened the road of a long-lasting Republic, the book explores some of the changes of the last fifty years and the tensions that are present within the constitutional text. In combining theoretical concepts of constitutional law with key contemporary and historical developments, such as the European integration, the response to environmental challenges, the practice of human rights and the pillars supporting French republicanism, this book offers varied and creative tools for a better understanding of the Republic of today.

Dr David Marrani is a Senior Lecturer in public law and comparative law at the University of Essex, UK. He lectures in particular on French constitutional law and comparative public law.

Routledge Research in Constitutional Law

Available titles in this series include:

Weak Constitutionalism
Democratic Legitimacy and the Question of Constituent Power
Joel I. Colon-Rios

Engineering Constitutional Change
A Comparative Perspective on Europe, Canada and the USA
Xenophon Contiades, Centre for European Constitutional Law

Freedom of Speech
Importing European and US constitutional models in transitional democracies
Uladzislau Belavusau

Post-colonial Constitutionalism in the Commonwealth
Peace, order and good government
Hakeem O. Yusuf

Dynamics in the French Constitution

Decoding French republican ideas

David Marrani

Routledge
Taylor & Francis Group

LONDON AND NEW YORK

First published 2013
by Routledge
2 Park Square, Milton Park, Abingdon, Oxfordshire OX14 4RN

Simultaneously published in the USA and Canada
by Routledge
711 Third Avenue, New York, NY 10017

First issued in paperback 2014

Routledge is an imprint of the Taylor and Francis Group, an informa business

British Library Cataloguing in Publication Data
A catalogue record for this book is available from the British Library

Library of Congress Cataloging-in-Publication Data
Dynamics in the French constitution : decoding French republican ideas / David Marrani.
  pages cm. – (Engineering constitutional change)
Includes bibliographical references and index.
ISBN 978-0-415-68371-5 (hbk : alk. paper) – ISBN 978-0-203-79865-2 (ebk : alk. paper)
1. Constitutional law–France. 2. France. Constitution (1958) 3. France–Politics and government–1958- 4. France–Politics and government–20th century. I. Title.
KJV4079.M37 2013
342.44–dc23
                                                                                    2013004289

ISBN 978-0-415-68371-5 (hbk)
ISBN 978-1-138-91881-8 (pbk)
ISBN 978-0-203-79865-2 (ebk)

Typeset in Garamond
by Cenveo Publisher Services

Contents

Acknowledgements   vii

Introduction   1

1   Nature and evolution of the Constitution of the French
Fifth Republic: reflections on semi-presidentialism   11

     1.1   A semi-presidential Constitution?   11
     1.2   Theoretical framework   12
     1.3   Original institutional arrangement and its evolutions   15
     1.4   'Elasticity' of the Constitution   24
     1.5   Towards a postmodern (or second modern) system of government?   35

2   The greening of the French Republic:
the constitutionalisation of the environment   37

     2.1   A new French bill of (environmental) rights   37
     2.2   The interesting historical development of the Charter   39
     *2.3   From an expected impact to multiple impacts on the
     French legal system   44*
     2.4   A 'greener' constitutional future   53
     *Appendix: Article 2 of the Constitutional amendment incorporating
     the Charter for the Environment into the French Constitution   54*

3   Human rights (in practice) and the French Republic:
the example of exclusion   56

     3.1   Preliminary remarks on exclusion   57
     3.2   Human rights in action   61
     3.3   Conclusion   70

4   The French Republic and its supranational offspring:
    the love–hate relationship between France and
    European law   72

    4.1 Introduction 72
    4.2 Position of European law in relation to the French Constitution 75
    4.3 Position of EC/EU law in relation to French statute law 79
    4.4 Recent developments 82
    4.5 Conclusion 84

5   Principle of indivisibility of the French Republic
    and the people's right to self-determination:
    the 'New Caledonia test'   87

    5.1 Introduction 87
    5.2 General context 88
    5.3 Administration of New Caledonia before the statute of 1999 90
    5.4 Administration of New Caledonia under the statute of 1999 94
    5.5 Is New Caledonia closer than ever to independence? 100
    5.6 Conclusion 106

6   The French Republic, its language and the paradigm
    of unity   108

    6.1 Introduction 108
    6.2 Monolinguism as an aid to the construction of France and the Republic:
    *   the myth of one language unifying internal minorities 113*
    6.3 From the affirmation of monolinguism to the recognition of pluri-linguism:
    *   the reality of pluri-linguistic (internal and external) minorities 118*
    6.4 Conclusion 127

Conclusion   129
Notes   133
References   175
Index   190

Acknowledgements

This work would never have been possible without the intellectual push of my dear friend Jacques Basso, Emeritus Professor at my alma mater the Faculté de droit, Université de Nice Sophia Antipolis, also former professor at the Institut d'Études Politiques of Paris.

I would like to express my gratitude to my colleagues at the School of Law of the University of Essex and particularly Richard Cornes, Maurice Sunkin, Brigid Hadfield and David Ong, but also Audrey Guinchard and Peter Luther. I am also indebted to Pierre Brunet and Pascal Richard and to my former assistants for their help, suggestions and encouragements. I wish to extend my thanks to Professor Leyland of London Metropolitan University and Professor Samuel of the University of Kent for reviewing this thesis.

I finally wish to give my special thanks to my daughters Giulia-Clara and Sadb for letting me work hours on this manuscript instead of spending time playing with them. I have also a thought for my parents, grandparents and great-grandparents and Cliona, and my dear friend Jean-Michel Urbani for 'sending me away' from my country years ago.

Introduction

FRANCE, MERE DES ARTS, DES ARMES ET DES LOIS,
TU M'AS NOURRI LONGTEMPS DU LAIT DE TA MAMELLE:
ORES, COMME UN AGNEAU QUI SA NOURRICE APPELLE,
JE REMPLIS DE TON NOM LES ANTRES ET LES BOIS.

J. Du Bellay, *Les Regrets*, XI

In 2008, France celebrated the fiftieth anniversary of the promulgation of the Constitution of the Fifth Republic.[1] It was also the year of the largest modification to the Constitution to date. On 12 July 2007, then President Nicolas Sarkozy announced what he called 'the need for changes';[2] the key term he used in this announcement was 'modernisation'. The year 2008 was therefore an ambivalent time: a time for celebrating one of the longest-lasting French Constitutions (only the Constitution of the Monarchy[3] and the Constitution of the Third Republic[4] survived more than fifty years) and a time in which it was more widely recognised that this established Constitution needed updating. Whether or not one agreed with President Sarkozy's desire to 'modernise' the institutions, and whether there was in fact a real need for modernisation of the Constitution itself, it is clear that 2008 witnessed a key moment in French constitutional history. However, the changing dynamics of the Constitution of the Fifth Republic have been neither the result of recent developments nor entirely the result of the 2008 constitutional act.[5] For a while now, the social, economic, environmental and historical contexts have influenced the Constitution to the extent that they have penetrated not only the text itself but also its spirit – the idea of 'the Republic' as it has evolved in relation to philosophy, which has made it what it means today.

First and foremost, the Republic may be linked to Plato and to the politics of Aristotle; this early philosophy sought to establish the best form of government. The two philosophers started their enquiries with an attempt to describe both pure and degenerate forms of government: the monarchy and tyranny, the aristocracy and the oligarchy, the Republic and democracy. Plato was seeking Justice,[6] which for him could only be found in what would be 'the good State', while Aristotle arrived at a definition of the 'ideal city', a place in which the best government would be found. This ideal space linked 'a city [that] is to be run well' and the Republic (of Plato).[7] The two philosophers differed in their account of democracy, however;[8] Aristotle considered the Republic a mix of two degenerate regimes – oligarchy and democracy.

Of course, they are not the only ones to have written on the Republic. Cicero, for instance, in *The Republic*, developed his ideas and what is important here appears to be virtue, which Cicero stated was an art that needed to be possessed and put into practice; he envisaged a theoretical but active virtue, with its most glorious activity: the government of the State. The Republic became an art – the art (or the science)[9] of managing the *res publica*. Cicero considered that the *res publica* was 'the thing' of the people, which was regarded as an ensemble of individuals associated by a pact of justice and a community of interests. For him, what differentiated the Republic from all other systems of government was the notion of virtue, which contributed to a fundamental separation of the two spheres of the Citizen and the mass of citizens. Furthermore, it contributed to the *summa divisio* between the private and the public spheres. Both the ensemble of citizens and the Citizen had their own space of movement. The Republic became the means to manage the business of the *res publica*, the public sphere.

This notion of virtue is also to be found in the work of Montesquieu; he believed that virtue was the major characteristic of the Republic. In his comparative work, he considered the republican state, the monarchic state and the despotic state. Montesquieu analysed what he called the 'laws' relative to the nature of each government and their principles: 'We shall examine this relation in each government, and we shall begin with the republican state, which has virtue for its principle.' By virtue, he meant 'in a Republic ... a very simple thing: it is love of the Republic; it is a feeling and not a result of knowledge; the lowest man in the state, like the first, can have this feeling.'[10]

Montesquieu considered virtue to be essential to the Republic in order to avoid corruption and, ultimately, despotism.[11] This feeling was shared by Rousseau, who believed that even though 'the maintenance of [French] virtue' was an 'extremely difficult' task, it 'would be necessary to maintain any successful republican government'.[12] This was premised on the new system of French government that began in 1792, which used virtue as its 'motor', as its (fundamental) principle. On 21 September 1792, monarchy, the system of government that had been operating for nearly one thousand years in France, was abolished. A proposal of Abbot Grégoire[13] was put to the vote and adopted: 'The national Convention decrees that royalty is abolished in France' (*La Convention nationale décrète que la royauté est abolie en France*).[14] Afterwards, acclamations of joy were heard – '*Vive la nation!*'[15] On 22 September, the Republic was proclaimed by the Convention. The act of proclamation, a solemn declaration, marked a change: it was a powerful moment and a powerful act, and similar proclamations would be used in many future declarations of emancipation.[16]

The French National Convention operated with a chronology that could compare to modern personal life and divorce proceedings: first we divorce and then we (sometimes) remarry. Of significance here were the two separate steps that occurred in quick succession. First, there was the abolition of the old order, the *ancien régime* (step 1), and then the proclamation of the new one (step 2). The Convention respected a (short) moment of transition but then things seemed to have happened very quickly, over a two-day period. Moreover, events began to accelerate and the Republic radically changed things, changed the past in two ways – by changing the time, starting a new era and opposing it to the 'vulgar era' of the previous regime, and by changing the head, the decapitation of the head: there was the virtual removal of the regime and the physical elimination of the King.

Time: the *Décret de la Convention nationale, concernant l'ère des Français*

Article 1 of the *Convention nationale* (a regulation passed on 5 October 1793, during the second year of the French Republic) stated:

> The era of the French is calculated from the foundation of the Republic, that took place on the 22 September 1792 of the vulgar era where the sun arrived at the real fall's equinox, entering the sign of Libra at 9 hours 18 minutes 30 seconds am, at the observatory of Paris.
>
> (*L'ère des Français compte de la fondation de la république, qui a eu lieu le 22 septembre 1792 de l'ère vulgaire, jour où le soleil est arrivé à l'équinoxe vrai d'automne, en entrant dans le signe de la balance à 9 heures 18 minutes 30 secondes du matin, pour l'observatoire de Paris.*)

The first major modification was the change made to names of days and months, and also to the numbering of years, to how years were counted from the moment the Republic was proclaimed. Two factors underpinned these changes. The first was hatred – of both the Church and the Monarchy – which made necessary the implementation of something 'new'. The second was to do with the scientific spirit of the time, as expressed in Diderot and d'Alembert's *Dictionnaire encyclopédique*. This scientific spirit accelerated the sense of rationality and uniformity by the creation of a 'new' year and a 'new' time; decimalisation played a key part here. The year was divided into 12 months of 30 days, a week being ten days (a decade). The hour was divided into ten parts, each of which was divided into ten parts and so on and so forth. One hundredth of the hour was a decimal, while one hundredth of a minute was a second decimal. More importantly, this created a new era and in the defining of this new era, the old era was negatively (re)defined. That is to say, before. Before the new era, there had been a vulgar era; after this came the era of the French. There was therefore a boundary and a rupture between 'before the Republic' and 'after the Republic'. The time after the foundation of the Republic became the era of the French, highlighting the importance of the people in this new political context, opposed to the vulgar era, the era of the kings. The date of 22 September 1792 became the birthday of this new era, the birth of the new time. Article 2 of the regulation specified that the vulgar era should be abolished. It not only created a separation between two periods, the era of the kings and the era of the French, it erased, *de jure*, the era of the kings. This 'virtual' elimination was repeated in the form of a second removal – the physical elimination of the King.

The regicide–parricide

The Republic physically removed and eliminated the head of state. It did so to such an extent that no future system was able to institutionalise a 'one person' head of state until the arrival of Emperor Napoleon I.[17] The head of state was not simply the symbol of the power of the French absolute monarchy, it was also the result of thousands of years of history. The removal of the King in the 'theatrical scene' of the revolution can be read in relation to Freud's myth of the primal horde: '[o]ne day the brothers who had been driven out came together, killed and devoured their father and so made an end to the patriarchal horde'.[18] The great leader was to be confronted by the anger of the sons: 'the primitive man [living] in small hordes ... under the domination of a powerful male, an individual who is "lord and father of the entire horde and unrestricted in his power", who is going to be killed by the sons who are united against him (the "expelled brothers").'[19] The sons committed parricide – a crime repressed by the worst penalties throughout the Middle Ages.[20] The new regime, the brothers in the revolution, had to remove the Father to become the new elite.

And so, French Republicanism was born. It was a blend of the philosophy of antiquity and that of the eighteenth century, a system of government that pursued 'the common good through popular sovereignty, liberty, virtue, mixed government and the rule of law'.[21] The 'French model' evolved over time towards the (ultimate?) design of the 1958 Constitution. Following this brief description of past events, it is useful to consider how they illuminate the present and contribute to the future. As the singer says: 'Marianne a 5 enfants, 4 qu'elle a perdu et 1 qu'elle ne reconnaît plus'.[22] The 'French model' developed over two centuries through a series of Constitutions. The first three Republics were established in reaction to a dying monarchy, either royal (the First Republic of the Constitution of 1793, the Second of 1848) or imperial (the Third Republic in the transition period 1870–5). The Fourth and Fifth Republics were established after the collapse of the preceding Republics, in 1946 and finally 1958.[23]

In 1958 a Republic of the new was established, that was to become a new Republic.

A Republic of the new

The end of the Fourth Republic

The first system of French government after the Second World War, the Fourth Republic, was established in 1946. It ended in May 1958 after a period of trouble that started in Algeria. On 13 May 1958, a coup was on its way in Algiers. The head of state President Coty appointed Pierre Pflimlin as the new head of government. Pflimlin was the leader of the centre-left French Christian Democrat party, the Popular Republican Movement (MRP), and he was in favour of negotiation with the Front National de Libération (FLN), the Algerian National Liberation Front. This provoked an insurrection among high-ranking military officers, like Generals Salan, Jouhaud and Massu the commander of the 10th paratroopers division, and politicians in Algiers. On 24 May, the paratroopers arrived in Corsica in preparation for the seizure of Paris and the removal of the government should General de Gaulle not be called to be in charge of the Republic. While preparations for their potential coup came 'closer' to metropolitan France, Pflimlin led the government of the Fourth Republic in the last days before its collapse and resigned on 28 May. The following day, President Coty asked General de Gaulle to take on the role of head of government as *président du conseil*, a function equivalent to that of Prime Minister. The situation was so bad that Coty specified that he would resign if the elected chamber did not support De Gaulle by a vote of confidence. His investiture took place on 1 June 1958, with the support of 329 MPs for to 224 against. The government that De Gaulle formed had fewer members than usual but included representatives of the four largest political parties as ministers of state.[24]

The government was faced with two tasks – one conjectural and the other structural. Conjecturally, the government had to end the troubles in Algeria and the political uncertainty facing the country. Structurally, the reform of the institutions of the Republic was at stake. As a consequence, two statutes with constitutional implications were adopted on 3 June 1958, one on constituent power, the other on the modification of the Constitution.[25]

The first statute adopted on 3 June 1958 concerned 'full powers' (*Loi accordant les pleins pouvoirs pour 6 mois*).[26] De Gaulle's government, the last government of the Fourth Republic, received full powers, including constituent power, similar to Marshall Pétain in 1940, the last head of government of the Third Republic. These 'full powers' were given to enable the Constitution to be modified by governmental regulations for a ten-month period, starting with the promulgation of the statute and subject to two conditions. The first was that the governmental regulations (*décrets*) passed by the government (named ordinances, *ordonnances*) had to be adopted by the Council of Ministers after advice received from the administrative supreme court, the *Conseil d'État* (unless emergency procedures had to be deployed).

The second condition was that government regulations should not cover certain areas, such as those reserved to the legislative power by constitutional tradition, the 1789 Declaration and the Preamble to the 1946 Constitution. The 'full powers' ended four months after the promulgation of the new Constitution (4 February 1959).

The second statute was the constitutional act (*Loi constitutionnelle modifiant la procédure de révision de la Constitution, prévue par l'article 90 de la Constitution de 1946*) of 3 June 1958.[27] This act aimed to amend the 1946 Constitution in order to allow changes to the procedure for amending the Constitution itself. The new version of article 90 of the 1946 Constitution established a 'fast-track' procedure to modify the Constitution of the Fourth Republic. The constitutional act set conditions of substance and form:

Conditions of substance

The government had to respect five fundamental principles in drafting the new Constitution:

1. The democratic principle – universal suffrage was considered the sole and only source of power.
2. The separation of powers – the French republican tradition of separation between executive and legislative powers had to be respected.
3. The government had to be scrutinised by parliament (a classic archetype of a parliamentary regime).
4. The judicial 'authority' (there is no recognition of the judiciary as a 'power' in the French republican tradition) had to be independent.
5. Relations between France and its 'associated people' (people from the French colonies) needed to be organised.

Conditions of form

Two conditions were posited:

1. The government had to consult a *comité consultatif constitutionnel* (composed of two-thirds of the MPs, which was put in place from 15 July 1958 to 29 July 1958) and the *Conseil d'État*. (The project was submitted to these bodies on 27 August 1958.)
2. The project of the Constitution had to be approved by the people by referendum. (It was approved on 28 September 1958 by 79.2 per cent of voters, and promulgated on 4 October 1958; it was published in the Official Gazette of the French Republic on 5 October.)

The original text comprised a preamble (with reference to the 1789 Declaration and to the Preamble of the 1946 Constitution) plus 92 articles.[28]

The text had (and still has) a specific order. For instance, the executive is positioned before the legislative: executive, respectively *titre* II President and *titre* III government and legislative, *titre* IV parliament (the 1946 Constitution positioned the President at *titre* V and parliament *titre* II). The text was 'efficient', short and flexible, using *organique* laws, which are statutes used to complement the Constitution at a later stage, without the need for constitutional amendment. De Gaulle presented the project on the 'symbolic' date of 4 September, commemorating the other mythical republics.[29]

What we know very quickly from the text is that this Republic is indivisible, secular (*laïque*), democratic and social. It ensures equality before the law for every citizen, regardless of origin, race or religion. It is a system of government that is supposed to respect all beliefs, with a Constitution that encourages gender equality in terms of access to electoral mandates and elective functions, together with equal access to professional and social representative organisations. The administration of the government is supposed to be decentralised, and the Republic has a language, French; its national symbol is the tricolour flag (blue, white, red) and its national anthem is *la Marseillaise*. The motto of the Republic is *Liberté, Égalité, Fraternité*, and its principle is *gouvernement du peuple, par le peuple et pour le peuple*. The Republic of the new quickly became the new Republic.

To a new Republic?

As mentioned above, in 2008 the Fifth Republic celebrated its fiftieth birthday. This has been a golden time for France, in which it has been possible to contemplate a stable and long-lasting system of government. It is worth noting that in terms of post-1789 France, the Fifth Republic is becoming the second longest Republican Constitution that the country has known. It is evident that the pre-1789 system of government was extremely stable, lasting for more than 1,300 years. After 1789, the move between democracy, monarchy, Republic and empire was rapid and characteristic of the forces involved. To summarise what happened during the years that followed the Revolution, it can be seen that a choice had to be made between a system with a head, and a system without a head (or with an extremely weakened head). What comes from the fiftieth anniversary of the Fifth Republic is primarily 'the return of the head'. It is more like a celebration of a fifty-year marriage: the event creates a time to reflect on the solidity of the settlement, to assess whether or not it was a good one. This is a very important point for France because the country was never able to achieve a good solid and lasting republican settlement after the revolution: the 1958 Constitution, however, seems to have succeeded in providing one. It is as if the contradictions of French constitutional history, with its pendulum movement between Republic and monarchy, either royal or imperial, had finally reached a consensus – an equilibrium between the 'rational-horizontal-egalitarian' enterprise that is the

Republic and the 'passionate-vertical-hierarchical' natural system that is the monarchy. The Fifth Republic is France in a state of grace.

First and foremost, what is new for this Republic is its stability. There has been no 'new regime' since 1958 although the Constitution has been amended many times, proving its flexibility. It may be said that the Constitution has remained that of the Fifth Republic even though the changes have sometimes been so radical that in the past the political elite would have declared a new Republic, the Sixth or the Seventh … But it was important to keep it as the Fifth, to show stability. In addition, it is a strong Constitution that permitted democracy to be truly practised as demonstrated by the *alternance*, the radical political change of 1981 when François Mitterrand was elected, or *cohabitations* between a President from a different political party his Prime Minister during the late 1980s and 1990s, for example. We have witnessed a slightly different evolution of this new Republic since 2007 with Presidents Sarkozy and Hollande. It has become the Republic of the spectacle and of the image, to the extent that President Sarkozy has been nicknamed the *télépresident*,[30] while President Hollande elected in 2012 is stuck in the tracks of his predecessor, either as someone copying his behaviour or as counter-model (*président normal*). The spectacle, the show, 'is nothing other than the sense of the total practice of a social-economic formation, its use of time' (*rien d'autre que le sens de la pratique totale d'une formation economique-sociale, son emploi du temps*) – or in other words, 'the historical movement in which we are caught' (*le moment historique qui nous contient*).[31]

The image is not simply that of the President appearing on television, the image is the 'imago' of someone looking in the mirror. In Lacanian theory, the reflection in the mirror indicates a unity of space and time, while the child thinks about him/herself as something composite, constructed of body parts. The image tests, simultaneously, the short-term, the immediate (present) reflection of the subject (the true image) with the image of the past (the mental image that the subject has of him/herself) but it also creates the idea of an aspect that will survive the initial experience and be remembered in the future. The mirror stage is in fact a process of ritual a young child undertakes when he wants to recognise himself in a mirror, with the approval of a third person, who provides a reference that frames the building up of the subject.[32] What is fundamental is the identity constructed in the reflection, in the mirror, which also influences the symbolic: 'The mirror stage is associated with the imaginary topology that exists prior to the symbolic register and yet is retrospectively constructed from it.'[33] In the case of the President, when the image is mixed with identification, and particularly with the paternal figure, we have an archaic image of a President who hides behind the uniform of a monarch. The imaginary is therefore a key element of the new Republic: it recalls the royal past.

However, the royal past and the contemporary use of the image by the President create a Republic of the short term, built on *le temps court*. And one may note the acceleration of time. Strangely enough, it has been during this perception of acceleration that the decision has been taken to shorten the presidential mandate, as if one wanted to emphasise the perception of time moving quickly. Furthermore, this will, in a way, place more 'stress' on the President because he will have only two consecutive mandates, if re-elected of course:[34] he will need to be faster, and stronger in reforming and modernising therefore attracting more anger and obstacles to his re-election. The spirit of the Fifth Republic is now 'presidentialism' – a sort of transplant from across the Atlantic. But it is also something that recalls the past, with the (unlucky) end of the Second Republic and its experience of the prince President.[35]

The bottom line is that the republican spirit of today resembles more than ever what Debord predicted when he declared that: 'The world already possesses the dream of a time, of which it must now possess the consciousness so as to really live it' (*le monde possède déjà le rêve d'un temps dont il doit maintenant posséder la conscience pour le vivre réellement*).[36]

In this book, I hope to contribute to a better understanding of the French Constitution. My contribution is neither a textbook on French constitutional law nor a new interpretation of this Constitution. Therefore the reader seeking a complete knowledge of French constitutional law or of the Fifth Republic Constitution may feel frustrated. What I propose is a collection of chapters that are looking at different elements of the Constitution of the Fifth French Republic. These elements, I am conscious, have been selected subjectively and my selection may in some ways be criticised, possibly because it may not reflect the mainstream work done on the matter. My idea, however, is to analyse critically some elements I consider fundamental not only to this Republic, but to republican ideas in France. This is an attempt to question the foundations of the Fifth Republic, considering both the 'old' and the 'new'. I particularly want the reader to grasp not only the dynamics and changes that occurred during the last fifty years of the Constitution but also the presence of older elements, sometimes archaic ones (from the time of the Revolution or even before), which create tensions within the constitutional text.

I have five main aims here. To begin with, I will examine a number of changes that have occurred over the last few decades. The work will sketch a movement that begins with a drift from a parliamentary regime towards a presidential system of government. In this movement, the head of state becomes the key to the new system, rebalancing it but also acknowledging the monarchical past. I then examine the turn towards human rights. For obvious reasons, human rights are central to the foundation of the Republic, as expressions of the Enlightenment and the Revolution. Yet they are also a twisted expression of French colonisation, which was considered as the means to export these human rights. I will then put forward a particular conception of French Republicanism, built on the idea of the 'one', on unity, which is embodied by the form of the State and the indivisibility of the Republic but it is also the catalyst towards a monolinguistic Republic. An important aim of this work concerns the reaction of the French Republic towards new regional and global developments, such as European integration and the response to environmental challenges, but it is also concerned with how the Republic is anchored in France's past.

The structure of this work reflects the main aims. The first chapter looks at the semi-presidential system of government and the evolution of the system during the fifty years of the 1958 Constitution. The second chapter explores the new rights added to the preamble, via a third bill of rights, the 2004 Charter for the environment; it examines the ways in which environmental issues affect the dynamic of the Constitution. Chapter 3 looks at human rights again, but this time examines their interaction with the text of the Constitution, analysing how the idea or concept of exclusion modifies what has been traditionally the idea of 'belonging' to the French nation. The fourth chapter explores the relationship between the French Republic and the European supra-national entity, looking at the difficulties caused by the integration of EC/EU legislation into French law. Chapter 5 is a reflection on the modifications made to the general administrative organisation of the French Republic. This chapter questions the basic principle of indivisibility as a theoretical foundation of the system. The final chapter examines another theoretical foundation of the system, connected to the previous one, commenting on the language of the Republic and the idea of unity.

1 Nature and evolution of the Constitution of the French Fifth Republic

Reflections on semi-presidentialism[1]

1.1 A semi-presidential Constitution?

Since 1789, the number of constitutional texts in France has reflected an ambivalence about the organisation of the polity. On the one hand, by transferring the onus of sovereignty from the monarch to the people (or what we could assume to be its theorised version, the nation) the governing body became a representative regime with an assembly as its main institution. 'Pure' and sometimes 'excessive' parliamentary systems of government were to be the basis of numerous French constitutional texts. On the other hand, the basic societal organisation, the tribal Indo-European society established through a Franco-Germanic hierarchical monarchic society, was present in many other texts. Ambivalence and discontent, a dialectical relationship between the two poles of the government of the French society could be resumed in the classical conceptualised expressions: parliamentary regime v. presidential regime. The Constitution of the Fifth Republic appears to be an attempt to reconcile the two opposed sides of 'how to govern a society'. The Fourth Republic, which failed to attract a wide consensus, was replaced after dealing (sometimes in a positive way) with decolonisation by the 'most monarchic' regime since the reign of Napoleon III and the Second Empire. It was a recurrent idea during the Third Republic that France has always needed a head. Charles Maurras was the leading figure supporting this claim, but the left wing of the time was also sharing this opinion, and later Duverger claimed, citing Maurras in *Échec au Roi*: 'The Republic is a woman without a head.'[2] This belief, embedded in the *ancien régime*, was obviously part of the background preparatory work on the new Constitution. As Professor Jean-Claude Casanova notes: 'The "real" father of the French Constitution is Charles Maurras, who is the "real" intellectual father of Charles de Gaulle, i.e. that France needs a head.'[3] The influence of Charles Maurras on Charles de Gaulle, founder of the Fifth Republic, cannot be dismissed. Neither can his influence on Mitterrand, De Gaulle's long-lasting political opponent, who not only became head of state under a Constitution that he vigorously criticised as a text permitting 'the permanent *coup d'État*',[4] but also its longest-standing President to date. Mitterrand noted in his first press conference that 'those institutions were a danger before me, they will be again after me. So far, I can accommodate myself to it.'[5] In doing so, he (re-)affirmed the monarchist characteristic of these institutions. Both De Gaulle and Mitterrand were educated under the Third Republic when the dialectic between monarchy and democracy was at its zenith; Maurras' ideas were crucial then. The ideological debate that marked the Third Republic, excluded for conjectural reasons from the constituent debate of 1945 to 1946 (after the Second Word War and the Vichy regime), reappeared in 1958 and was transposed in the text of the Constitution of the Fifth Republic. The structural debate of 'who should govern' formed part of the preparatory debate for the drafting of the new Constitution and it is present in the text itself. It is also present in two major modifications that took place in 1962 and 2000, although less evident in the 2008 amendment.[6]

In this chapter, I wish to demonstrate the tensions within the text of the Constitution, characterised by the constitutional amendment that concern the President. I will start by looking at the theoretical framework to consider how the current semi-presidential system sits between the parliamentary and presidential versions; I will then analyse the constitutional arrangement at the origin of the Constitution and how it evolved, before looking into the dynamics of the Constitution as it now stands.

1.2 Theoretical framework

As I will be considering the Constitution of the Fifth Republic, I will work from the hypothesis that the system in place since 1958 has been a mix of parliamentary and presidential regimes. I will look, therefore, at some broadly accepted definitions of these regimes.

If we follow the classic approach elaborated upon by Sartori, there are three prototypes of systems for government: the parliamentary regime, the presidential regime and the semi-presidential regime.[7]

1.2.1 Parliamentary regime

According to Sartori, the prototype for a parliamentary regime is the UK's 'Westminster system', although it can also be seen in France in the Constitutions of the Third and (to some extent) Fourth Republics. The system is mainly known for the way the main powers collaborate. The primary characteristic of the parliamentary regime is that the institution itself – parliament – is sovereign. There is a transfer of sovereignty from the people or the nation towards the legislative institution of the governing body. The parliamentary system, in fact, 'demystifies' the people or nation as sovereign: the institution becomes the perceived sovereign. Another characteristic is that the parliament is democratically elected. There are different ways to recruit members of the legislative institution, according to the election laws of a country of course. For instance, the UK operates the majoritarian voting 'first-past-the-post' system to recruit members of parliament while the French Third Republic operated variations of proportional representation.

The head of government is also leader of the political party or coalition leading the lower chamber. Indeed, under constitutional convention, the leader of the party or coalition of parties with the greatest number of seats in the House of Commons becomes Prime Minister.[8]

If we now look at a 'politico-legal' reading of the system, we find that there is no proper separation of powers but rather a collaboration between the executive and legislative bodies. Consequently, it may be assumed that most of the time the executive can pass any laws it wants to under this system, reinforcing the primary characteristic of the sovereignty of the institution of parliament.

Finally, the government is accountable to the national parliament that checks its work through tools like the vote of confidence, and as 'counter-party' the executive may be allowed to dissolve parliament. This double-sided mechanism, which is understood as the core of this system of collaboration, is in fact rarely activated because of the close relationship between the executive and the elected members of the lower chamber.

1.2.2 Presidential regime

Sartori considers the 'Washington system' to be a prototype of a presidential regime, although two French examples, the 1791 Constitution and the Second Republic, could also be considered.

Under the presidential system of government, the President is directly elected or nominated but can also be, in some cases (like the 1791 French Constitution), a hereditary monarch. The legislative assembly or assemblies is or are normally directly elected. In the USA, the two chambers are directly elected, although what is 'represented' in each chamber is different (people and member states). Under the 1791 French Constitution, and the 1848 Constitution, an unicameral assembly was directly elected.

The system's main characteristic is that of a 'strict' separation of powers. Therefore in this model of strict separation of powers, the link between the executive and legislative bodies is said to be minimal. Indeed, the President and the executive are not 'controlled' by the legislature but directly by the people. Thus the President and the executive cannot dissolve the assembly or assemblies.

1.2.3 Semi-presidential regime

Sartori defined the Fifth French Republic as a prototype of a semi-presidential system of government. He described it as a system comprising a head of state with a head of government incorporated in a bicephalous ('two-headed') executive, and a parliament with a least one directly elected chamber. It is interesting to analyse what the literature has defined as semi-presidential and what criteria have been retained. In the current literature on semi-presidential systems of government, different conditions are found to describe the system.

Sartori considered four conditions:

- The head of state has to be directly or indirectly elected.
- The head of state shares power with the Prime Minister as the executive is bicephalous.
- The head of state is independent from the legislative power but cannot govern alone. Directives can be given and the government is supposed to apply them, hence the national parliament plays a noticeable part here.
- The Prime Minister is independent from the head of state and dependent upon the parliament: this variation depends on the majority supporting the action of the Prime Minister.

Duverger,[9] who was one of the first to undertake a study of semi-presidential systems, specified that a system of government could be considered as semi-presidential if:

- the head of state is elected by direct suffrage;
- the head of state has considerable powers;
- the Prime Minister and the government 'mirrored' him, acts under a separation of powers and may remain in office only if parliament does not show any opposition to them (in other words if it is 'Orleanist'[10]).

Elgie has given the most recent explanation,[11] in which semi-presidential means that:

- there is an elected fixed-term President;
- the Prime Minister is accountable to parliament;
- the dual executive interacts on an outgoing basis.

In order to consider further existing semi-presidential regimes, I wish to look more closely at the account made by Duverger. Duverger, who studied the semi-presidential system of government and conceptualised it in *Échec au Roi* ('checkmate'), shows that there is a scale of semi-presidential regimes ranked according to the powers given to the President. He classified seven countries, primarily through their constitutional texts (a 'theoretical approach') and, secondly, by examining what was really happening (a 'practical approach'). Duverger found that Finland had the widest powers given by a Constitution to a head of state. France ranked in only sixth position according to the 'theoretical approach' (that is according to the powers of the President listed in the Constitution). In terms of the 'practical approach' (what was happening in reality), however, France came first and Finland second. What separates the two is minute as in both cases the President affords great autonomy vis-à-vis the other institutions. For Duverger, the Finnish Constitution dissociated more the President from the government than the French Constitution. This confirmed Sartori's belief that the Constitution of the Fifth Republic was the prototype of the semi-presidential system of government.

In fact, looking at the evolution of the Constitution since 1958, it is noticeable that the French semi-presidential system is strongly based on how the President is recruited, on the absence of political accountability, and on the respect of the 'synchronisation' between the President's majority and that of the lower chamber of the French parliament, the *Assemblée nationale*. It is then obvious that the key institution of the Constitution of the Fifth Republic is its President. The first evolution to be considered then should be the change in how the President was recruited, as organised by the 1962 amendment of the Constitution. The second should be the change brought about by the 2000 amendment, made in relation to the President's mandate.

1.3 Original institutional arrangement and its evolutions

The 'establishment' of the dying Fourth Republic called on General De Gaulle in order to 'save the country'. He was in charge of organising a new institutional arrangement and designing a new Constitution. In an important postwar presentation, the Speech of Bayeux (16 June 1946[12]), he declared that it was necessary for the country to have a head of state who would be above the political parties. This idea, as we have seen, was the product of a certain ideology and the historical background of the Third Republic, but it became more important because of De Gaulle's experience of wartime and was forged as part of De Gaulle's response to the defeat of France. He believed that the outcome would have been different if a strong leader had led the Republic. De Gaulle was 'the man who won the war', a legendary figure, and he had a certain idea or vision of France: France, as Maurras said, needed a leader and the President, within that logic, had to be strong.[13] The person leading the Republic had to be a strong figurehead. That said, though this description may have fitted well the person of De Gaulle, it was not clear whether the idea of a strong figurehead would survive De Gaulle and last over time or not: ultimately, what needed to be strong was the institution of the head of state. Articles 2 and 3 of the constitutional act of 3 June 1958,[14] the guidelines for the redaction of the new Constitution, were instrumental in defining this future architecture. Article 2 specified that the executive body had to be separated from the legislative body. Separate specialised bodies would be entrusted with specific functions. Article 3 specified that the government would be scrutinised by the parliament. If the Speech of Bayeux was a declaration with strong monarchist undertones, the *Loi constitutionnelle* (3 June 1958) was not. It was evident that the new Constitution would organise a parliamentary system of government, not a presidential one. The institutional balance found in the project of the Constitution, which would be adopted, was a living proof of this statement: there were to be two indirectly elected institutions (the President and the upper chamber of parliament, the *Sénat*[15]) and a directly elected institution (the *Assemblée nationale*), which would be the body representative of the nation.

1.3.1   A parliamentary system with some 'presidential features'

Therefore, we may want to ask this simple question: Is this 1958 Constitution radically different from previous ones? The Fifth Republic Constitution established a system of government similar to those of the Third and Fourth Republics. As observed by John Bell, '[The Constitution] was meant to establish a parliamentary regime, perhaps more strictly organised than before, but a parliamentary regime nevertheless.'[16] 'Similar', of course, does not mean 'the same'. Many clues in the text of the Constitution show a drift towards a presidential system. For example, the Third Republic was a parliamentary system. It had a bicameral parliament with both chambers having equal powers. The Fourth Republic was also parliamentary, but had a truncated bicameral system: the 1946 Constitution was a settlement, a compromise between an 'assembly government' and a full bicameral system. The lower chamber was strong and the upper weak. The Fifth Republic was designed with a bicameral and (more) egalitarian parliament. The two chambers, lower (*Assemblée nationale*) and upper (*Sénat*), do not have equal powers but the *Sénat* is 'more powerful' than the upper chamber under the Fourth Republic Constitution. This does not mean that the system is closer to the presidential prototype described by Sartori, but it shows that the regime was designed to put some distance from the 'assembly government' of the Fourth Republic. The Fifth Republic completed and perfected the introduction of the so called *État de droit*. A hierarchy of norms was established, placing the Constitution at the apex of the pyramid of norms. Acts of parliament were formally placed under the Constitution and constitutional control was introduced to enforce the established hierarchy. Statute laws, under the rule of the Constitution of the Fifth Republic, became subordinated to the Constitution. In 1958, constitutional control could only operate 'at the bill stage', on the *proposition de loi* (a bill initiated by members of parliament) or the *projet de loi* (a bill initiated by government); therefore it could not take place on 'an act'. It somehow kept alive the myth of the law as the supreme expression of the general will.[17] The 'real' or efficient constitutional control was extended by the 2008 amendment which introduced a priority preliminary ruling on the issue of constitutionality, an ex-post control, in its article 29.[18]

What is truly interesting in the Constitution is how the extent of the changes has permeated the structure of the text itself and how the layout of the constitutional document reveals that something has been altered. If the Fifth Republic established the institution of head of state, so did the Constitutions of the Second, Third and Fourth Republics. But the text of the Constitution of the Fifth Republic was the first to position the executive power before the legislative power. Articles concerning the President were positioned in the second section, *titre II*, just after the first that concerns sovereignty. Articles regarding the government followed in section III, while those concerning the parliament were relegated to the fourth section. Even in the original version of the Constitution, in 1958, many strong new presidential discretionary powers were incorporated, which hinted at a move towards a presidential regime.

1.3.2 *Presidential discretionary powers*

The Constitution contained (and still contains) two types of discretionary powers: express and implied.

1.3.2.1 *Express presidential discretionary powers*

Article 19 outlined eight areas where the President can act independently. These are articles 8 (paragraph 1), 11, 12, 16, 18, 54, 56 and 61.

As far as the parliamentary regime is concerned, articles 8 (paragraph 1) and 12 are significant. Article 8 concerns the appointment of the Prime Minister, whom only the head of state can appoint. The President does not have to follow any rules or guidance. This can be said to depart from the model of the parliamentary system of government, such as Westminster's. The French President can appoint whomever he wishes to the post of Prime Minister, without limiting his choice to the leader of the party or coalition of parties with the majority in the lower elected chamber. Article 8 is the constitutional basis for the appointment and dismissal of the Prime Minister. This may be done 'a volo'. That said, if the President appoints the Prime Minister, the Prime Minister remains closely connected to the lower chamber of parliament and needs to be at least supported by its majority. If the Prime Minister does not have the support of both institutions (President and parliament), there could be considerable political issues. Without the support of the lower chamber, the Prime Minister would not be able to introduce any legislation, even if the President supports him or her. Therefore the Prime Minister cannot afford to be without presidential support, but neither can he or she risk losing parliamentary support. As developed later, until recently, this constitutional arrangement offered the strong possibility for the President and the lower chamber to be politically separate. It was 'simply' a mechanical consequence of the difference of terms: one was elected for seven years, the other for five. There was a risk of losing the majority at the National Assembly because of elections normally planned for the end of the five-year period, or if the President decided to dissolve the National Assembly, which can be done under article 12. After certain formalities (including consultations with the Prime Minister and the President of the two chambers), the President may dissolve the directly elected chamber of parliament. Article 12 was used, for example, by Mitterrand in 1981 and 1988 to allow the synchronisation of the parliamentary majority with the presidential majority. Jacques Chirac used article 12 in 1997, aiming to gain an increased support, even though the lower chamber was not hostile to the President at all. Unfortunately, the majority returned was then opposed to the President. The use of articles 8 and 12 has been very important in the changes towards the presidentialisation of the regime. It was not the case with article 18 until 2008. Article 18 is perhaps less important but it has always been linked to the parliamentary regime: the head of state could not be physically present in parliament. It allowed the President to address the chambers through a message read out on his behalf. Although article 18 used to forbid the President from physically attending a session of parliament, this was modified in 2008.[19] This could be considered to have been a major (symbolic) step towards a presidentialisation of the regime.

In addition, the new Constitution gave the President many more important attributions. For instance, the President was given the power to 'consult' the sovereign directly, bypassing the institution in charge of the legislative power and allowing the people to directly 'enact'. Indeed, according to article 11, the President may use a referendum in a discretionary manner after a formal proposal from either the government or the two chambers of the parliament. Article 11 was used and some say abused. De Gaulle himself considered his own interpretation of article 11 several times, and it became instrumental in the way he dealt with the institutions.[20] Furthermore, we found very interesting article 16 which deals with emergency powers. For Agamben, 'the state of exception is regulated by Article 16'.[21] It gives full powers to the head of state if the institutions of the Republic, the independence of the Nation, the integrity of the territory or the execution of any international engagement are in danger. Article 16 was used controversially by De Gaulle from April 1961 to September 1961 after an attempted coup in Algeria. The President kept article 16 in force although the rebellion was quashed in a few days. During that time, many powers were transferred to the President including law-making powers. It was never used again, although according to Agamben, there is in fact no need to use such an article as the state of exception 'has gradually been replaced by an unprecedented generalization of the paradigm of security as the normal technique of government.'[22]

Finally, articles 54, 56 and 61 deal with the *Conseil constitutionnel*. Article 54 and 61 address the power given to the President to refer a 'bill' to the *conseil* in order to check whether or not the statute will conform with the Constitution,[23] while the President, under article 56, has the power to appoint the President and three members of the *Conseil constitutionnel*.[24]

In addition to the express powers we find those that are implied.

1.3.2.2 Implied presidential discretionary powers

Further to attributions listed under article 19, the Constitution gives other discretionary powers to the President. I would particularly like to note those under article 15, which entrusts the leadership of the army to the President and grants him the discretionary power to use French nuclear weapons.[25] Other powers that imply discretionary elements are article 7 (the President may have the power to resign and force a new election – useful in time of political uncertainty) and article 9 (the President chairs the Council of Ministers, i.e. where and when the presidential initiative is transformed into future parliament 'bills'). Finally, article 5 gives a general power to the President as guarantor of respect for the Constitution, the efficient functioning of public powers, and the continuity of the State, together with the independence of the nation and the integrity of the territory. Of course, these powers should be carefully read in the light of the political accountability of the French head of state.

1.3.3 The importance of the political accountability of the President

Under article 68 of the Constitution of the Fifth Republic, the President benefits from criminal immunity (except for crimes of high treason). It can in fact be said that the President benefits from three types of 'absence of accountability': for civil or criminal wrongdoings and political accountability. In matters of civil liability, the President cannot be held accountable for any damages he causes. In matters of criminal liability, he cannot be charged with a crime (except that of high treason). In matters of political accountability, the President is accountable to no one. That said, political accountability is always supposed to be an obligation for an elected representative. It is standard practice for a member of parliament, in a parliamentary regime, to be held accountable to the electorate during his or her mandate. But there is no mechanism in the Constitution that holds the French President accountable. If one looks back at the original version of the Constitution, the 1958 text, the design of the political institutions clearly intended to put in place a parliamentary system of government. Therefore the traditional parliamentary mechanism that the head of state had to have all his acts countersigned by the head of government or a minister accountable to parliament was in all minds: this was the tradition of the Third and Fourth Republics. We have seen that in 1958, the President was given discretionary powers by the Constitution. These are attributions that could be exercised without being politically accountable to anyone or anything, in the traditional meaning, unless, of course, an election was called, and the President would lose popular support. This political 'absence of accountability' of the President was justified by the tradition and the character of the parliamentary system of government (as set up in the *Loi constitutionnelle*, 3 June 1958), and the principle of immunity, particularly in political terms, was maintained by the original version of the 1958 Constitution. But this particular point was at stake when the Constitution was modified, that is when the discretionary powers given by the 1958 version of the Constitution 'clashed' with the 1962 and other amendments touching on the election and the mandate of the head of state: the election by universal suffrage was the first major evolution, reinforced by the 2000 amendment modifying the length of the term of office.

1.3.4 *The major issues of the presidential election and mandate*

The two major modifications of the Constitution concerning the President occurred in 1962 (election by the people) and 2000 (mandate aligned on that of the deputies).

1.3.4.1 *The President elected by the people*

The Constitution was amended in 1962 to allow the President to be elected directly by the people and no longer by an enlarged electoral college. This was the direct influence of De Gaulle, who was perceived as the man who won the war and stood up not only to the enemy but also to the allies as an incarnation of the country, of France. In a way, the Constitution was designed by De Gaulle for De Gaulle, but it had to be able to last after De Gaulle. When he was the victim of the *Petit Clamart* terrorist attack on 22 August 1962, he decided that the time had come to make further constitutional provision for the President.[26] De Gaulle knew he was a strong figurehead but was worried this characteristic was too much attached to his person. The question then was what would happen to the next President, to his successors? Would he or she be a strong figurehead with a practice of the Constitution similar to De Gaulle's or should the Constitution institutionalise a strong President? De Gaulle answered that question by proposing a modification of the Constitution that institutionalises strong leadership. When he became President in 1958, under the original version of the Constitution, he was without doubt a strong figure holding the position of head of state in a parliamentary system of government. He wanted to add something to this arrangement, however – something that had monarchic inspiration: the 'head' that for Maurras was missing would be back. In consequence, De Gaulle seized the opportunity of a terrorist attack to introduce an amendment to the Constitution. It was in fact a very simple text, only modifying article 6 of the Constitution, simplifying its wording. The new article would state simply that the President would be elected directly by the people for seven years.

The system moved from two indirectly elected institutions that were supposed to contain the directly elected assembly under a parliamentary regime. A new institutional balance resulted: there would be, after this reform, two directly elected institutions – the President and the National Assembly – and one indirectly elected – the Senate.

In 1965, the first election was held after the amendment had been passed. This was the first change in how the President was recruited under the Fifth French Republic. The people elected De Gaulle for seven years.[27]

Between 1958 and 1965, even though the system of government was fully parliamentary, the Prime Minister was already 'the thing' of the President. This was mainly due to De Gaulle's personality, his charisma, but also due to the personalities selected as Prime Ministers, all very close personal allies to the General (Debré, considered to be the drafter of the Constitution; Pompidou, who managed the Anne de Gaulle Foundation for Down's Syndrome named after the daughter of De Gaulle; Couve de Murville, who joined De Gaulle in his 1943 adventure). In 1965, the President became considered as representative of the Nation (without *legally* being so).[28] This revised institutional arrangement granted the President a stature similar to the National Assembly. The President was now at the same level as the lower chamber of parliament: the President gained legitimacy.[29] In fact, this was a personification of the function of head of state, because perhaps in a monarchist way, the President became somehow the incarnation of the State or at least an institution that reminded the people of the person of the monarch – the strong paternal figurehead of the Indo-European tribes.

The 1962 constitutional amendment therefore modified the original institutional equilibrium of the Constitution. It increased the 'intensity' of legitimacy and at the same time forced De Gaulle to find a way to control the function of the President by creating a new balance. In what would be called a *gaullienne* reading of the Constitution, he considered that he, the President, was accountable to the people, while, in parallel, the Prime Minister was accountable to the elected assembly, which was itself accountable to the people. If the parliamentary system of government organised how parliament may hold the government accountable, the evolution of the Fifth Republic Constitution meant the President had to be accountable too. De Gaulle initiated a new practice: he used the tool of the referendum as an instrument of political control of the legitimacy of the President. A 'yes' at a referendum would be considered a vote of support while a 'no' would be held as a vote of sanction equivalent to a non confidence that would trigger the resignation of the President. His intention was to make the President accountable to the people while the government was accountable to parliament. In 1969, de Gaulle proposed a reform of the Senate and local governments (notably with the creation of regions). He explained as he did for every referendum organised during his presidency that if the 'no' vote should prevail, he would resign.[30] He used his interpretation of the Constitution for the last time: the referendum returned a majority of 'no' votes. Consequently, the President resigned. No other President has employed this reading of the Constitution. All successors of De Gaulle have limited themselves to the letter of the text. The major problem after him was not only the continuity of the presidential function but also its control. Indeed, as mentioned above, in the 1958 text, the role of President did not carry any political accountability. The problem was to find the right balance between the immunity of the President, his direct election by the people, and the discretionary powers granted by the

Constitution to the head of state. This become increasingly important as the presidentialisation of the system went further in 2000.

1.3.4.2 The presidential mandate aligned to the deputies' mandate

The seven-year tenure had been a tradition since the beginning of the Third Republic. The 'President monarch' elected for seven years was introduced by law on 20 November 1873, which amended the Constitution of the French Third Republic. The President, Maréchal de Mac Mahon, was elected as temporary caretaker of the function of head of state until the promised restoration of a monarch during the troubled times that followed the end of the Second Empire. The *septennat* was set up to allow one of the possible pretenders to the throne of France to become king. There were two such pretenders, the 'legitimiste' Comte de Chambord, Henri V, grandson of the last king (and brother of Louis XVI), Charles X, and the 'Orleaniste' Comte de Paris, grandson of King Louis-Philippe I, monarch under the July Monarchy. Chambord was supposed to be crowned but refused at the last minute to enter Paris in a carriage flying the tricolour flag – a symbol related of course to the Revolution. The monarchists, leading the French parliament at that time, decided to prorogue the mandate of the President to seven years, via the 1873 amendment, hoping that by then Chambord would have died, leaving the Comte de Paris as the unique successor. The tenure of seven years was therefore strongly linked to the monarchy. It remained the tenure chosen by De Gaulle for the new Constitution.

The 1958 Constitution was supposed to function according to the ideas of De Gaulle. That meant particularly that there should always be a perfect coherence between the majority in the National Assembly and the President. It was sensible for De Gaulle to have the two institutions elected by the people (whether or not we consider their status as representative of the nation) in the hands of the same political party or coalition. This was defined as the *fait majoritaire*, the *gaullienne* reading of the Constitution. The *non gaullienne* reading of the Constitution would be the *cohabitation*, a period when President and Prime Minister would be politically opposed. This theoretical situation became a reality and occurred in 1988, 1993 and 1997. The cause was identified as arising from the difference in mandate (President seven years; National Assembly five years). There was therefore strong support to shorten the mandate in order to (re-)establish a connection between the majority in parliament and the President. This was considered as conforming to the spirit of the Constitution. The Constitution was therefore modified in 2000 to bring back its original spirit.[31] It was designed to avoid the President and the Prime Minister standing on different political sides. As mentioned, the Prime Minister has always been a close ally of the President but is traditionally also closely linked to the lower chamber of parliament: the Prime Minister needs the support of both. To avoid any 'non-synchronisation' or *cohabitation*, and to enforce strong presidential leadership, it was decided to decrease the duration of the presidential mandate to five years. In doing so, it aligned both tenures of directly elected political institutions – the President and the lower chamber of the French parliament.

The underlying idea was to find a compromise between a 'President monarch' (which was used to qualify the head of state since 1958[32]) and, as Jospin commented during the 1995 campaign for the presidential election, a 'President citizen'.[33]

Since 1958, the opposition had often commented on the length of the presidential mandate. The 1968 left-wing parties made a clear reference to a five-year mandate, so did the 'common programme' of the Left in 1972.[34] In 1973 President Pompidou proposed an amendment to the Constitution. The project was supported, in accordance with the Constitution, by the majority of the two chambers, but because it was clear that the necessary qualified majority of 3/5 would not be reached to finalise the change, the procedure was not completed. At the beginning of the 1980s, proposition 45 of candidate Mitterrand's *'110 propositions'* manifesto related to the change of the presidential mandate.[35] President Mitterrand seemed to have forgotten that point after his election. During an interview given on 28 April 1985 at *Télévision Française 1* (TF1), he commented on the shortness of the seven-year mandate.[36] Not only he did not try to modify the mandate but he also ran for re-election and was the only President to serve for 14 years. During the 1995 presidential election, the candidates took opposing views on the issue of the length of the mandate. Jospin supported a five-year term while Chirac was against it. On 5 September 2000, Valéry Giscard d'Estaing introduced a proposal to alter the Constitution by modifying the length of the mandate, which was approved by President Chirac the following day in the name of modern democracy: President Jacques Chirac relied on populist formulations: 'seven years is too long', 'five years is more modern'.[37]

In fact, the duration of the mandate was only one side of the concern here. It had, indeed, to be considered together with the other side of the problem: the lower chamber of parliament and the duration of the mandate of the deputies. In fact, the two sides were linked in order to provide for what I wish to call a force synchronisation. During the *travaux préparatoires*, it was forecast that the system might move towards a presidential system of government, while retaining a parliamentary aspect, mainly due to the accountability of the Prime Minister to the *Assemblée nationale*. This constitutional amendment took place during the long cohabitation that started in 1997 as we will see in the development below. It was the third since 1981. For the purists, this was not right. As Massot stated, 'the instauration of the five year term of office *quinquennat* should allow a return of the initial conception of the Fifth Republic as it used to operate from 1962 to 1986'.[38]

The then Minister for Justice Guigoux had to support the bill in parliament. She argued that modifying the mandate of the President meant not only modernising the function of the office of the President but also at the same time modernising democracy. She mentioned that, primarily, this modification would allow the French people to elect their President more often. The *rapporteur Larché* mentioned De Gaulle's methods and referred to them as a justification for 'something to be done':[39]

> Except while facing elections, the President is controlled only on its own initiative. This was the practice repeated by General De Gaulle through the use of dissolutions and referendums, sometimes contested, with as ultimate consequence, his departure in 1969.

Minister Guigoux also referred to the need for a more coherent system. She suggested that five years would be closer to the general trend in neighbouring European countries, and would harmonise the domestic mandates through the imposition of a ordered relationship organised between the three institutions of head of state, government and National Assembly. Indeed, only Italy and Ireland have a President elected for seven years, and in many countries, the MPs' mandate is four or five years. Minister Guigoux used the example of the House of Commons, here reminding the National Assembly that from the 1716 Septennial Act to the 1911 Parliament Act, it was elected for seven years, leading to Rousseau's declaration that 'the English people are free one day every seven years'.[40] Obviously, the French people should be free at least one day every five years!

To sum up, this amendment was about 'coordination', 'coherence', 'harmonisation' and 'stability' between the mandates of the head of state and that of the deputies. The institutions had to function 'normally', in the way they had been designed, that is in a semi-presidential way, but without using a *gaullienne* reading (control from the people of a President with political immunity). In a way, the 2008 modification reinforces presidentialisation by limiting the number of consecutive mandates. I will not develop it here because it is not as radical as the previous two reforms. That said, it is obvious that the limitation to two consecutive mandates refers to the way the mandate of the US President is organised under the Constitution of the USA, the model for Sartori of presidential system of government. However, so far it does not seem to have had any major impact on the institutional arrangement and does not seem to contribute to the same extent as the other amendments to the changes of the Constitution.

1.4 'Elasticity' of the Constitution

These two significant modifications to the Constitution created space for major changes in the functioning of the institutions. The question of synchronisation and non-synchronisation of the office of the President and the Prime Minister became an important issue, in some ways more psychological and political than legal. I will therefore present a taxonomy, organised around what I believe to be the most relevant changes in the Constitution of the

Fifth Republic, with regard to its semi-presidential characteristic – the 1962 and 2000 revisions: pure synchronisation, non-synchronisation and forced synchronisation.

1.4.1 Preliminary remarks on the variations in synchronisation of the President's majority with that of the National Assembly

On 21 December 1958, the first presidential election under the new Constitution, De Gaulle was elected by an enlarged electoral college, mainly composed of members of parliament. After the 1962 amendment, the President was elected by direct universal suffrage, the Electoral College becoming the largest possible in a modern democracy: the people. Because of the bicephalous characteristic of the executive under the Constitution of the Fifth Republic, and due to the new balance within the constitutional arrangement after 1962, the issue of the synchronisation of both President and lower chamber of parliament both directly elected by the people, became topical. The Prime Minister, who had usually been a close ally of the President, needed a majority in the lower chamber, to be able to introduce successful legislations. Duverger wrote that the majority is originally formed around the head of state and the President is normally the party leader. If this is not the case, then the party leader should be the Prime Minister.[41] Duverger also predicted that a different majority in the directly elected chamber would oppose the President. This would be evident and apparent within the 'two-headed' executive. After 1962, two types of situations are found: the period of constitutional ('normal') functioning under the *fait majoritaire* (a majority in the two directly elected institutions) and the period of ('abnormal') functioning under *cohabitation* (literally living together; it is used here to characterise a 'two-headed' executive with two opponents). As discussed, the *fait majoritaire* was always considered the right way the Constitution should work, the *période normale*. By qualifying that functioning of the Fifth Republic as the 'normal' reading of the Constitution, it was clear that the other way, the *cohabitation*, was the 'abnormal' one. This dichotomy between normal and abnormal became a real issue. It became obvious that the question was one of synchronisation and non-synchronisation within the executive. It seems clear from the positions taken and the constitutional consequences, i.e. the two revisions touching article 6 in 1962 and 2000, that normality and abnormality constituted an important argument for the political elites and the commentators, while being absent from the 2008 revision. One may therefore look at a pure synchronisation as the way the Constitution should operate, a 'good' reading of the Constitution, while cohabitation should not be normal, and must be a 'bad' reading of the Constitution, a non-synchronisation. As a result, the situation had to be brought back to normality, even if it was by force.[42] The Fifth Republic was supposedly ill and the remedy was to enforce synchronisation.

1.4.2 *Pure synchronisation*

The *fait majoritaire* is a result of the direct election of the President and a majority that clearly support him in the other directly elected institution, the lower chamber of the French parliament. It is supposed to be the 'normal' functioning of the institutions. As we have seen, the Constitution stated that the presidential term of office was seven years until 2000, and the National Assembly members' term of office was five years. The 'two-headed' executive was in a peculiar position within the institutions.

In a situation of *fait majoritaire*, there is a pure synchronisation reflecting the semi-presidential character of the system. There have been three periods of pure synchronisation since 1958:

- 1958–86: De Gaulle's first and second terms, Pompidou and Valéry Giscard d'Estaing presidencies, Mitterrand's first term until the 1986 general elections, the beginning of the first cohabitation;
- 1988–93: Mitterrand's second term, until the 1993 general elections, the beginning of the second cohabitation; and
- 1995–7: Chirac's first term until the 1997 general elections, the beginning of the third cohabitation.

But we do have different types of pure synchronisation according to the variations in its substance.

During the period 1958–65, synchronisation was a consequence of the strength of the first President De Gaulle as a figurehead. The President was not directly elected by the people. It was simply the combination of De Gaulle as candidate and an enlarged electoral college that resulted in a parliamentary regime and a strong leader. During De Gaulle's second term, Pompidou, Mitterrand first term pre-1986, Mitterrand second term pre-1993 and Chirac first term pre-1997, this was reinforced by a change of Electoral College. As previously mentioned, the 1962 amendment replaced the enlarged electoral college by 'the people'. This was analysed by Duverger and Sartori as being the prototype of a semi-presidential system of government. In this system, the President and the Prime Minister are connected. The Prime Minister is more 'the secretary of the President' than 'a creature of the French parliament': less independent from the President and more independent from the parliament than in a classical parliamentary system. The bicephalous executive functions like one head: it is synchronised. These different periods saw a strong President with a weak Prime Minister, while Valéry Giscard d'Estaing's situation was unique. Giscard d'Estaing was not a Gaullist but a centrist. He had to face Chirac as chairman of the new Gaullist party, the *Rassemblement Pour la République* (RPR),[43] and appointed him Prime Minister in May 1974. This situation did not last long and Chirac resigned in August 1976, leaving the President with a weak leadership. Raymond Barre became Prime Minister; he was neither a member of parliament nor the leader of the coalition, although he was known to have centre-right ideas; he was an academic, whom Valéry Giscard d'Estaing considered to be 'the best French economist, at least one of the foremost'.[44] This example confirms the idea of the President being the leader who sits above the political parties. The President does not need to appoint a strong figure from the majority but may choose as Prime Minister anyone he wants, accentuating the perception of the head of government as a simple secretary of the President. Barre remained Prime Minister until the loss of the presidential election in 1981.

The head of state in a situation of pure synchronisation is a strong leader rather than the politically neutral head of the classical parliamentary system of government, sometimes considered an *arbitre*, a referee rather than a leader. The President is involved in policy-making, although he may use his Prime Minister as an intermediary between himself and the people or the MPs. This may contribute to a rather inverted reading of what is happening. The President is supposed to preside, i.e. to be the mind, while the Prime Minister is supposed to execute, i.e. to read the mind of the President and speak about it to his government: it is a system that should be simultaneously presidential and parliamentary. In fact, the President becomes the real and unique motor of the executive. He defines the programme of 'his' government, even though articles 20 and 21 of the Constitution state that the 'the government shall determine and conduct the policy of the nation' and 'shall direct the conduct of government affairs', not the head of state. During the 1958–9 period of trouble in Algeria, Debré, who was then Prime Minister under De Gaulle, took the side for a French Algeria. When it became clear that De Gaulle was no longer strongly supportive of the idea of a French Algeria, Debré had to follow his leader and had to advocate for an independent Algeria.[45] The President after 1962, receiving greater legitimacy from direct election, was supposed to sit above all partisan games and to refrain from entering the political arena. The Prime Minister was supposed to be the one in the political game, working and being seen fighting. But by becoming the real actor of the executive, the President was coming under pressure. He was seen as making all the decisions and getting involved in politics. It became more complicated and more difficult for some presidents to be re-elected. For instance, Valéry Giscard d'Estaing was not re-elected in 1981. On the contrary, Mitterrand in 1988 and Chirac in 2002 were re-elected after a period of non-synchronisation.

Strong leadership is linked to the increase in legitimacy brought by direct election. It forces a reading of the Constitution that differs from its (parliamentary) letter. It is even more evident in the case of the 'Father' of the French Constitution. Some have claimed that De Gaulle's use of article 11 (in 1962 and 1969) for instance was illegal.[46] But he could do this because he was strongly supported. Strong leadership contributes to a modification of the classic function of the government. In fact it affects the classical parliamentary way that government operates.

Indeed, regarding the presidential powers exercised on the advice of the Prime Minister or the government, the practice of *fait majoritaire* modifies the reality of the Constitution, inverting the meaning of the articles' wording. In relation to the wording of article 8, paragraph 1, which concerns the resignation of the Prime Minister, there is no mention of interference by the President. But it is well known that it is always the head of state in practice who forces the head of government to resign. For instance, Michel Debré offered his resignation to General de Gaulle many times but the General did not accept. He finally asked Debré to resign in April 1962.[47] Article 8, paragraph 1 is worded in such a way as to suggest that the Prime Minister will issue a letter of resignation and the President will accept it. In reality, it has been said that the President asks the Prime Minister to prepare this letter when first appointed.[48] Chirac left in 1976 but would probably have been asked to leave by Valéry Giscard d'Estaing, and the letter would have been drafted at the time of his appointment in 1974.

Similar comments can be made on the use of article 11. According to the text, the government is supposed to advise the President on holding a referendum (although not on a constitutional amendment, which is dealt with, normally, in article 89), but in fact all referenda to date have been initiated by the head of state.

Outside the scope of presidential discretionary powers, the President needs the government and/or the Prime Minister to act legally. Indeed, it is well known that countersigning presidential documents in a period of *fait majoritaire* is not a problem because there is no opposition within the Council of Ministers. It is the core of the bicephalous organised executive. Both heads sign the acts of the executive during the meetings of the Council of Ministers. In 'synchronised functioning', the two heads have similar wills and present unified opinions. This of course differs from the practices of the former Republics, where the President was not associated with the important decisions. There is no ambiguity here: the head of state is the decision-maker and the Prime Minister follows.

The appointment and dismissal of government members, under article 8, paragraph 2, is presented as something the President does with the help of the Prime Minister. In fact, in the *fait majoritaire*, the head of state chooses the ministers and removes them, not the Prime Minister. The same may be said about article 13, paragraph 1, of the Constitution, or the understanding of articles 15 and 21. Article 13 states that government regulations are taken during the Council of Ministers. The initiative is left to ministers and the discussion is collegial, with the President only signing government regulations. In a situation of *fait majoritaire*, the President interferes. This is due to the absence of separation between President and government in that situation: the President truly decides. It was clear in the case of Debré and De Gaulle on the matter of Algeria for instance. Every decision and all initiatives were coming from De Gaulle, to the extent that when De Gaulle modified his view on whether Algeria should remain French or not, Debré had to adapt and comply.[49] On article 15 and 21, it was noted above that the President is the head of the army, but the Prime Minister (and in some respects the Defence Minister) also shares competences in this area. In a situation of *fait majoritaire* the latter are mere executants of the presidential will and lose all freedom to act on their own initiative. That is not the case in a period of non-synchronisation.

1.4.3 *Non-synchronisation based on political factors*

Non-synchronisation occurs when the directly elected head of state and the majority of the directly elected lower chamber are from different political sides. *Cohabitation* is the opposite to *fait majoritaire* and, in that situation, the system of government is closer to a prototype of the parliamentary system of government. Professor Chapsal, in her comments on cohabitation stressed that:

> Everything seems to indicate the President of the Republic behaved like the Queen of Great Britain, that it was impossible for him to do otherwise and that the mechanism of the Fifth Republic fell from presidentialism to parliamentarism.[50]

It seems that the matter is somewhat mechanical, or simply a question of timing. Again, the President's term of office was seven years and that of the other directly elected institution, the National Assembly, was five years. In a classical parliamentary regime, the term of office of the head of state does not really matter vis-à-vis that of the head of government. Indeed, in a system that has no two-headed executive, there would be no problem with a lower chamber shifting to the opposition, because a divergence of political opinion between the head of government and a President would not really matter. In the case of the Fifth Republic, the bicephalous executive makes the political opinions of the two executive heads extremely important. In situations of non-synchronisation, the Prime Minister is either the leader or a strong figurehead for the party or coalition leading the directly elected chamber. In that case, the two-headed executive is no longer synchronised. The non-synchronisation may appear to disrupt the system and to be incoherent according to the strong leadership 'atmosphere' established by De Gaulle (hence the comments made on the qualification of normal and abnormal functionings of the Constitution). Then again, even with a President confined to his constitutional powers, because of the direct election, the Head of State remains a strong leader, the figurehead, the incarnation of the country. This theoretical situation nearly became a reality in 1967 and 1978 before becoming actual reality in the 1980s and 1990s.

It was expected that the March 1967 general election would be won by the opposition and that a majority hostile to De Gaulle would be returned, though in the end a very small majority supporting the President was elected. In 1978, everyone was waiting for the Left to win the general election. If it was clear in 1967 that De Gaulle would not remain President if he had to face a hostile National Assembly, Valéry Giscard d'Estaing was prepared to remain in place and therefore to create an opportunity for the first instance of non-synchronisation. Losing a general election demonstrates that a party and somehow its leader has lost the support of the people and that there is a disenchantment with how the country is ruled. De Gaulle would certainly have resigned, respecting 'his' interpretation of the Constitution and the will of the people. What is striking here is how the two dates of March 1967 (general elections) and May 1968 (the events) relate.[51] One may analyse this relation through the notion of rigidity: no political change might trigger the people to protest and march the streets. Then again, as the executive was facing a time of uncertainly, one may have considered a resignation, even without 'losing' the general election that would perhaps have brought about a left-wing President. Of course, this left-wing President may have needed to accept governing alongside an opponent assembly. But this is of course only a supposition. The only comment that remains to be made about this 'missed' cohabitation is the necessity for equilibrium within the institutions. The price to pay for absent cross-party dialogue, perhaps for real democratic debate, is the outburst of public demonstration: the people protest when confronted by the absence of mediation the political institutions are supposed to bring. The second possibility offered by non-synchronisation is an executive with two opposing leaders. It did not come about in 1967, nor in 1978, although the President was ready for non-synchronisation. The first occurrence of two opposing leaders came about in 1986, followed by two variations in 1993 and 1997.

1.4.3.1   A left-wing President facing a right-wing Prime Minister for a short period of time

The party of President Mitterrand lost the general election twice, each time within two years of the end of his term of office. On 16 March 1986,[52] Mitterrand lost the support of the lower chamber; the general election was won by a right-wing coalition (the RPR–UDF) led by Chirac. Mitterrand did not resign but appointed Chirac as head of government, who remained in place until the presidential election of 1988. The general elections of 21 and 28 March 1993 also returned a right-wing majority. The Parti Socialiste (PS) won only 56 seats (17.5 per cent of the vote). During this period 1993–5, Mitterrand appointed Edouard Balladur – Chirac preferring 'semi-retirement' to prepare for the presidential elections of 1995.

1.4.3.2   A right-wing President facing a left-wing Prime Minister for a long period of time

Chirac won the 1995 election. He had strong support from the National Assembly which had been elected in 1993. He could contemplate another three years at least without any political problem. However, in 1997, Chirac decided to dissolve the National Assembly and called for a general election. He subsequently lost his supporting majority. This triggered the beginning of the longest period of non-synchronisation, 1997–2002. Lionel Jospin became Prime Minister and remained in this position until the 2002 presidential election.[53]

Political disagreement within the executive may have an impact on constitutional practice in many ways. The functioning of the Constitution described in situations of synchronisation is mirrored in non-synchronisation: the President loses many of his powers. In any case, strong presidential leadership remained on matters of external sovereignty. Diplomatic matters and defence are part of the so called 'presidential domain'. This was certainly the case during the ongoing crises in Lebanon and Chad in 1986. But President Mitterrand certainly emphasised the pre-eminence of the President in regard to international relations. He was in charge of the many external crises such as the withdrawal of French soldiers from Lebanon and the arrival of soldiers in the Gulf region in 1987. Mitterrand was the main actor in these crises, not his Prime Minister Chirac. Under article 13, paragraph 1, the President may decide to block the work of the government by using constitutionally discretionary powers to sign delegated legislation *ordonnances*. François Mitterrand decided to refuse to sign three *ordonnances*.[54] This non-synchronisation creates an interesting situation that departs from the constitutional *gaullienne* vision of the Fifth Republic. That said, the forecast risk of a major institutional crisis under non-synchronised functioning of the institutions did not prove to be real. There were political tensions and uncertainty but the Constitution was proven at that time to be simultaneously rigid and yet flexible in its application. The Constitution was to remain an optimum text for a French Republic, in comparison to the other four, allowing *alternance* in 1981 and allowing a dissonant executive in 1986, 1993 and 1997, proving at the same time its solid but flexible nature in resisting a reading which was not the one intended in 1958.

Cohabitation has been characterised as being a strange situation in the institutional arrangement. It was a move from a sort of non-institutional equilibrium during synchronisation (a time when we see the people/nation as the sole counterweight of the power when the two directly elected institutions are from the same political side), to an institutional equilibrium (non-synchronisation, when the counterweight is formed within the executive itself). The non-synchronisation is in fact the return to a parliamentary system of government that, incidentally, provides for more influence of the people. One may see at least one obvious result of non-synchronisation: the electorate sees a tangible consequence of its will at the end of election day: it sees a change. Non-synchronisation may therefore characterise what the philosopher Alain considered as power against power.[55]

Strangely, and perhaps against all odds, the consequence of an apparent non-synchronised functioning of the institutions is the evidence of a more democratic functioning of those institutions. Perhaps *cohabitation* may have been the victim of comments touching more the individuals in charge than exclusively the institutions. For instance, the relationship between Chirac and Valéry Giscard d'Estaing between 1974 and 1976 was very turbulent. One may attribute this to a non-synchronisation within the executive. A similar explanation may be given to the relationship between Mitterrand and Rocard between 1988 and 1991.[56] But these types of non-synchronisation have more to do with a problem of personality rather than an institutional non-synchronisation in times of *cohabitation*. Indeed, what has always been important was that non-synchronisation was presented as an abnormal situation, a situation that needed to be identified and dealt with, hence the changes that occurred in 2000.

We should emphasise again the aspect of normality and abnormality here. A 'normal situation' should characterise the 'normal' reading of the Constitution. Therefore, an abnormal situation is the one of non-synchronisation. It may be easy to characterise the differences between synchronised and non-synchronised situations by this simple statement: a synchronised situation is a reading of the Constitution that conforms to General de Gaulle's interpretation while a non-synchronised situation is simply a reading of the Constitution that conforms to a parliamentary system of government. What is perceived as a normal reading of the Constitution negatively defines the other reading, the abnormal one, and then implies that the abnormality should disappear: no one wants to discuss it and everything has been done to redress it, through forced synchronisation.

1.4.4 Forced synchronisation based on a constitutional amendment

The motivation behind the modification of the Constitution in 2000 was clear: to avoid at all costs all non-synchronisations. This change focused on the mandate of the President, reducing it to five years to align it with the tenure of the members of the National Assembly. In that respect, it was necessary, after the 2000 amendment, to alter the end of the term of office of the deputies. As explained, the French parliament may legislate to complete the Constitution through *loi organique*, special statutes that detail particular articles of the Constitution. In 2001, it was decided to extend the term of office of the deputies by eleven weeks, to allow legislative elections to take place after the presidential election.[57] Article L.O. 121 of the *Code électoral* was modified consequently. The general elections were planned a few weeks before the presidential election, on 24 March 2002, and the presidential election was to be held on 14 or 21 April 2002. The spirit or logic of the institutional arrangement was carefully considered.[58] In the light of the 2000 constitutional evolution, it was considered illogical to set the elections for directly elected members of parliament before the presidential election. The *Conseil constitutionnel* was consulted on the matter.[59] It has been clear from the beginning of the Fifth Republic that the presidential election is the key moment of French political and constitutional life: 'because of the place of the election of the President of the Republic by direct universal suffrage in the functioning of the Fifth Republic'.[60] It was explained that it was logical for the general election to follow the presidential one, in accordance with the 'normal' reading of the Constitution that implied the requirement for a *fait majoritaire*. In fact, 'it was desirable that the presidential election precedes, as a general rule, the legislative elections and that this rule should be applied to the presidential election foreseen in 2002.'[61] Everything was organised to obtain a synchronised chronology: first electing the President, then electing the National Assembly. That said, some possibilities for non-synchronisation were more or less disregarded, for instance the dissolution of the Assembly and the resignation or the death of the President.[62] But these possibilities were deemed to be somehow limited and without any major effect on the President's strong position. Indeed, only the President would be able to activate the end of the synchronisation, those reinforcing its power. In addition, even if a non-synchronisation did occur, it would be limited to a short cohabitation. Since 2002, this has led to a forced synchronisation.

This is the new situation, the situation of all presidents since 2002. In 2002, Chirac was elected with a very large majority because he was facing the extreme right candidate Le Pen. A 'republican front' was built around Chirac that would also lead to the success of the right at the 2002 general election. An ally of the new President, Raffarin, became Prime Minister. He was definitely the secretary of the President and not a strong personality. The bicephalous executive was back to 'normal'. Even when De Villepin was appointed after the defeat of the referendum on the European Constitutional Treaty which cost Raffarin his job, the functioning of the institutions was strongly semi-presidential. The only opposition the President had to face came from within his own supporters. Future President Nicolas Sarkozy took over the presidential party and became its leader while being a member of the government, although not its chief. Further examples of pure synchronisation are of course 2007 and 2012. When Sarkozy was elected President in 2007, journalists and scholars very quickly named the newly elected President the 'hyper-President' or 'omni-President'.[63] Sarkozy, who was a young President, contrasted with Chirac in many ways, primarily because he was younger and adopted a different style. Badiou, a French philosopher, was sarcastic about the Chirac years in an article published in *Le Monde*, comparing Chirac to Brezhnev.[64] Chirac was pictured as the caretaker of the system rather than someone who took action. This particular method of ruling made him look like a President of the Third or Fourth Republic, closer to the pure French model of a parliamentary regime, but at the same time it made him very distant and more like a monarch. But this is also a way of dealing with the forced synchronisation that resulted from the 2000 revision. Sarkozy declared not long after his election that 'Je l'avais rêvé, je le mets en œuvre'[65] (I dreamt it, I will do it), and the message is, further, that 'he will do it'. He mentioned that he would take decisions – hence the journalists' nicknamed him 'hyper-President', 'omni-President' or even, for some scholars, 'téléprésident', someone who has taken over all the media and is governing through the permanent use of radio and television. But if one looks at this way of conducting the State as corresponding to an excessive *gaullienne* reading of the Constitution, then the very proactive behaviour of the President served to increase this perception. Both the 2007 and 2012 presidential elections were followed, of course, by the legislative elections, and because of the closeness of the two, no one would have predicted a sudden reversal of the majority over this period. President Sarkozy led his UMP party to a massive victory in the lower chamber of the French parliament while François Hollande had the PS and other left-wing parties including the ecologists in the same position in 2012. The majority returned in both directly elected institutions was naturally similar in both cases. But even though this was a result of the 2000 amendment, it was done artificially by a little twist in the chronology of the two elections. It seems that the newly elected Presidents had their own, somewhat similar, interpretation of the (new) reading of the text. Notably, both Presidents obliged all appointed ministers to face the public vote. As the presidential and general elections are now 'locked', the Presidents appointed their governments after the presidential election. The new ministers were forced by the Presidents to campaign to get a seat in the lower chamber of parliament. One minister, the former Prime Minister under Chirac and Mayor of Bordeaux, Alain Juppé, lost in his attempt to be elected deputy. He had to resign from his position of minister.[66] Juppé clarified the new rule: 'I will present as soon as tomorrow morning my resignation to the President and the Prime Minister.'[67] He returned as Foreign Secretary at the end of the President's term. It was the same for the government of J. M. Ayrault in May 2012.[68] The practice introduced by Sarkozy has then been respected, though not his attempt to open the government to non-members of the UMP or close allies. Sarkozy asked eminent figures of the opposition to join his team at different levels. Firstly, he appointed some as members of government. The best example of this opening up is the appointment of Bernard Kouchner as Minister of French Foreign and European Affairs, assisted by Jospin's ex-cabinet director, Jean-Pierre Jouyet. But also to be found here are the former national secretary of the socialist party (PS) Eric Besson (*Secrétaire d'État à la Prospective et l'Évaluation des politiques publiques*), and the President of Emmaüs, Martin Hirsch (*Haut commissaire aux solidarités actives contre la pauvreté*). Secondly, Sarkozy appointed the socialist Didier Migaud as Chair of the Finance Commission. Also, Sarkozy put others forward as candidates for a variety of positions (the former socialist finance minister Strauss-Kahn was appointed Chair of the IMF; former socialist education and culture minister Lang was made vice-chair of the *Comité de réflexion et de proposition sur la modernisation et le rééquilibrage des institutions de la Vème République*;[69] Jacques Attali, one of Mitterand's ex-counsellors, was appointed Chair of the *Commission de réflexion 'pour la libération de la croissance française'*). In addition, Sarkozy decided to work on the reform of the institutions, to 'modernise' them. The *Comité de réflexion et de proposition sur la modernisation et le rééquilibrage des institutions de la Vème République* was officially set up by the President on 18 July 2007. The committee delivered its report on 30 October 2007, which included 77 propositions. President Sarkozy conducted a constitutional revision that was approved by the parliament meeting in *Congrès* on 21 July 2008.

The synchronisation, forced by legal means, by legal texts, appears to have been 'corrected' by the will of the newly elected Presidents. Since 2002, two ways have been found to deal with it. The first is 'attentist'. This characterises the 'non-action' of Chirac. It positions the President closer to the neutral personage of the Third and Fourth Republics while allowing a strict interpretation of the revised Constitution. The second way is 'proactive'. This characterises the energetic reading of the Constitution practised by Sarkozy and followed to some degree by his left-wing successor Hollande. The President is or at least appears to be 'doing something' all the time or nearly all the time (like F. Hollande).

In conclusion, it seems that this situation cannot be left to the letter of the text of the Constitution. In its current version, after an amendment drafted during the non-synchronisation period to avoid the 'abnormality' of the 'non-synchronisation', the Constitution forces a democratic game that might destroy democracy by concentrating all the institutions in the hand of the presidential party. What was perhaps not foreseen was the eventuality of trouble with the Senate. The Senate changed political side in 2011 after the senate elections as the majority returned was a left-wing one. The French parliament then had one chamber from each political side, creating a nice balance in the legislative body. But even after the victory of the left in 2012 (in the presidential and general elections), troubles in the Senate have not eased because of a more than usual fragmented left-wing majority. Of course, under the current Constitution, the Prime Minister is accountable only to the National Assembly and not to the Senate. Therefore a Senate in the hands of the political opposition affects neither the political institutions nor the dual executive, in the same way as it would if the National Assembly was. That said, should a non-synchronisation occur, the opposed Senate is poised to delay the legislative process.

1.5 Towards a postmodern (or second modern) system of government?

This chapter has analysed the true nature of the Fifth French Republic through the revisions, evolutions and dynamics of the Constitution. To conclude, the functioning of the Constitution of the French Fifth Republic does not match the intention of its creators. On the one hand, 1958 was to be the start of a system with a President monarch, a referee, *un arbitre*, legitimated by strong constitutional presidential powers, together with a parliamentary regime aided by a rationalised parliament and a strong Prime

Minister. Oscillating between synchronised and non-synchronised situations, the original logic saw the head of state becoming a leader, moving to a more 'normal' parliamentary regime President (although conserving certain strong powers on everything that touched the external relation, and strongly resisting the will of the Prime Minister on every possible occasion).

There is no doubt that the French head of state is one of the most powerful positions given by any Constitution currently in force. However, it remains the strong leadership of a State in transition. Three factors may help to illustrate this view.

First, the emergence of a transnational society in Europe is contributing to a radical change in the structure of the relationship between the people or nation and its governing body. Second, the French Republic has been facing structural economic problems for decades, which undermine the way the system has recently developed. Third, there is a clear decline of the nation-state concept, and of the parliament as the real legislative body – particularly the elected chamber as an institution that clearly represents the people.

There is also, finally, the deeply rooted reference to the leader, the 'father of the horde', of 'the group'. Since the decapitation of Louis XVI, there has been a succession of political systems of government oscillating between having a strong leader and not. Particularly since 1870, the position of the leader has been dramatically diminished by successive constitutions. De Gaulle believed in following the path of 'restoring' the authority of the leader. Rather than 'really killing' the head of state, in a democratic society the head of state has to be symbolically 'killed' via regular elections. In that respect the 1962, 2000 and, in a way, 2008 amendments of the Constitution meant that the people would have more opportunities to do so. The 2008 change goes even further, obliging the 'father' to step down after ten years. We might have to watch the future carefully to see whether or not the 'circulation' of Presidents happens in reality, as if it does not, 'the group' may not be happy and show its discontent as it did in 1968 and 2005. De Gaulle when re-elected in 1965 replaced himself; 'the group' protested in 1968. Chirac, re-elected in 2002, again replaced himself; 'the group' protested in 2005.

The difficulty in relation to the Constitution of the Fifth Republic lies in merging and linking every aspect of French history. It is a text of consensus – a settlement where the position of the leader is similar to that of a clan that recalls the memory of a strong figurehead, power and God, while the parliament remains the rational institutionalised democratic side of the Republic. It is a difficult game that has proved so far to have been, nevertheless, long lasting. In this chapter, I have analysed one of the main features of the Fifth Republic Constitution, the semi-presidential system of government. I have considered how the system has evolved since the promulgation of the Constitution in 1958. In Chapter 2 I propose to explore the new rights added to the preamble, with the 2004 Charter for the Environment as an illustration of the way environmental issues affect the dynamic of the Constitution.

2 The greening of the French Republic

The constitutionalisation of the environment[1]

2.1 A new French bill of (environmental) rights

In 2005, France completed the long and interesting process of elaboration of a new 'bill of rights' which was then incorporated into the material Constitution via a constitutional amendment. On Monday, 28 February 2005, the Fifth Republic Constitution was modified. Two texts were presented on the same day to the members of the French Parliament meeting in its 'constitutional' form, the *Congrès*.[2] The first constitutional bill contained four articles with a proposal for the modification of articles 88-1, 88-5 and title XV of the Constitution.[3] The second bill concerned the introduction of a reference to the *Charte de l'environnement*, the Charter for the Environment,[4] in the Preamble of the Constitution.[5] The two proposed amendments were very interesting in their nature, substance and outcome. The first bill was submitted as a prerequisite to the referendum on the ratification of the Treaty establishing a Constitution for Europe. This first modification of the Constitution was successful,[6] the European Treaty was dramatically rejected by the French people.[7] The second modification also passed.[8] I aim here to show that the outcome of this amendment was indeed very successful, creating a nice symmetry with the resounding failure of the former amendment. In this chapter, I will discuss the evolution of the expected outcomes of the Charter, and highlight its unforeseen but arguably welcome implications.

The constitutionalisation of environmental issues has been considered in many international and European constitutions. If we concentrate only on European constitutions,[9] we find a rather eclectic catalogue of levels of consideration given to environmental issues. The Spanish Constitution, for example, recognises, in article 45, the right to enjoy an environment appropriate to the development of the person, and the duty to preserve it. It places a general duty on public authorities to have this principle respected and through article 53, the duty is extended to the legislative power.[10] In the Italian Constitution we find a broader style of protection, through the fundamental right to health encapsulated in its article 32. While the Portuguese Constitution presents a right to have one's health safeguarded (article 64), and a right to a healthy and ecologically balanced human environment (article 66), both articles include detailed mechanisms to defend these rights.[11] The German Constitution considers, in article 20a, the fundamental protection of the basis of life,[12] while the Greek Constitution lists, in article 24, many considerations for the environment, the primary one being inserted in the beginning of paragraph 1: the protection of the natural and cultural environment constitutes an obligation of the state.[13] What is primarily noticeable here is the proposed method of including environmental issues within the constitutional texts. An environmental 'bill of rights' does not appear to have been the way chosen by any other European country except France and this will be examined in detail later.

France has often been seen as leading the debate in the promotion of rights, as it did in the eighteenth century with the Declaration of the Rights of Man and of the Citizen, and in the nineteenth century with its *Code civil*. With the Charter, France has entered a new era in its arrangement of its constitutional norms. In Europe, it has more or less become classical nowadays to see Constitutions generally 'located' at the apex of the hierarchy of norms while a mechanism of validity obliges inferior norms to respect superior ones. Supreme or constitutional courts ensure the respect of the fundamental norms by inferior courts and frame the work of the legislature. The Fifth Republic Constitution followed that trend while departing from those of the previous Republics in two ways that are of interest to this chapter: first, the weakening of the Parliament, and second, the creation of a constitutional court, the *Conseil constitutionnel*. The two combined meant that the Constitution was put at the apex of the hierarchy of norms in France. As previously mentioned, since 1958, a bill can be referred to the *Conseil constitutionnel* for constitutional control.[14] Since 1971,[15] the *Conseil constitutionnel* has extended its jurisdiction beyond the articles of the Constitution. It recognised as part of a *bloc de constitutionnalité*[16] a corpus of constitutional norms, the Preamble of the 1958 Constitution, itself referring to the former declaration of rights, and public and civil liberties.[17] As it stands, an addition to the Preamble is sufficient to extend the *bloc de constitutionnalité*, i.e. the constitutional norms. This is precisely what has been done by the 2005 constitutional amendment. From that point, the reference to the Charter in the Preamble, as it does for the other bill of rights (the 1789 Declaration and the 1946 Constitution Preamble),[18] allows the *Conseil constitutionnel* to review the constitutionality of a statute. Bills containing provisions which could be in breach of the Charter will be censured and never enacted. This is also the case of promulgated statutes since the 2008 constitutional amendment. Finally, one could foresee a great development of the entire framework of French environmental law. The addition of a new 'bill of rights', consecrating environmental issues in the Constitution, was supposed to change and influence the legislative quality of the acts of the French parliament, mainly as an instrument of constitutional control. What is very important in matters of constitutional rights is how these can be enforced. Indeed, declarations of rights are of course a right step forward for a governing body. That said, even though these are important, having one or more mechanisms to give them concrete protection is a more efficient way to ensure respect for the rule of law. It now seems that the influence of the Charter has surpassed all hopes. After an interesting historical development, what was supposed to be a rather dull document, a mere addendum to the French Constitution, appears to have had a far greater impact than was initially expected.

2.2 The interesting historical development of the Charter

The Charter had a rather unusual conception. The other two French bills of rights were adopted by representatives of the nation assembled in constituent form without much preliminary consultation. Both were 'top-down' documents, designed by a certain political elite and driven by political and philosophical considerations of the time. In the case of the Charter, a mixed procedure was used, with 'bottom-up' elements associating citizens with the process.

2.2.1 On the elaboration of the Charter

President Chirac was the initiator of this new 'bill of rights'. During his first term of office,[19] he indicated in a speech in Orleans in 2001 his desire for an environmental Charter.

> 'A new and vast ambition is imposed on everybody, and particularly on us: to make France a new crucible of this new ethic and new way of life for the 21st century. To enshrine a humanist ecology at the heart of our republican pact.'[20]

During the 2002 presidential election campaign, environmental protection was one of the major issues of Chirac's candidacy. Five points were particularly developed in his programme. Primarily, Chirac presented the preparation of a Charter for the Environment that would rest upon the Constitution and would comprise five fundamental principles: prevention, precaution, responsibility, integration and, finally, information and participation. Then there was the idea of the creation of a departmental minister of ecology and sustainable development, making sustainable development an important mission of the State. In addition, Chirac proposed the creation of a World Environment Organisation that would be able to act as a counterweight to the World Trade Organisation (WTO). Furthermore, he then suggested special procedures for regulating the introduction of Genetically Modified Organisms (GMOs), similar to those used in the pharmaceutical industry. Also mentioned was the more specific issue of burying power lines, and finally the teaching of ecology, or perhaps more accurately an ecological consciousness, in schools.[21]

Immediately after his electoral success in 2002, President Chirac began the implementation of his programme. On 5 June that year, the elaboration process of the Charter was launched. The process itself would turn out to be a peculiar one in the French context. Three weeks later, on 26 June, a commission was established under the authority of the Prime Minister. Professor Coppens, a scientist, was appointed as chair of this committee to supervise the proceedings.[22] From October 2002 to April 2003, national and local public consultations began through the use of surveys, Internet fora and webchat services. From January to March 2003 proper *assises territoriales*, local meetings, were organised.

On 8 April 2003, the Coppens Commission produced a draft of the Charter which was submitted to the government as a working document. This draft proposal of a constitutional bill was adopted in the *Conseil des Ministres* on 25 June 2003 and sent to parliament for adoption.[23] The bill was then successfully passed in the National Assembly on 1 June 2004,[24] and in the Senate three weeks later on 24 June.[25] On 18 February 2005, President Chirac initiated the final part of the process for a constitutional amendment by convening the *Congrès*, which subsequently approved it while modifying the Fifth Republic Constitution on 28 February 2005.[26]

Not only the design of the Charter but also its position within the constitutional norms had a symbolic significance. The Charter was written and approved as a separate text, which was then referred to in a constitutional amendment. Furthermore, reference to the Charter was not introduced in the articles of the Constitution but in the Preamble of the Constitution. Both the 'how' and 'where' were a clear statement of the wish for continuity in the French tradition of a written 'bill of rights'. The constitutional history of France shows a long list of new 'bills of rights' inserted at the beginning of the text (the First and Fourth French Republics for example) or within the text (the Second French Republic) of the French constitutions. In 1958, the idea was to present a concise text with the ability to 'open it up' and amend it where necessary. The text was mainly organising the political institutions. This was necessary after the collapse of the Fourth Republic. The Fifth Republic Constitution did not present a Preamble with a 'bill of rights'. The constituents in 1958 chose instead to make a reference to historically important bills. Even if the Preamble and the articles of the Constitution are both considered by the *Conseil constitutionnel*[27] as being 'the' constitutional norm, it would have been possible to place the Charter within the corpus of articles of the Constitution itself. However, inserting it in the Preamble was instead chosen, maintaining the wishes of the original constituents of 1958.

The Charter is the first 'bill of rights' that has been developed since 1946. It has now become a 'third pillar' of rights. Environmental rights are now enshrined within the Preamble of the French Constitution (and in consequence within the French constitutional norm) with the idea that these constitutional rights are rights of man. The Preamble, like the Constitution, is simple and precise. The rights of man are those of the liberal rights of the 1789 Declaration. The socio-economic rights of the 1946 Constitution Preamble and the environmental rights of the Charter for the Environment of 2004 complete the 1789 Declaration. The Charter is an investment in and for the future, a sort of 'short circuit that opens the present on the future',[28] to use an expression of Gilles Deleuze. The Charter is supposed to help us now to build a better future. Indeed, the philosophical substance of the Charter is very significant.

2.2.2 On the philosophical substance of the Charter

Theoretically, two major philosophical currents have contributed to the environmental narratives: the 'biocentric deep' ecology and the 'anthropocentric humanist' one. As explained by Dominique Bourg, there are three scenarios of socio-political organisation. The first is considered to be a fundamentalist scenario based on biocentric deep ecology. The second and the third scenarios are, on the contrary, anthropocentric humanist ones. The second or authoritarian scenario prescribes 'a tyranny benevolent and well informed'[29] while the third or democratic scenario follows the sustainable development framework defined by the Brundtland Report. The will of the constituents in 2005 was for the Charter to complete the 1789 Declaration. As such, it ensures the continuity of the French liberal tradition. The objectives, rules and rights of man listed in its seven *considérants* and ten articles therefore illustrate the humanist side of the document. In considering this, the *beau texte*, the 'nice text', requested by President Chirac definitely departs from the 'deep ecology' and its fundamentalist scenario.[30] Indeed, President Chirac considered that 'To choose humanist ecology, that's a step towards putting man at the centre of all projects and that allows him the responsibility of his destiny.'[31]

The clues that may help us to look at the Charter as anthropocentric is the reference made to mankind (*homme* and *humanité*), the description of the environment as a common patrimony of humanity, the wording similar to that used within the Universal Declaration of Human Rights,[32] and, finally, the mention of sustainable development incorporating Principle 1 of the Rio Declaration. There is, of course, the will of the constituents to create a liberal document that would tend to follow the democratic scenario. If we further analyse the five points that Chirac listed in his speech in 2002, two contain insights that are strongly open to the dialectic of the anthropocentric movement of political ecology. The first point is the teaching of ecology at school and the other is the writing of the Charter itself. Translated into the scenarios of political ecology and linked to the French republican tradition, the teaching relates to the authoritarian scenario, while the idea of a 'bill of rights' relates to the democratic scenario.[33]

2.2.2.1 *Education*

Education has always been considered a very high priority in France strongly related to the French Revolution and national unity. The French Revolution was primarily conceived as a 'revolution of the mind'. And indeed, it was a necessity for the republicans in 1789, to ensure for the continuity of their ideas, to affirm and reaffirm these permanently. The 1791 Constitution (the first post-revolution Constitution) considered education as fundamental. Undeniably, education was considered the foundation stone of the republican future, underpinning language and nationalism. One nation, one language. So to unify the nation, and to provide a single communication medium for the French revolutionary army, all local dialects had to disappear. Public education was linked to the unity of the French nation via the French language. One may therefore understand why education has always been an exclusive competence of the central State.[34] As a consequence, it was never transferred to sub-national (local) authorities, and it was always an aid to the dogmatic development of French republicanism. Historically, it was at school that the ideas and ideals of the Republic were (and in a way still are) taught through an official curriculum, preached by the primary school teachers, the *instituteurs*, elements of a monolithic centralised system of education.[35] The *instituteurs* have always been ambivalent, part teacher, part 'soldier'. Their function is broader than simply teaching. Education for the Republic is something crucial that propagates the humanist ideas of the Revolution. As Charles Péguy claimed, the *instituteurs* became the representatives of humanity, *représentant de l'humanité*. But, during the French Third Republic, they were also known as the *hussard noir de la République*, a metaphor of the Napoleonic soldiers that was applied to the teaching staff of the Republic.[36] In fact, the teachers were in charge of educating the minds of new generations, as the Republic came from the French Revolution, the revolution of the mind. But educating the mind for the French Third Republic meant creating the ultimate republican, even if it could be seen as a rather authoritarian creation of a republican culture. Military discourse and the violence of imposing French as a unique language made education in some ways authoritarian. The Charter incorporated education and formation in article 8 and the promotion of a sustainable development in article 6.[37] Chirac's proposal made during the 2002 campaign was to introduce the teaching of ecology at school. Even before the Charter was crowned as a constitutional text, its philosophical principles became a reference for the French department of education.[38] During the summer of 2004, instructions were given to civil servants in charge of education from *recteurs d'académie* (chief education officers) to head teachers of primary and secondary educational institutions on the application of article 8 of the Charter to 'generalise the education on the environment for a sustainable development from the academic year 2004'.[39] Environmental education (the programme 'EEDD') became a main priority and a fundamental public policy of the French Republic and is now considered an important part of the curriculum of French primary and secondary schools.

Hence, environmental issues now form part of French republican values that have to be taught to future generations. So, according to the tradition of 'metaphoric military aspects of education' (only primary and secondary education), the French Republic is pushing, forcing, environmental issues on the youngest members of the population. One may consider this a noble act, but it may also be said that this implies an authoritarian vision of environmental protection when linked to the French educational tradition. There is, therefore, in the discourse of the candidate Chirac a contradiction. While it respects the French liberal tradition and strongly roots the Charter in the anthropocentric scenario, it falls between an authoritarian and a democratic approach.

2.2.2.2 *Writing the Charter*

As mentioned, in Chirac's programme for the environment, the Charter was meant to take into consideration five 'environmental principles' (prevention, precautionary, responsibility, integration, information and participation) that philosophically relate to the Brundtland Report.[40] The incorporation of the Charter into the constitutional norms of the Fifth French Republic intended that these principles, and particularly the prevention principle and the precautionary principle, were to be elevated from legal rights to constitutional rights. The anthropocentric Charter introduced a hierarchy in environmental principles. The prevention principle is now considered an objective of constitutional value while the precautionary principle is the (unique) principle of constitutional value. It seems that since 1982, the *Conseil constitutionnel* refers to *principes à valeur constitutionnel* and *objectifs à valeur constitutionnel*. For Professor F. Luchaire, the principles of constitutional value are directly applicable and can be invoked by an individual before a court while objectives of constitutional value are imposed on the legislative power but are never directly invoked before a court.[41] The precautionary principle is set at the top of the hierarchy. It is considered specifically in article 5 of the Charter as a 'principle' (principle of constitutional value) and has been a part of the French legal order since 1992, after the 'integration' of Principle 15 of the Rio Declaration into French law.[42] Article L.110-1.1° of the Environmental Code considers that under the precautionary principle

> The absence of certainty, based on current scientific and technical knowledge, must not delay the adoption of effective and proportionate measures aiming to prevent a risk of serious and irreversible damage to the environment at an economically acceptable cost.[43]

The precautionary principle also receives a proper definition within the Charter.

> Even if scientific knowledge is uncertain where damages occur which could have serious and irreversible effects on their environment, public

authorities shall within their own domains of competences, apply the precautionary principle through the implementation of procedures for the evaluation of risks, and the adoption of provisional and proportionate measures in order to prevent the damage occurring.

As such this declared right is more a duty of public authorities, with a limited scope. As stated, the procedure of evaluation of risks and the adoption of provisional and proportionate measures should avoid the occurrence of damage. What is rather interesting is how the text of the Charter is balanced here. The principle of constitutional value – the precautionary principle – concerns only public authorities. This diminishes its scope dramatically. Article 3 of the Charter outlines the prevention principle without referring to it as a 'principle'. (It is instead considered an objective of constitutional value – see Table 2.1 below.[44])

> Everyone shall, within the limits imposed by Statute Law, prevent possible damages to the environment one may create or, failing that, limit their consequences.

However, its scope is very large as it appears to apply to everyone, blurring in that case the border between right and duty, as does also the new responsibility objective (article 4):

> Everyone shall contribute to repairing damages one causes to the environment, within the limits imposed by Law.

If we look at articles 3 and 4, the two 'objectives of constitutional value', responsibility and the precautionary principle, are not as explicit and developed as the 'principle of constitutional value', the prevention principle, included in article 5. Then again it may be noted that there is a different scope, which balances this lack of precision. The two articles mention 'everyone shall' and therefore are applicable to everyone, again blurring the thin line between rights and duties. In concrete terms, if one uses the example of GMO experimentation, there is a strong possibility an experiment conducted by a public authority may be considered in breach of article 5 but not if it is conducted by a private company.[45] The Charter was never meant to be only a philosophical document. It was supposed to be a concrete legal text that only concerns a bill submitted to constitutional control and not any other type of legal action. In fact the philosophical document proved to be more complex than expected and its legal outcome more wide reaching.

2.3 From an expected impact to multiple impacts on the French legal system

During the legislative debate, members of the assemblies predicted that incorporating a new bill of rights into the numerous French constitutional

Table 2.1 Effects of the Charter

Political effects/unclear legal effects	Declaratory effects	Preamble paras 1, 2, 4 and 5
	Operational effects	Preamble para. 3 Articles 8 to 10
Clear legal effects	Objectives of constitutional values	Preamble, paras 6 and 7 Articles 1 to 7
	Principle of constitutional values	Article 5

Source: N. Chahid-Nouraï, 'La portée de la Charte pour le juge ordinaire', *AJDA Chroniques*, 2005, p. 1175 (trans. and ed. the author).

norms would increase the scope of constitutional control. This was the first bill since 1946, a bill that would be added to the other two. It was a complex bill, not only declaring at the same time rights and duties but also considering new areas of rights protection. The belief was mainly that the scope of control of the *Conseil constitutionnel* would be enlarged. This was a consequence of the idea that the Preamble of the Charter was specifically supposed to serve as a guide for control. There has been, in fact, a diversity of impact during the first years of application as authors commented that some articles (like articles 8, 9 and 10) would have no legal effects, while articles 1 to 7 would.[46] The diversity of impact is strongly related to the differences in the substance of the rights incorporated in the Charter (see Table 2.1).

2.3.1 *Political effects/unclear legal effects*

President Chirac, in his speech on the first anniversary of the promulgation of the Charter, spoke precisely about the difference between unclear and clear legal effects. On political/unclear legal effects, Chirac mentioned article 8 and discussed its educational importance. He declared that:

> Because it engages our future, the Charter needs to be known by everyone but first by the youngest. It will be studied at school, within an educational programme on environment, generalised since 2004.[47]

The Charter is a document with broad aspects, the primary one being that of a guide for institutions, particularly the French parliament and government. The political/unclear legal effects of the Charter are seen a priori, in the decisions, acts and during policy-making processes of the administration.[48]

> At large, the Charter for the Environment demands all public policies to integrate the need for sustainable development and must be taken into consideration throughout the preparation of texts.[49]

What the scholars have described as political/unclear legal effects are followed by what may be defined as clear legal effects.

2.3.2 Clear legal effects

It was manifest from the start that the principles of the Charter were always meant to guide the legislative power in its law-making process because of the structure of the hierarchy of norms imposed by the 1958 Constitution, combined with constitutional control through the *Conseil constitutionnel*.

> The *Conseil constitutionnel* [...] examines bills voted by the parliament through the principles of the Charter. And these principles guide the work of the government during the elaboration process of the projects of law. I think particularly about the future law on GMOs or those transposing the environmental liability directive.[50]

The Charter became a new instrument for the control of the constitutionality of bills as expected, but it also became a document used in traditional civil and administrative litigation.

2.3.2.1 Charter and constitutional control

Since the 2005 constitutional amendment, the reference to the Charter in the Preamble allows the *Conseil constitutionnel* to review the constitutionality of a bill by reference to it.[51] Furthermore, it has been argued that article 1 of the Charter, which proclaims that everyone has the right to live in an environment that is balanced and respects health, constitutes a *liberté fondamentale*, a fundamental freedom.[52] Bills containing provisions which could be in breach of the Charter will be censured and never be enacted as law. On the other hand, proposals (or projects) such as that for an eco-tax could be put forward without risking censure as was the case in the eco-tax project.[53] Indeed, in 2000, the *Conseil constitutionnel* ruled that a proposed eco-tax did not conform to the Constitution. It considered that this tax did not respect the principle of equality in relation to public charges. Of course, in the 2000 ruling no reference was made to the Charter for the Environment of 2004 as the Charter was only incorporated in 2005.[54]

An example of this occurred on 26 October 2005, when a statute, which adapted communitarian law, brought into force the dispositions of the Charter in areas concerning the evaluation of impacts on environmental projects as well as access to information. Future projects under statutes governing water and aquatic environments, on national parks and natural maritime parks, on GMO, on transparency and security in nuclear areas, and on the management of radioactive materials and wastes will all have to take into account the principles of the Charter. Furthermore, article 6 of the Charter promotes respect for sustainable development in all new pieces of legislation. It operates like a 'green' tutor during the legislative process, ensuring the 'green' quality of any pieces of legislation through their respect for environmental rights and duties.

Since 2005, many references to the Charter have been made during the process of constitutional control. As mentioned previously, in the landmark 1971 decision incorporating bills of rights into the Constitution,[55] the *Conseil constitutionnel* exposed its reasoning in the case of constitutional control involving the Preamble of the Fifth Republic Constitution (rather than the Constitution itself): the council expressly referred to the Constitution and its Preamble, then they recognised that the Preamble was incorporated into the constitutional norms, and finally they associated it in the single term 'Constitution'. In the following decisions it was therefore only necessary to consider the Constitution without specifying which particular texts or parts of the constitutional norms the council was considering (the Preamble or the articles). The implied use of the Preamble became the normal way of exercising constitutional control. Therefore we are facing a similar operation here in the case of the Charter. Two methods of using the Charter by the *Conseil constitutionnel* can be found chronologically, one express, one implied.

EXPRESS USES OF THE CHARTER

In March 2005,[56] two citizens were concerned about the legality of preparatory documents to the referendum authorising the ratification of the treaty establishing a Constitution for Europe. They decided to contest the legality of a regulation, the presidential *décret* of 9 March 2005 that triggered the submission to a referendum, which had to be scrutinised by the constitutional council. The bill was considered by the two citizens to be contrary to article 5 of the Charter.[57] It was a strange idea indeed to refer to the Charter for such a matter. But the two thought that the Treaty was indeed contrary to the Charter and then considered rightfully that they should mention it. It was therefore not a surprise that the *Conseil* held that it was not relevant to mention the Charter and did not, in this case, scrutinise the alleged non-conformity of the statutory instrument.[58] 'Considering [...] that in any case, the treaty establishing a Constitution for Europe is not contrary to the Charter for the Environment of 2004'.

It was a tremendous opportunity for the *Conseil*. By expressly declaring that the statutory instrument conformed to the Charter, the *Conseil* considered it part of the Constitution, as it had previously in 1971. The only problem in this case was that in its ruling, the *Conseil* solely considered the position of the Charter but did not substantially consider the Charter itself. Nonetheless, this was subsequently achieved.

In April 2005,[59] on a bill concerning the creation of a maritime register, the Charter was referred to explicitly in paragraphs 13, 36, 37 and 38 of the decision. It is particularly interesting that in paragraph 13, the applicants listed in detail 'parts' of the Constitution they wanted to use and included article 6 of the Charter that is concerned with the development of a culture of sustainable development in public administration. The *Conseil constitutionnel* then commented on this question in the argument laid down in paragraphs 36 to 38. It was argued that the bill was not contrary to article 6. Paragraph 37 is probably the most important one, as it firmly stated that the application of the dispositions of article 6 had to be left to the discretion of the legislature.

> Considering that following the dispositions of article 6 of the Charter for the Environment of 2004: 'Public policies must promote sustainable development. For this purpose, they conciliate protection and valorisation of the environment, economic development and social progress'; it is a power for the legislature to determine, in the respect of the principle of conciliation laid down by those measures, the terms of its implementation.

In July 2005,[60] a bill was discussed on the energy policies of France. It was of course the ideal forum for environmental protection to be considered. As such, the Charter was referred to by some of the opposition members of parliament who decided that the bill did not conform to the Constitution. Indeed, applicants were trying to get the bill declared incompatible with the Constitution and used, in their argument, the principle of equality enshrined in article 6 of the Charter to try to convince the constitutional council.[61] The *Conseil constitutionnel* here again considered that the bill did not infringe article 6.[62]

These last two cases offer a good illustration of the constitutional importance of the Charter as a tool in the interpretation of a bill in comparison to the first case. Indeed, we can see from these that the Charter, as was intended during the process of its elaboration, has been directly used as a legal tool in the process of constitutional control. However, as well as these express uses, implied uses of the Charter can also be found in the assessment on the conformity of bills relating to environmental issues.

IMPLIED USES OF THE CHARTER

Although a decision of April 2005 may be the first attempt at an implied use of the Charter,[63] it was certainly used in December 2005[64] during the discussion of the finance bill that concerned the credits allocated to ecology and sustainable development.[65]

Since then, the implied use of the Charter in matters of constitutional control seems to have been the preferred approach, thus following the traditional fashion since 1971 of operating constitutional control based on the Preamble. Then again this has proved to be more difficult to recognise as no major pieces of legislation relating to environmental issues were brought before the *Conseil constitutionnel* in 2006 and early 2007, except perhaps the decisions of 30 November 2006[66] on a bill relating to the energy sector and that of 22 February 2007[67] on a bill relating to the development of the area of *La Défense* in Paris.

The predicted outcome of constitutional control was both quantitatively low and qualitatively important. This is perhaps why it is interesting to show that in addition to the aforementioned, the first two years of operation of the Charter have seen an unpredicted development of its use by the lower courts.

2.3.2.2 *Charter and administrative and civil/criminal litigation*

If constitutional control was the most definite expected outcome of the Charter, it was somewhat surprising to find it used by French courts. The Charter did, in fact, also provide guidance for the courts under the supervision of the supreme court of the administrative justice system (the *Conseil d'État*) and the supreme court of the civil and criminal justice system (the *Cour de cassation*). It is indeed interesting to note that some lower courts of the two judicial systems have used the Charter in the same way as the constitutional council. This outcome was most unexpected and transformed the Charter into an operational document.

The *Conseil d'État* was not a novice in environmental protection. The precautionary principle in its legislative version has long been a reference point for judicial review in France. Since the transposition of some principles included in the Declaration of Rio into French law, the precautionary principle has been applied in administrative decision-making.[68] The administrative courts were using the precautionary principle in its statute law 'format', a sort of 'legislative right', in areas such as GMOs[69] and insecticides[70] before extending the scope of control to general environmental protection and public health. Many examples have been seen particularly in the area of GSM (mobile phone) antennas, as for instance in a case before the *Cour Administrative d'Appel (CAA) de Marseilles*[71] in 2002 relating to the matter of a planning permission granted to a GSM operator for a mast that was contested for health reasons. The permission was granted and then contested before the lower administrative court which confirmed the permission. It was then quashed on appeal before the *CAA* on the basis of the precautionary principle. In the same year, in a similar matter, the *Conseil d'État* suspended a decision to refuse permission to erect a mast, referring to the precautionary principle.[72] In this case, the supreme administrative court applied the precautionary principle in a narrow sense rather than in a broad sense because the court, on the basis of expert evidence, did not consider that the mast was a proven health risk. Now, following the constitutionalisation of the Charter and specifically the precautionary principle, a local authority must consider the possibility of health risks in its decision, 'even if scientific knowledge is uncertain'. If a decision is then considered by an administrative court the uncertain character of a health risk will provide fundamental grounds for the court's ruling. Hence, the Charter creates a 'shock' in the public sphere, firstly by renewing the 'spirit' of the precautionary principle, and secondly by inserting in the highest legal position a 'bill of rights'. The unforeseen wider scope of the Charter was immediately seen by environmental associations, ecologists and activists.

In April 2005, a local administrative court, the *tribunal administratif* of *Châlons-en-Champagne*, was given the task of checking an alleged breach of civil liberty committed by an act of the *préfet de la Marne* (this is the representative of the central state in one of the administrative units of Metropolitan France, namely the *département de la Marne*).[73] The *préfet* decided to authorise a rave party on a former military field of the airport of Marigny, which is considered of high environmental value.[74] This decision was challenged by several environmental groups, which considered that it was against a fundamental freedom, namely the right to environmental protection.[75] These groups asked the judge using a *référé liberté*, an emergency summary procedure, to suspend this permit. The procedure of *référé liberté* that was used implied the existence of a fundamental freedom.[76] It is a summary procedure used when a public authority or a private organisation in charge of operating a public service has allegedly breached a fundamental freedom in one of its decisions.[77] The judge considered in its *ordonnance* dated 29 April 2005 that the administrative decision of the *préfet* had to be suspended on the basis of article 1 of the Charter.[78] The Charter was recognised here as containing fundamental freedoms considered being of constitutional value.[79] The summary procedure was confirmed by a judgment dated 4 May 2006 in the same jurisdiction.

In addition, the Charter was used as an instrument against the re-introduction of bears in the Pyrenean areas.[80] Twenty-six parties, including six French local authorities, i.e. five *communes*, one *département* and 20 farmers' associations, argued that the decision by the Minister for Ecology and Sustainable Development for the introduction of five Slovene bears in order to repopulate the Pyrenees should be suspended. One of the grounds on which the challenge was upheld was that the participation principle enshrined in the Charter had not been respected because the appropriate consultation with the local population had been partial and limited to a certain area in the Pyrenees. This case was the proof that the Charter could be used outside the predicted limited scope of constitutional control. As stressed previously, constitutional control that was supposed to be the sole point of the Charter has now evolved. In this case, the farmers tried to use the Charter to prevent the reintroduction of the bears, making their own use of the Charter for their own benefit. It was obvious to the court that the farmers were doing so and their action was unsuccessful.

The *Conseil d'Etat* has been employing a rather indirect, perhaps limited, way of applying the Charter. In February 2006, on the same day, two cases used references to the precautionary principle of 'constitutional rights'.[81] Both parties in both cases were arguing whether or not the precautionary principle had been breached by the defendant. The different outcomes had nothing to do with the application of the Charter; rather, the most crucial point here was the utilisation of the precautionary principle as a ground to seek administrative justice. What is evident in administrative justice is that the lower courts are less reluctant to consider environmental issues than the highest court. Indeed, the *Conseil d'État*, in its first rulings after the Charter was integrated into the Constitution, restricted the Charter's use.[82] The supreme administrative court therefore remained within the scope of its function to control legality (in opposition to the function of the *Conseil constitutionnel* which controls constitutionality). If the Charter has become a legal instrument that can now be considered in any administrative court, what the courts will make of this instrument remains unclear. As mentioned, the precautionary principle may well now be a legal basis for the arguments of defendants, while the *Conseil d'État* may be willing to consider the legality of administrative decisions towards articles 1, 2 and 6 of the Charter. Then again, it is normal for the supreme administrative court to analyse only the legality of an administrative decision rather than its constitutionality.

The Charter has had an impact on the civil and criminal courts as well. Environmental law in France has always been considered a special branch of the *droit administratif*. As a consequence, environmental issues were absent from civil and criminal courts. The reclassification of certain environmental rights at constitutional level created a certain dynamic in these courts. The Charter was immediately seen as an 'operating bill' that enshrines rights that have to be protected. It may be interesting to analyse how legal actions brought against activists attacking experimental GMO were considered before and after the approval of the Charter. On 25 July 2004, the first national meeting of the *Faucheurs Volontaires* resulted in the neutralisation of a GMO seed plantation.[83] In 2004, 222 activists were involved and were convicted by the *Tribunal Correctionel of Toulouse*, a criminal court of first instance. On appeal, the *Cour d'Appel de Toulouse* gave prison sentences to eight activists and awarded damages.[84] This case was the first to reach the level of the supreme court of the civil and criminal justice system.[85] The defendants were trying to get the judgment of the *Cour d'Appel de Toulouse* quashed on three grounds, including that the court did not analyse their facts in the light of the Constitution and particularly the newly adopted Charter. The argument used by the defence was the possibility the Charter offers to deny criminal responsibility to somebody acting under the principle of 'defence of necessity'. This was prompted by the new developments and the reasoning used by two criminal courts, the *Tribunal Correctionel d'Orléans* in 2005 and the *Tribunal Correctionel de Versailles* in 2006 (see below). The *Cour de cassation* in 2007 rejected every argument, including the one developed on the basis of the Charter.[86] '[…] Judges have justified their decision […], the Charter for the Environment shall not be invoked, in this case, as a basis for the "defence of necessity".'

The *Tribunal Correctionel de Riom* in 2004, followed by the *Cour d'Appel de Riom* one year later, came to a similar conclusion. The *Tribunal Correctionel de*

Riom could not employ the principle of 'defence of necessity' in the trial, but could do so at appeal level, because it took place after the modification of the Constitution incorporating the Charter, although relating to facts dating back to 2004. It meant that the Charter could not be relied upon at that time and therefore the decision of the first court was confirmed. The *Tribunal Correctionel de Clermont-Ferrand* and the *Tribunal Correctionel de Lille* both in 2005 gave a prison sentence and awarded damages against, respectively, 12 and 11 activists (there was no appeal in either case).

The two cases which started after the modification of the Constitution (if we exclude the one that went through all the appeal and cassation processes) are more important, at least in terms of legal construction and reasoning, and prove a difference of impact. The *Tribunal Correctionel d'Orléans* on 9 December 2005 released 49 activists involved in destroying a field of GMO crops on an experimental site belonging to Monsanto. The activists were accused of committing serious damages on goods belonging to someone else, a criminal offence,[87] and were asked to pay a sum in compensation for the civil offence. The court analysed the imminent and actual danger, together with the necessity of the action taken by the activists and finally the proportionality of the means used by the activists. The court considered that there was no criminal offence committed as the activists were in a 'defence of necessity'.[88] Furthermore, the court mentioned that the ECHR article 2 (right to life) had now an equivalent in domestic law through the Charter. It was then mentioned that the 'defence of necessity' was justified as a consequence. The Monsanto company appealed the decision, which was quashed in 2006. The *Court d'Appel* considered that there was no proof of any imminent or actual danger. As such, the Court decided that what had been done by the activists was not necessary. The Court finally added that the defendants could not sustain that they had no other possible course of action, while remedies offered were multiple and that an authorisation of dispersal given to Monsanto was quashed by the *Conseil d'État*.[89]

Furthermore in 2006, the *Tribunal Correctionel de Versailles* used similar reasoning to its counterpart in Orléans. Nine activists, who destroyed a field of GMO crops, were accused of committing damages on properties belonging to persons involved in a public service,[90] and were asked to pay a sum in compensation of the civil offence. The qualification of the offence committed was slightly different to the previous case as INRA (the National Institute for Agricultural Research), a 'public scientific and technical establishment under the joint authority of the Ministry for Higher Education and Research and the Ministry for Food, Agriculture and Fisheries',[91] was involved.[92] The Court held that there was no criminal offence again on the grounds that the activists were acting in a 'defence of necessity'.[93] Furthermore, the Court's reasoning combined the ECHR articles 2 and 8, right to life and right to the respect for a private life, with the right to a healthy environment. Finally, it declared that the right to a healthy environment had now an equivalent in domestic law through the Charter. The Court then considered that use of the 'defence of necessity' was justified. The *Court d'Appel de Versailles* in 2007 quashed this decision. The same justification was proposed here. It was considered that there was no proof of any imminent or actual danger. Once more, the Court decided that what had been done by the activists was not necessary.

To resume, it can be argued that there are no differences here between cases in administrative or civil/criminal courts: the higher courts have taken a conservative traditional approach that considers the Charter solely as a document for constitutional control (and therefore under the remit of the constitutional court). In contrast, the lower courts have been involved in a progressive development. They have departed from classic reasoning and allowed for wider applications of the Charter.

2.4 A 'greener' constitutional future

This chapter has looked at the constitutionalisation of environmental rights and how it affects the 1958 Constitution. In 2005, with the extension of the scope of constitutional review via the Charter for the Environment, an increased consideration of environmental issues in French law was foreseen. However, it has developed beyond all odds during the first years of enforcement. Constitutionalisation of rights in a non-flexible written legal Constitution such as the French one allows for a greater protection of rights. It could be said that the constitutionalisation of environmental rights in fact demonstrates the emerging constitutional law of the environment. That said so far only articles 1 to 4 and 7 have been invoked in the context of the constitutional control a priori and with the new procedure of *question prioritaire de constitutionnalité* (QPC) a posteriori. The *Conseil* went further in its use of the Charter, for example in considering the creation of a new carbon tax.[94] In the case in which the *Conseil* had to consider the new law relating to GMOs,[95] it specified that the ensemble of rights and duties declared in the Charter had constitutional value. It recognised that the rights and freedoms guaranteed by the Charter were also rights and freedoms guaranteed by the Constitution and as such were susceptible to be invoked in the QPC procedure that allows the *Conseil* to control the conformity of a promulgated act to the Constitution. This procedure was used in many 2011 cases brought to the constitutional council.[96] It seems that the 'greening' of the Constitution has truly begun with some great impacts.

The Charter was the result of the will of President Chirac and developed into a national document the people were supposed to embrace. The document was formally raised to the status of the highest law of the land. Technically, it was only supposed to be a document enshrining environmental issues in an ageing Constitution. To some extent, the Charter was designed to be placed on the walls of public services offices and official buildings like a new 1789 Declaration. The outcome, we have seen, is radically different. The Charter is utilised as a real 'bill of rights'. Even when the Charter could have been considered a document presenting only some general statements, the *Conseil* worked to identify the prescriptions contained in these general statements. For instance, the rights and duties stated in general terms in articles 1 and 2 of the Charter were interpreted as a requirement for everyone of a duty of care against environmental damage. Not only was its status as an interpretative tool for the *Conseil constitutionnel* confirmed but also the competence of the legislator in the implementation of the principles of the Charter of the Environment was affirmed. It then became evident that the Charter was more than this, that it was also an 'active' legal tool that could be used by individuals who have concerns about environmental issues. The Charter protects against the use and abuse of the environment by (all) humans for the sake of humanity. Technically, there has been a normative increase in the Constitution. In practice, what was expected was clearly modest compared to what has actually happened. The effects have been broader than mere constitutional control: the Charter is fostering a culture of constitutional rights protection that is new and has a massive influence on how the Constitution will now be apprehended. The culture of rights protection seems to be the correct development of the culture of rights declarations. The French republics have been tremendous regimes for declarations of rights as we will see in the following chapter.

Appendix: Article 2 of the Constitutional amendment incorporating the Charter for the Environment into the French Constitution[97]

Article 2: the Charter for the Environment of 2004 is thereafter drafted:

> The French People,
> Considering,
> That resources and natural equilibrium have conditioned the rise of humanity;
> That the future and the very existence of humanity cannot be dissociated from its natural environment;
> That environment is the common heritage of the human race;
> That humans increasingly influence living conditions and their own evolution;
> That the biological diversity, the blossoming development of person and the progress of human societies are affected by some modes of consumption or production and by excessive exploitation of natural resources;
> That preservation of the environment has to be sought on the same level as other fundamental interests of the Nation;
> That in order to ensure a sustainable development, choices made to answer current demands should not compromise the capacity of future generations and of other Peoples to satisfy their own needs;

Proclaim:

Art. 1. – Everyone has the right to live in a balanced environment which respects health.

Art. 2. – Everyone shall take part in the preservation and improvement of the environment.

Art. 3. – Everyone shall, within the limits imposed by Statute Law, prevent possible damages to the environment one may create or, failing that, limit their consequences.

Art. 4. – Everyone shall contribute to repairing damages one causes to the environment, within the limits imposed by Law.

Art. 5. – Even if scientific knowledge is uncertain where damages occur which could have serious and irreversible effects on their environment, public authorities shall within their own domains of competences, apply the precautionary principle through the implementation of procedures for the evaluation of risks, and the adoption of provisional and proportionate measures in order to prevent the damage occurring.

Art. 6. – Public policies must promote a sustainable development. To this purpose, they conciliate protection and valorisation of the environment, economic development and social progress.

Art. 7. – Everyone has a right, within the conditions and limits of Law, to access information relating to the environment in the possession of public authorities and to participate in the public decision-making processes which have an impact on the environment.

Art. 8. – Education and training on the environment have to contribute to the exercise of rights and duties listed in the present charter.

Art. 9. – Research and innovation should contribute to the preservation and the improved development of the environment.

Art. 10. – The present Charter inspires European and international action of France.

3 Human rights (in practice) and the French Republic

The example of exclusion[1]

In this chapter I will consider human rights again but not the 'new' rights, rather the 'old' traditional rights. Because the republican ideas are also about fraternity, as the motto of the republic states, I will look at human rights in practice and from a different angle, considering the very complex case of non-nationals, the excluded, rather than looking at simple cases of French citizens' rights. Considering the case of France in relation to exclusion and human rights seems contentious at first sight. How can we contemplate France being in breach of human rights legislation while the 1789 Declaration can be considered to be one of the first serious attempts to protect those rights? In viewing the attempt to export the 1789 Declaration by those who also wanted to export the French Revolution, a contradiction comes to light. At the same time that France was bringing 'light' to others, it was enforcing it through colonisation. The modern resonance of this contradiction is, broadly speaking, immigration and how it links to human rights. This is a tale of people who came (and still come) to France, invited or not, decided that it was the place they wanted to be, to belong to, but are now treated as 'outlaws' and have become excluded from mainstream society in this place that is supposed to be a republican model.

Two situations have to be considered, *de jure* exclusion and *de facto* exclusion. *De jure* exclusion may be looked at through its impact on an individual's human rights. But the rigid notions of nationality and citizenship, linked to the notion of statelessness, do not seem to apply, broadly speaking, to the new forms of exclusion. The example of France is, of course, relayed by the media as being a problem affecting only North Africans from the former French colonies who are seeking a better future in France. Indeed, 28.8 per cent of immigrants come from the Maghreb and 12.9 per cent from countries formerly under the administration of France.[2] However, *de facto* exclusion has a wider scope. Many Asians, for example, have been affected by the problem without the spotlight of the media (14.1 per cent of non-national immigrants are from Asia).[3] On the other hand, new legal developments and particularly the changes implemented by the Sarkozy administration (new immigration law, new ministerial department on immigration and nationality, 'positive' immigration, quotas, the idea of a Mediterranean Union ...) operate as an ambivalent normative approach, creating exclusion and limiting its impact.

According to a recent report, in 2004 4.9 million immigrants resided in France, which represents 8.1 per cent of the population. The number of immigrants from Africa and Asia had increased from the last survey (in 1999), while the number of European immigrants had fallen from the 1945–1970s period.[4]

3.1 Preliminary remarks on exclusion

Exclusion refers to the verb to exclude. Exclusion is not really a wall but rather a door between two spaces. The door opens from one space into the other, in both directions, and in a way it links to an event, the act of moving from outside to inside. The event in our specific case is the movement of population from one place to another. When the door is opened, the event takes place. When the door is closed, the event is blocked and cannot happen. What conditions the relationship between the two spaces is based on history and politics, and is regulated by law. The law here has been the gatekeeper since 1945, when the first French ordinance concerning non-nationals was enacted.[5] Exclusion has an ambiguous meaning. It means to forbid the entering of something, to prevent the event from happening. In that case, those who are outside cannot come in: the door is shut. It also means to remove something or someone. Exclusion is a door that we close after sending people out. We remove someone we do not want to stay in.

The theme of exclusion in France is articulated logically (from a civil law tradition perspective) around nationality, citizenship and immigration. However, this is the problem of immigration that initiates the issue of exclusion. One wishes to pass through the door and to create the event of coming in. An immigrant will come and want to stay. The first exclusion will be from nationality, and then from citizenship. It is necessary to be a French national to have political rights. But it may be possible to merge the two issues. From nationality, the theme of exclusion develops with citizenship. It then 'positions' itself between nation and state: statelessness, *a-patride*, relates to the absence of *patrie*, 'fatherland', that is a problem concerning a community, the nation, rather than the absence of state. It is then a problem of belonging to a nation, even though we can affirm that there is a semantic slide here, due to the use of nation instead of *patrie*, 'fatherland', which is a much more emotional concept. The pace of opening the door between what constitutes the French space and immigrants has been codified in the *Code de l'entrée et du séjour des étrangers et du droit d'asile*.[6] Article L.111-1 CESEDA considers the quality of foreign individuals in a very simple manner: those are not French nationals because they are either with, or without, a foreign nationality. This definition seems to work rather well in relation to a person being without French nationality, although we can find many cases of the impossibility of being either deprived of French nationality or offered French nationality. We can also argue that the absence of French citizenship granted to individuals living in France may be considered as an exclusion, a *de jure* one. We could also consider, like the German sociologist Ulrich Beck, that the Nation State concept is missing one of its constituents – the Nation – because of the dissolution that is particularly clear at the continental European level that brings a trans-national society.[7] This could affect the intensity of the separation between nationality and citizenship concepts, and modify the perception of 'what is what'. That said, what is at stake is principally to define those who enter the French territory with or without the right to do so and overstay. Since 1985, with the Schengen Agreement and the Treaty of Amsterdam, the matter is not only a solely French concern; it is the problem of another space, the Schengen space.[8] Meanwhile, France remains strongly protected by its constitutional norms. These are highlighted by the *Conseil constitutionnel* in its landmark 1993 decision that containing immigration flux is legitimate.[9] After one of the first 'undocumented' (*sans papier*) protests (the occupation of Saint Bernard Church in Paris), the highest administrative court (*Conseil d'État*) ruled in 1996 that the French administration had the right to regularise the situation of a non-national, to modify their situation from undocumented to documented. Interestingly, an internal document *circulaire* of the French Home Office of 13 June 2006 established the conditions for the (exceptional) regularisation of school children and their families if they were resident in France for at least two years prior to this date.[10] Of course, the texture of the problem of opening the doors to other/s resides in the quality and the perception of otherness. And this does concern France as a former imperial entity. Immigration is therefore, to a large extent, a problem of the past that comes into the present. The migrants are mainly people who used to be within the French colonial space and it concerns France in its post-colonial dynamic. The centre is still attracting individuals from outside, and because the feeling in the centre is that the door should be shut and remain shut, the situation of *de facto* exclusion has arisen, a situation that is a very interesting case study because it highlights tensions between constitutional rights and fundamental freedoms and their practice.

3.1.1 *On post-colonial constitutions*

Two constitutions have been in force in France since 1945, that of the Fourth Republic (1946) and that of the Fifth Republic (1958). The left-wing-inspired Fourth Republic Constitution took into consideration the characteristics of the colonies but collapsed from its incapacity to provide adapted management for the French empire. The Fifth Republic Constitution did something quite similar but achieved decolonisation. The legacy of the Fourth Republic Constitution is, mainly, its Preamble that the Fifth Republic constitutional text has now reified. As one of the three French bills of rights enforced under the 1958 Constitution (the one concerned with socio-economic rights), the Preamble of the 1946 Constitution, paragraph 4, considers France as a welcoming and safe place. It states that: 'Any man persecuted in virtue of his actions in favour of liberty may claim the right of asylum upon the territories of the Republic.' This article is the continuation of a long-lasting tradition making France a *terre d'accueil*. The 1946 Constitution Preamble is about opening the door, but not at any cost, and only when it is necessary. This principle has been organised by the CESEDA and given a specific constitutional recognition by a decision of the *Conseil constitutionnel*.[11] The same ruling held that the principle enshrined in paragraph 4 had to be organised by statute laws and international conventions, that is by legal instruments situated in the hierarchy of norms in place since 1958, under the constitutional text. At the same time, post-colonisation consequences are represented here: casual and exceptional immigration, all at once, organised and protected. One should not forget that the period since 1945 had seen an increase in immigration. The period of the 1950s–70s was characterised by European immigration (mainly from Spain and Portugal), while since the 1970s, immigration has been from Africa (and particularly North Africa) and Asia. If the period of the 1950s–70s has something to do with the attraction of an economically successful France, from the 1970s, immigration was much more profoundly linked to the post-colonial situation, where certainly the centre of the former empire was the place to go. The perception of the two postwar waves of immigration has created a myth of 'the good' immigrant (European immigration) and 'the bad' immigrant (African immigration).

3.1.2 *On the legal framework*

My emphasis here will be on attempting to show how the French Declaration of rights operates to protect, or not, non-nationals on French territory. As previously explained, the Fifth Republic Constitution has organised a political system that departs from the previous Republics by the strict implementation of a hierarchy of norms and the creation of a constitutional court. The two combined meant that the Constitution was to be the apex of the hierarchy of norms in France. As I mentioned, the hierarchy is protected by the *Conseil constitutionnel*.[12] The council has developed since 1971 a material Constitution, extending its jurisdiction above the articles of the Constitution.[13] The *Conseil constitutionnel* recognised as part of the constitutional norms (*bloc de constitutionnalité*) the Preamble of the 1958 Constitution, itself referring to the former Declaration of rights, and public and civil liberties.[14] This complex, interrelated network of texts has clearly been useful since 1958. Constitutionalisation was found to be the best protection of human rights that were in the past protected by subordinate legislation. As stressed by Renucci, European human rights have rationalised constitutionalism in Europe but there remains the question of the disparity of application of conventional norms.[15] Indeed, France does not appear to have given the broader recognition to conventional rights that they needed. Furthermore, international instruments, generally, have been considered to be situated under the Constitution but above normal statute law.[16] Even if the *Conseil d'État* and the *Cour de cassation*, have reaffirmed the supremacy of the Constitution over every other text, the recognition of the significant place of European law, whether communitarian[17] or conventional,[18] was recognised in 2007 by the *Conseil d'État*.

In the matter of immigration, it seems, prima facie, that more than the 'classic' constitutional norms are involved. The landmark 1993 *Conseil constitutionnel* decision DC 93-325 *Maîtrise de l'immigration*[19] listed norms that may be linked to *de jure* or *de facto* exclusion, from 'pure' statelessness to classic immigration, starting with pure constitutional norms, incorporating many international and sub-constitutional instruments.[20] While one may find the list a rather interesting didactic tool, operating as a guide for those who need to know where to find legal instruments applicable to non-nationals, it may not be as simple as it seems. In paragraphs 2, 3 and 4 of the ruling, the constitutional council went on to develop its argument on the constitutional norms applicable to the control of the statute on immigration, the object of the constitutional control. The *Conseil* primarily reaffirmed the absence of 'principle' (*principe*) or 'rule' (*règle*) of constitutional value giving general and absolute rights to non-nationals to enter or stay on the national territory. It then specified that it will only consider statute laws with what are considered to be constitutional norms that may include, for a particular case, the spirit of an international convention. The *Conseil* then affirmed a number of freedoms and fundamental rights recognised in everyone living in the territory of the Republic: individual freedom and security, including the right to come and go; freedom of marriage; the right to live a normal family life; the right to social protection and to proper access to justice to protect these rights. Finally, the *Conseil* reaffirmed the right to asylum. Again, France was thinking of itself as a place where the door is always open to those who need shelter. But increasingly, if individuals allowed under the 'shelter' of the *terre d'accueil* were fine, the door had many more limitations: entrance and the right to stay on French territory is not a general and absolute right.

It may be argued that the constitutional norms applicable to *de facto* (and *de jure* in a way) exclusion are now involving more international documents than the traditional constitutional norms. One must not forget the importance of the Constitution and how the entire domestic order derives from the Constitution. The main bills of rights of 1789 and 1946,[21] because of their constitutional level in the hierarchy of norms, appear to be the most important documents. They have the particularity to be deterritorialised. The rights considered by the two bills apply to humans generally and not specifically to the 'French'. That said, the 1789 Declaration is about the rights of man and citizens. As such, the reference to 'man' is not a link to nationality, but 'citizen' relates it to *de jure* exclusion. The 1946 bill of rights moves towards a complete 'humanisation' of rights. Perhaps because it was a postwar Declaration, it concerns every human being, as expressed in its introduction. In 1789, France had not started its vast qualitative expansion. I mean here the export of the 1789 ideals, and therefore the rights defined, concerned solely the French, even though this was not specified. The 1946 bill refers to the people who had been colonised, recognising many specific rights, or rather specifying that the rights granted to French people would be extended to other populations. In the meantime, it reaffirmed the rights of 1789, ambivalently considering, as a consequence, the notion of the 'citizen'.

What these bills of rights are about is primarily equality and non-discrimination. All rights granted to nationals are also available to non-nationals, as upheld by a 1990 ruling of the constitutional council[22] and confirmed by the landmark 1993 decision in paragraph 35: 'The exclusion of foreigners lawfully residing in France from the benefit of supplementary allocation, [...] contravenes the constitutional principle of equality.'

Excluding non-nationals legally residing in France from benefits is against the constitutional principle of equality as defined by the Constitution, and particularly against the 1946 bill of rights as held in the 1990 ruling, paragraphs 24, 25 and 26.[23]

Primarily, the focus was to close the door to avoid further movements in both directions: no more people in (immigration zero), no more people out (migrant would become French). This was an attempt to 'rationalise' immigration (that is also being exacerbated by the idea of quotas) and to make migrants 'French', by magic.

3.2 Human rights in action

A non-national, from outside an EU-member state, may visit France for three months. After that time, the non-national may remain on the territory if documented (article L.311-1 CESEDA). Article L.311-2 details the different types of authorisation required to remain on the territory:

- temporary stay – 1 year (may apply for residence card);
- resident – 10 years (automatically renewable);
- competences and talents – 3 years (can apply for residence card);
- retired – 10 years (renewable).

The question of human rights here is more a question of individuals and family who want or need to stay in France than a question of how they come in. But because of the transversal aspects of human rights, it is not certain that *de facto* exclusion only concerns undocumented non-nationals, although there is a strong probability that the reality of exclusion will be exacerbated if the non-national is non-documented. That said, even a documented national may suffer from *de facto* exclusion. Exclusion has become something from the past that has emerged in the present. It is a problem of temporality that has a socio-economic dimension.

Let us consider non-nationals moving to France. In my opinion, modern and postmodern immigrations have more to do with economic issues than political ones. Furthermore, if it were for political reasons, the 'France *terre d'accueil* apparatus' would certainly operate immediately to support the claims of migrants. I believe it is therefore not at stake here. A migrant moving to France and who wishes to remain in France would, it is evident, want to 'make a living' in France. His or her[24] main concern, after wishing to live a normal family life, would then be to be able to work; everything else seems subordinated, logically, to work. It concerns the Constitution in its socio-economic dimensions through the socio-economic rights protected by the 1946 Constitution Preamble are all more or less connected to employment. The health system, for example, requires individuals to work in order to benefit from any protection. In that sense it is not the *de jure* exclusion that is important but the *de facto* one. An additional comment I wish to make here is that scholars recognise that non-nationals staying in France benefit from rights that are protected, and that protection should prevent them from *de jure* and *de facto* exclusions. Interestingly enough, the only specific right granted to non-nationals – the right to family reunification – concerns not individuals but families as a whole. As such, the right of family reunification goes well beyond the *de jure/de facto* borderline, but also beyond the actions of the debate on entering the territory and remaining there.

3.2.1 *A few words on the sole non-national-specific rights: right to family reunification or grouping*

Topically, as seen in ECJ/EUCJ cases, the right to family reunification is by far the most common way of entering French territory.[25] According to the 2005 INED report, 64.74 per cent of immigrants from the Maghreb entered on this basis.[26] We should 'read' those data and the EU cases together, in the light of article 8 of the ECHR, and particularly consider the discrepancy in interpretation of this article between the two European top courts,[27] while analysing the 1946 Constitution Preamble, paragraph 10, which states, 'The Nation shall provide the individual and the family with the conditions necessary to their development.' It is the 'French' legal basis for family reunification. Then again, the *Conseil constitutionnel* has specified that the legislative power has competence to define the many conditions of organisation of this right (hence the importance of the CESEDA). Since the 1978 GISTI case,[28] it is understood as a *principe général du droit*, a translation of the right to live a normal family life, proclaimed later by the 1993 ruling of the *Conseil constitutionnel*, and developed more precisely in a 2005 ruling: 'La procédure de regroupement familial est une garantie légale du droit des étrangers établis de manière stable et régulière en France à y mener une vie familiale normale' ('The procedure of family reunification is a legal guarantee of the right of non-nationals established in a stable and regular fashion in France to live a normal family life').[29]

Family reunification allows documented non-national migrants to be in France with their families. Article L.411-1 CESEDA,[30] as amended by the statute of 24 July 2006, provides that any non-national who has regularly resided in France for 18 months (12 before 2006) may apply for family reunification. The family must prove that they have sufficient financial resources (although since 2006 social welfare payments are no longer taken into account in the calculation of those resources), decent accommodation and the family must not already be on French soil. The authorisation to enter the French territory is given by the state representative in the *département* (*Préfet*), after verification that the conditions of accommodation and financial resources are fulfilled by the applicants although this may change. Family reunification cannot be considered for common law partners (*concubins*) and may not be successful if a divorce procedure is filed. Finally, family reunification can only apply to children under the age of 18.[31]

3.2.1.1 *Recent trends concerning the right to family reunification*

A 2007 statute[32] was supposed to be the last 'chapter' of the modification started by the Sarkozy 1 and 2 Statutes.[33] Chapter 1 concerned immigration of families and integration. The system is supposed to operate as follows: the family gets temporary documents before getting permanent ones, and should, all being well, be granted French nationality as a final point of the process. In brief, the statute aimed to absorb migrants – to help migrants to become French nationals:

Temporary permit → Permanent permit → French nationality

This process is, *de jure*, no longer based on the unilateral action of the state but on a contractual relationship between the immigrants and the state, which is new in public law and particularly in matters concerning issues such as nationality and citizenship, i.e. to determine who are associated to the social pact that is the French Constitution. Under the articles of the 2006 Sarkozy 2 statute, *the contrat d'accueil et d'intégration* became compulsory on 1 January 2007. *De facto*, there is an obviously unbalanced situation regarding the parties to this contract. The State is clearly in a dominant position and this may leave the migrants with no choice but to accept any conditions laid down by the State that conform to EU legislation.[34] Of course, this is also a matter of implementation of the Constitution, particularly the 1946 Constitution Preamble, paragraph 10 – the constitutional basis for family reunification. The new conditions are:

- knowledge of the French language, for all migrants over 16;
- knowledge of the core values of the French Republic;
- requirement of a minimum income for all migrants; and
- training on the rights and duties of parents in France, particularly for parents of children benefiting from family grouping.

Many regulations came into force to clarify some of the statute propositions. A 2008 decree concerned the preparation for integration into France of foreigners that would like to remain in France.[35] The French language level and the knowledge of the core values of the Republic are assessed.[36] The former *Agence nationale de l'accueil des étrangers et des migrations* (ANAEM), now the *Office français de l'immigration et de l'intégration* (OFII) is in charge of setting the levels directly or for contacting local agencies to do so.[37] Furthermore, if the level is not satisfactory, the same agencies will have the task of training the candidate. The logic underpinning this new legislation and regulation is to choose the candidates and to get 'the best ones', using the contractual relationship as a new way of organising migrant entry and rights to stay. The right to family reunification or grouping seems the sole non-national specific right. Some authors considered that it is a civil and political right,[38] but it may also be labelled a socio-economic right, as defined by the 1946 Constitution Preamble. I use family reunification for the purpose of introducing the following socio-economic rights that I wish to consider in relation to *de facto* exclusion. The right to family reunification has been and continues to be modified, as have been the rights I now want to consider.

3.2.2 Socio-economic rights

As mentioned, one of the main concerns for non-nationals living in France is employment. Article 1 of the 1958 Constitution states the general protection against discrimination, while article 1 of the 1789 Declaration defines the general principle of equality or right to equality: 'Les hommes naissent et demeurent libres et égaux en droits'. The 1946 Constitution Preamble, paragraph 5, considers that no workers may be discriminated against because of their origins. Therefore a constitutional right to protection against any type of discrimination exists under the 1958 Constitution. This right is not limited to nationals only. A ruling in 2000 of the constitutional council reminded us of the obligation for the legislature to fix the fundamental principles of labour law and particularly the application of paragraph 5 of the 1946 Constitution Preamble.[39] In addition, the new article L.1132-1 of the *Code du travail* (modifying article L.122-45), modified in 2007–8 to transpose European legislation,[40] states that no individuals may be discriminated against on the basis of origin, gender, morality, ethnicity, nationality, race, political opinions, union activities or religion. The wordings of the new article particularly insisted on the direct or indirect character of the discrimination in relation to access to employment, to employment itself, and to professional training and working conditions, all related to the principle of equality or right to equality defined in the Constitution, notwithstanding that it may be curtailed (for specificity or necessity of the job, for example). That said, the *Code du travail*, article L.5221-5, states that a foreigner can only work in France if he or she has received a priori an authorisation to do so.

The problem of employment is therefore mainly an issue of whether or not someone can enter the French territory and be documented rather than one of pure discrimination. Of course, someone who is documented, and came either through the family reunification channel or through any working migrant schemes, will not encounter any legal difficulties in finding employment because proof of employment would have been one of the main legal requirements. According to the *Code du travail*, article R.5121-11, a non-national may either be living outside France, wish to come (*introduction*) to France, or may be in France and hoping to be allowed to remain in the country (*changement de statut*). It then seems more complicated for overstayers to work than for documented non-nationals. However, article L.311-2 and 3 CESEDA seem to imply that undocumented non-nationals may be granted authorisation to stay on French territory. Then again, CESEDA, article L.313-10, does not separate documented non-nationals and work permits for non-nationals; the issue of employment is once again crucial. But the trend is to list jobs in areas for which there is no high level of competition. One 2007 *circulaire*[41] explained the new system of authorisation for non-nationals, based on a list of jobs and divided according to French counties. The practice was criticised by the then *Haute autorité de lutte contre les discriminations* (HALDE).[42] HALDE saw two reasons to criticise.[43] First, the way to implement the 2007 *circulaire* remains vague and appears to be discriminatory because it is based on criteria that imply a selection of non-nationals; within the category of non-nationals, it discriminates among non-nationals, excluding Algerians and Tunisians covered specifically under bilateral agreements.

That said, one should not forget that even though being documented is not at all similar to being undocumented, an undocumented individual will or should still be protected by constitutional rights, like the right to education and the right to health protection.

3.2.2.1 Education

Here again, a combined reference may be made to article 1 of the 1958 Constitution and article 1 of the 1789 Declaration. However, socio-economic rights seem to give further details than what can be derived from the general principles of (or right to) equality and protection for discrimination. The 1946 Constitution Preamble, paragraph 13, highlights that the nation guarantees to everyone equal access to education:

> The Nation guarantees equal access for children and adults to instruction, vocational training and culture. The provision of free, public and secular education at all levels is a duty of the State.

Consequently, there should be no discrimination between nationals and non-nationals on the matter of education. This also applies to discrimination between those who are documented and undocumented. The right to education, understood as a right to access the public service of education, appears to be an instrument against exclusion particularly important for the

French Republic.[44] Furthermore, between six and 16 years old, education is compulsory (*Livre* I, *Titre* III, Ch. 1 *Code de l'éducation*). Therefore all children, including children of foreign origin, must go to school (article L.131-4, *Code de l'éducation*) but situations are different for children below the age of six and older than 16.

UP TO THE AGE OF SIX

Under the combination of statute laws, of the 1945 Order and of rulings of the *Conseil d'État*, together with the *circulaires* of 6 June 1991 and 20 March 2002, the registration of a child in a primary or secondary school and higher education institution cannot be subordinated to the presentation of permits and should not consider, in any circumstances, the age of the pupils. However, an authorisation is needed to register a child going to primary school, and one source of difficulty appears to be the delivery of the registration certificate by the local mayor for children between three and six going to the French equivalent to reception year or Montessori (*école maternelle*) (article L.113-1, *Code de l'éducation*). This certificate has to be given to the school director to allow the child to enter the school and it is the duty of the mayor to provide that certificate; reticence or resistance may from time to time slow the proper application of this right.

AFTER THE AGE OF 16

The *Conseil d'État* ruled that a decision to deny access to education to a child between 16 and 18 had to be justified.[45] Under CESEDA, article L.313-7,[46] a temporary student resident permit may be granted to a non-national in secondary school or higher education, under the sole condition of sufficient resources. The French administration has discretionary power to grant the same residence permit without the condition of sufficient resources being fulfilled if the non-national has been studying in France without interruption since he or she was at least aged 16, is now in higher education and has entered the French territory legally. The number of students who entered the territory legally is indeed quite high (40,218 or 19.4 per cent of entries in 2005, including 45.7 per cent Asian and 14.23 per cent from the Maghreb).[47]

The 2006 *circulaire* of the French Home Office set up conditions for the (exceptional) regularisation by a *Préfet* of school-age children and their families if they are resident in France for at least two years from 13 June 2006.[48]

The principle of automatic regularisation after ten years of stable residency in France, organised in 1998, was repealed. But the French home secretary considered that 'Cependant, j'ai bien conscience que le retour dans le pays d'origine après 10 ans de séjour illégal en France est parfois inconcevable' ('I am conscious that returning to the country of origin after staying illegally for ten years in France is inconceivable').[49] The idea of 'regularisation' of families, that is of documenting those families with children that are of school age, appeared contrary to the general policy of immigration control during the period of the Chirac 2 and Sarkozy presidencies. However, the media coverage of families affected by these new measures forced the government to issue a *circulaire* on 31 October 2005 that proposed a moratorium until the end of the 2006 school year.[50]

Confronted with a possible increase in tension at the end of June 2006 (with the development of surveillance committees, the organisation of godfathers/mothers of children likely to be removed because their parents would be, and calls from associations to hide children), the *Ministère de l'intérieur* decided to draft two new *circulaires* concerning the undocumented *sans papiers* families with children in school. In particular, prefects have been ordered to carefully consider applications from families with particular difficulties. The 2006 *circulaire* offered families (including single-parent families) with at least one child in school since September 2005, the possibility of returning to their country of origin as a general rule.[51] If the families rejected this offer, a new assessment of their situation to allow them to remain in France on an exceptional and humanitarian basis would be proposed as an exception. That said, if families did not accept a return to their country of origin, these undocumented non-nationals would be granted an exceptional resident permit (*carte de séjour temporaire mention 'vie privée et familiale'*).[52] Four types of situations were foreseen by the French home office:

- non-nationals totally outside the scope of the *circulaire*, but still 'in a way' within the normal scope of French legislation on non-nationals, such as individuals regularly on French territory waiting for family reunification with a spouse irregularly on the territory, asylum seekers, single persons or couples without children, non-nationals, the 'Dublin convention' and so on;
- non-nationals within the scope of the *circulaire*, that is families irregularly on French territory with school-age children, who could pretend to fill all the criteria: these would be documented;
- non-nationals within the scope of the *circulaire*, who could not pretend to fill the first criteria (this meant the first two criteria were recognised as the most important): these would not be documented;
- non-nationals within the scope of the *circulaire*, that is families irregularly on French territory with school-age children, who could pretend to fill the first criteria but not that of integration: these would not be documented during summer 2006 but may be exceptionally considered under the new legislation.

What this account of the law touching on the right to education opened to 'all' tells us about the French Constitution is primarily that the rights that are enshrined in this Constitution are well known and may be used efficiently by 'all'. It also tells us about education as the most advanced republican tool for the production and reproduction of an enlightened nation, a republican nation that does make 'others' part of it. The right to education goes very deep. It concerns whoever is in the French republican space, and whoever arrived in this space may want to use this right to be kept in. It therefore tells us about the attraction of the Republic, how it wants to recreate itself, how it wants to produce republican minds and how the Republic also tries to protect itself from the powerful tools that are human rights. The *Réseau éducation sans frontière* (RESF) association and the CIMADE officially contacted the HALDE in July 2006 about the un-egalitarian condition of processing the application of regularisation by prefects.[53] The example of the *circulaire* illustrates perfectly the traumatic ambivalence of human rights here in general under the 1958 Constitution and the right to education notably. It is a document that is only an instrument of communication between the central authority and the external services of the central authority. The 2006 *circulaire* was only a document informing the prefects of what they had to do and gave them an (official) interpretation, according to legislation on the subject, without creating any additional rights. But because it links individuals to constitutional rights it becomes a much more important document than French public law seems to recognise. The right to education has therefore been an important topic in immigration policy in the last few years. The other area of concern was the right to health.

3.2.2.2 Health

Here again, reference may be made to the 1958 Constitution, article 1, and the 1789 Declaration, article 1. However, in a similar fashion to the other rights considered here, socio-economic rights seem to have further detailed implications than those immediately evident from the general principles. As mentioned above, the 1958 Constitution, through its Preamble, integrated the 1946 Constitution Preamble that enshrined socio-economic rights. Its paragraph 11 highlighted that it was the duty of the Nation to guarantee health protection to everyone:

> It shall guarantee to all, notably to children, mothers and elderly workers, protection of their health, material security, rest and leisure. All people who, by virtue of their age, physical or mental condition, or economic situation, are incapable of working shall have to the right to receive suitable means of existence from society.

This solution has something of an application of the general principles of or right to equality and non-discrimination. This right is, of course, also guaranteed by the 1948 Universal Declaration of Human Rights and the 1962 International Labour Organisation Convention 118 concerning equality of treatment of nationals and non-nationals in the area of social security, ratified by the French Republic in 1974.[54] As already mentioned, fundamental freedoms are guaranteed to nationals and non-nationals without discrimination. Furthermore, the constitutional council in 1990 specifically considered the protection against discrimination between French people and non-nationals in the matter of social welfare benefits.[55] Here again, human rights in the Constitution, becoming constitutional rights, have a power to transcend situations. Individuals are subjects, not simply nationals, not simply citizens. In true French republican fashion, those rights exceed the traditional limits of the Constitution.

3.2.2.3 *French national health insurance* (Sécurité sociale)

Under the 1958 Constitution, statute law remains the instrument organising the right to health codified under the *Code de la Sécurité Sociale*.[56] As stated in the constitutional norms, a non-national may be part of the French national health insurance but only under certain conditions organised by statute law. Indeed, the general condition is whether or not he or she is documented with regard to the relevant legislation.

Non-nationals have a right to benefits such as health, maternity and death insurance.[57] That said, they need to be regularly documented to benefit from these rights.[58] This is based on a condition of residency that the individuals should be able to prove.[59] There are many additional restrictions. Indeed, also excluded are undocumented non-national beneficiaries (*ayants-droits*) over the age of 18 of a documented national.[60] However, concerning social benefits, there is no discrimination based on nationality. But all individuals, nationals or non-national, have to work to receive these benefits – hence the importance of employment.[61] Indeed, all social benefits from the *Sécurite sociale* are open to all non-national workers and their beneficiaries (*ayant droits*), but are strictly linked to residency conditions. (This condition does not apply to social welfare benefits for retirement, e.g. pensions.)[62]

Individuals living in France are affiliated to the *Sécurité sociale* (*régime général*), including its overseas departments, in a stable and regular fashion.[63] The condition of residency is slightly more complex for non-nationals.[64] They are affiliated if they reside in France for at least three consecutive months (not applicable to non-national asylum seekers or to non-nationals admitted in order to seek refugee status) and if they conform to the legislation on non-nationals remaining in the country. Social services have the obligation to check that non-nationals are documented before paying benefits.[65]

In addition, benefits available to families with children are attached to particular conditions such as residency.[66] A non-national (including a child over the age of 18 of a non-national) may get social benefits if he or she can prove documentation (with documents similar to the ones listed under article D.161-25-2).[67] It is also the same for child beneficiaries of non-nationals.[68]

3.2.2.4 *CMU and AME*

The *Couverture Maladie Universelle* (CMU) and *Aide Médicale de l'État* (AME) (Universal Sickness Cover and State Medical Assistance) are health protection systems designed for those who cannot be covered by the general social security system. The CMU, set up in 1999 (and in force since 1 January 2000), comprises basic cover and complementary cover.[69] The basic CMU opens access to health insurance and the complementary CMU gives some additional benefits, such as free access to GPs and hospitals. It is open to anyone who is without employment (a condition to access, as explained previously, the French social security system) but can demonstrate stable and permanent residency. Non-documented non-nationals may not be covered under this system. It is supposed that undocumented non-nationals may only be allowed medical care under a special regime, namely the 'medical help' scheme AME. The *Livre* II *Code de l'action sociale et des familles*, which codified the Finance Acts 2002 and 2003,[70] subordinated the attribution of AME to undocumented non-nationals to a permanent residency condition of three months, except in the case of an exceptional decision by the minister in charge. Then again, the *Conseil d'État* held that the statutory instruments taken in application of this statute were illegal because they did not respect article 3-1 of the *Convention relative aux droits de l'enfant*.[71] As a consequence, non-national children may seek medical care without taking into consideration the condition of residency. The *Fédération internationale des ligues des droits de l'Homme* (FIDH), together with the *Ligue française des droits de l'Homme* (LDH) and the *Groupe d'information et de soutien des immigrés* (GISTI) formally complained on 3 March 2003 before the European Committee of Social Rights (ECSR). They stated that the AME and the CMU were contrary to the European Social Charter, ratified by the French Republic on 7 May 1999. It was alleged that the AME and CMU were contrary to articles 13 (the right to social and medical assistance) and 17 (the right of children and young persons to social, legal and economic protection) and article E (the prohibition of all forms of discrimination in the application of the rights guaranteed by the treaty) of the Charter because it would deprive a large number of adults and children with insufficient resources of the right to medical assistance. In 2004, the ECSR in *International Federation of Human Rights Leagues (FIDH)* v. *France* ruled that there was a violation of articles 13 and 17 of the Social Charter. The French authorities changed their original view by adopting circular DHOS/DSS/DGAS No. 2005-141 of 16 March 2005.[72] This circular interprets the code in such a way that there is now defrayal of the costs of urgent care delivered to undocumented non-nationals resident in France and non-beneficiaries of State Medical Assistance.

3.3 Conclusion

In this chapter, I have described rights guaranteed under the 1958 Constitution and provided an illustration of the reality of their practice. I have specifically considered immigration and exclusion to test the limits of the protection offered. I have therefore not looked at the situation of nationals here but rather at the extreme situation that may be found on the French

Republic territory, that of undocumented individuals. Immigration and exclusion are topical problems that demonstrate the tension and movement operating in the Constitution. As explained by Sophie Boyron: 'A "new citizen" seems to be emerging from the amended Constitution.'[73] The French bills of rights have worked to help tackle the major issues surrounding immigration and exclusion but have not been able to provide perfectly coherent answers to all problems. They have created a legal arsenal of rights that are granted to citizens and non-citizens, but in the meantime the collapse of meaning of the term citizens into 'men' and the use of the word individual as an umbrella to cover national and non-national have proven to be both very intellectually elaborate and at the same time very complex. I focused on the right to education as defined in the Constitution knowing how important it has always been for both individuals and the Republic itself. It is mainly around education that the apparent conflict revolves between the French state and the undocumented non-nationals who want to remain in France. One may want to analyse, for instance, the reactions triggered by the adoption of the *circulaire 'Guéant'* limiting foreign students working in France after their graduation.[74] The *sans papiers* and generally the issue of exclusion are only extreme examples of how far you can interpret a text on fundamental republican issues: to breaking point, that is to the limits of republican ideals. Indeed, while the right to education was designed to foster 'good' republicans, with the right to education the *sans papiers* have sometimes been able to find a loophole to fight the French administration because it was for them the ultimate chance to remain in France.

In the light of recent developments, it is clear that the ideas and ideals of the Revolution 'in practice' remain ambivalent. Perhaps the *sans papiers* are here to remind the Republic of its core values ... It is a reality that the French bills of rights have developed protections not only for nationals and citizens, but for men and women, for individuals and families of different origins, national or not, undocumented or not. But in practice, what the Constitution provided is a screen against the true incapacity it has demonstrated to reconcile so far the 'old' citizen with the 'new'. That includes the development of the European dimension which will be the subject of the following chapter.

4 The French Republic and its supranational offspring

The love–hate relationship between France and European law[1]

4.1 Introduction

After analysing the movement in the system of government of the Republic, and how human rights affect its development, I wish to concentrate in this chapter on the issue of Europe, taking again a peculiar angle, considering the challenges the Republic faces in its European adventure.

Love and hate are well-known concepts of psychoanalysis. Freud found a perfect illustration of the ambivalence of love and hate in the case of Hans: 'There was a fear of his father and fear for the father. The former was derived from his hostility towards his father, and the latter from the conflict between his affection which was exaggerated at this point by way of compensation, and his hostility.'[2] An internal fight forced Hans to alternate between hitting his father's hand (hate) and then kissing his father's hand (love).[3] 'Hitting' and 'kissing' the European Union or EU may well be a useful analogy for what has been happening in the relationships between France and the European supranational entities it helped to create many years ago.

Many commentators have now written and/or spoken about how the people of France, the sovereign people, rejected the treaty establishing a Constitution for Europe on Sunday, 29 May 2005.[4] It was, however, not the first time that the French have rejected a European treaty. During the French Fourth Republic, on 30 August 1954, the National Assembly rejected a draft bill authorising the President of the Republic of the time, Vincent Auriol, to ratify a treaty establishing the *Communauté européenne de défense* (CED). While the rejection was voiced in two different ways, the outcome was the same. There is in France, and probably in many other member states (in light of what happened on many occasions in Ireland[5]) a permanent fight between the 'sovereignists' and the 'federalists', the people who are afraid of 'losing their soul' and those who think a supranational project is not a myth. In fact, we find here a profound example of the fight between the concepts of nation state and cosmopolitan society so present in contemporary constitutions. Indeed, many French believe that the presence of France in Europe should be without loss of its (perhaps again, here, mythical) 'power' or nation-state status. Even if the results of 29 May 2005 have to be relativised,[6] one must remember that the blocking of the Common European Defence treaty in the 1950s halted European integration until the Single European Act (SEA) 1986.

If one can analyse democracy in a modern state as being solely about government by representative, in contrast to government by referendum (the 'principle of popular government'),[7] it seems more and more obvious that we are in fact living in systems whereby an elected elite rules the people who chose it. It can be said that the people and its elected elite share a common feeling about Europe. Indeed, the people of the French Republic as a group are not alone in fearing changes brought about by European integration. If France has been one of the main initiators of European integration through the establishment of the European Coal and Steel Community (ECSC), Euratom and the former EEC, then the country's political and legal establishments, the elected elite, have shown constant resistance to the legal output of this organisation. It is notable that integration of European laws into the French legal order has always been a difficult task.[8] All the original foundation treaties were signed and ratified during the Fourth Republic, but the European Community (EC) system developed mainly under the Fifth Republic.[9] The dialectic between the belief in the EC as a simple international organisational system with integrated institutions, and the recognition of the system as supranational, or as having 'traditional intergovernmental – supra-national/neo-functionalist – neo-realist polarities',[10] brought many complex issues into the French legal order, which I intend to summarise in this chapter. Primarily, the objective is to look at how EC/EU laws fit within the domestic legal order. Particularly, the 'qualification' of international or transnational law has significance in this debate. For a long time it seemed that the postwar French Republics did not consider EC/EU laws as transnational but rather as international.[11]

4.1.1 *Remarks on the hierarchy of norms in the French legal order*

Under the 1946 Constitution (Fourth Republic), international treaties and agreements were supposed to be at the same normative level as domestic statute law. But there was nothing to give clarity in resolving questions of conflict within the hierarchy of norms, for reasons such as the absence of a strict hierarchy, the importance of acts of parliament and the relative position of the Constitution, and the lack of proper constitutional control under this Constitution. On the contrary, the Preamble of the 1946 Constitution, now considered part of the current constitutional norms of the Fifth Republic, implied that international laws took precedence over domestic ones. The Preamble proclaimed in paragraph 14 that the Republic conformed to all aspects of international public law and, in paragraph 15, that under the condition of reciprocity, France consented to limit its sovereignty.[12]

In 1958, the text of the Fifth Republic Constitution not only consecrated a hierarchy of norms as we have seen but established that international norms have a position that is both infra-constitutional (situated under the Constitution) and supra-legislative (situated above an act of parliament) in the newly defined 'French' hierarchy of norms. The Preamble of the 1958 Constitution considered not only this matter, taking into account the statements in the 1946 Constitution Preamble, but also article 55 of the 1958 Constitution. Article 55 provides that international treaties, correctly approved and ratified, have an authority superior to statute law, on the condition of reciprocity, which is understood as the correct application of those treaties by the other parties.[13]

The intention of the elites drafting the 1958 Constitution was to protect its internal order from any loss of coherence. To do so, they deliberately established a structure that had been absent in the previous (Fourth Republic) Constitution. The ordering of the system of norms was considered broadly in its domestic aspect, but while the 1958 Constitution clarified the position of international law in relation to statute law, nothing was clearly defined regarding the relationship between the Constitution itself and international law.

It is worth stating that the Fifth Republic is the first French regime to establish a proper hierarchy of norms, with the Constitution at the apex of the domestic implementation of a coherent hierarchy built on 'Kelsen's pyramid' of norms. It is also the first proper attempt to organise a control of constitutionality, the corollary of the system of norms, in order to enforce respect of the hierarchy thus organised.[14] Indeed, the *Conseil constitutionnel* was set up to scrutinise the constitutionality of statute law. The key question is, in the logic of the 'pyramid', that of the validity of norms. If the position of international law in the hierarchy appears clear, it is not absolute. Article 55 of the 1958 Constitution does not define the temporality of the norm, which means that it fails to elucidate whether or not an international norm is valid indefinitely in the French legal order. The consideration of space (can a norm from 'outside' be considered 'inside' the system?) becomes a problem of time. In consequence, interpretation of article 55 has swung between a positive and a negative reaction to this problem. Can a subsequent statute repeal a previous international norm or, on the contrary, do we have a situation where the previous norm, because international, always takes precedence? Then again, article 55 focuses on international norms broadly speaking. It does not differentiate between international 'worldwide' and international 'regional'; it does not precisely make reference to communitarian or conventional European laws. These norms are truly ambiguous: at the same time international laws with strong substantial effects, but with different legitimacy and different values. Article 55 also refers to treaties and not to secondary legislation (such as directives and regulations), which could be considered to be transnational law. Regulations normally have a direct effect without the need to use domestic law to transpose them into the national/ domestic legal order. From the moment of their official publication, regulations become part of the French legal order. Directives are the source of further problems, as specific national legislation or regulations have to be passed to execute the transposition of EU norms.[15]

There has been an increasing problem in the interpretation of article 55 of the 1958 Constitution, mainly due to a doubling of the volume of norms coming from 'outside' the domestic order. Primarily, there has been a dramatic inflation of the volume of general international norms. The increase in multilateral treaties has made it more difficult to verify the application of treaties by other parties; consequently, it has increased the problem of reciprocity. This situation has rendered complex, even quasi-inoperative, any control of validity of an international norm entering the French legal order. There has also been an increase of transnational norms because of the multiplication of treaties establishing transnational institutions, which receive power to control the application of those treaties and receive power from these treaties for the creation of norms. The 1957 Treaty of Rome is, of course, an example of this kind, with its increased transnational law-making process through the subsequently developed doctrines of supremacy and direct effect.[16]

This point confirms what Ulrich Beck refers to as the second phase of modernity. Law in western European countries has become transnational.[17] It makes this issue of the position of EU law in the French legal order important to be addressed but difficult to resolve. However, there is also an attempt to prevent the EU from having *carte blanche* over the domestic legal order. In this chapter I will try to demonstrate that there has been an evolution in the integration of European law into the French legal order under the 1958 Constitution that illustrates the thesis of a second modernity, as Beck presents it. Firstly, I will analyse the position of EU law in relation to the French Constitution and then in relation to domestic statute law, taking into consideration, in both cases, the balance between the international nature and the transnational nature of European law. In other words, I will consider the prorogation of the production of norms by the nation state, and the push towards the production of transnational norms. Finally, I will look at the latest developments in the context of the French Fifth Republic.

4.2 Position of European law in relation to the French Constitution

France is considered to be a dualist state. In this respect, international law needs to follow a two-step procedure to be integrated and incorporated into the French domestic legal order.

France also follows the principle of *pacta sunt servanda* (agreements must be kept). As upheld by the *Conseil constitutionnel* in the 1992 Maastricht I, II and III decisions,[18] the principle of *pacta sunt servanda* is now considered to have constitutional value, which constitutes a French commitment to its international obligations.[19]

In France, the hierarchy of norms and the organisation of the *état de droit*, the French equivalent to the rule of law, allows the *Conseil constitutionnel* to scrutinise the constitutionality of treaties (under articles 54 and 61 of the 1958 Constitution). Article 55 indicates that international treaties are infra-constitutional and, as already mentioned, EU law does not have a special position in the norms considered by the Constitution so the problem has to be analysed through generic international law. The issue here is not how the constitutional review of a treaty is organised, but whether EU treaties hold such importance that they have to be considered differently from 'traditional' international treaties. In fact, and to summarise, could the constitutional council have the authority to review domestic statute law by reference to a treaty rather than the Constitution? The answer was negative. Did it change? It is still not clear but we have witnessed an evolution from resistance, through precedence and, finally, to harmony.

4.2.1 *Resistance*[20]

As discussed in Chapter 1, a return to the leadership of De Gaulle in 1958 saw the political system moving from parliamentary to semi-presidential. Strong political leadership brought a strong sense of the 'defence' of national law in reaction to the new EC (at that time) system. In fact, until 1975, the three highest courts of the French Republic opposed any intrusion of European legislation into the domestic legal order.[21] The constitutional court and both the administrative and judicial supreme courts refused to allow communitarian or conventional laws to take precedence: the intention was to prevent an undermining of French law.

The *Conseil constitutionnel* did not recognise itself as having the authority to review a law by reference to or against a treaty. In a landmark ruling in 1975[22] concerning the legalisation of abortion, *interruption volontaire de grossesse* or *IVG*, the *Conseil constitutionnel* reminded us of the scope of its control. The *Conseil* had to consider a statute legalising abortion. Opponents argued the possibility that the statute was contrary to the European Convention on Human Rights (ECHR). The *Conseil* reaffirmed that it could only verify the conformity to the Constitution of a bill by reference to the constitutional norms. What was meant to be reaffirmed by the *IVG* case was that treaties have no constitutional value.[23] As a consequence, in 1975 the *Conseil constitutionnel* refused to scrutinise the conformity of a statute to the ECHR, considered here as a model of transnational norms. It was a clear demonstration that this type of international law was not part of the constitutional norms. By analogy, if the *IVG* case concerned laws resulting from the 'other' set of European laws, the conventional ones, it meant that all international instruments – EC treaties and secondary legislation included – were a type of 'general' international law and as a consequence their substance was not constitutional.

In this ruling, the *Conseil* did not depart from a strict literal interpretation of the text of the Constitution. It is clear that nothing was said in the text that could confer constitutional value on international law. On the contrary, what was obvious was that international law has always been situated above statute law; *IVG* is a reminder of that point. In its interpretation, the *Conseil* solely considered the hierarchy imposed by the Constitution. But with the evolution of European integration, European laws may have been affected in different ways than the more 'general type' of international norms. The *Conseil* left the burden of deciding on this matter to other courts.

4.2.2 Collaboration

In a 2004 decision,[24] the *Conseil constitutionnel* attempted to develop a different position. The Conseil was supposed to scrutinise the conformity to the 1958 Constitution of a parliamentary bill on the digital economy (*loi pour la confiance dans l'économie numérique*), tranposing the Electronic Commerce European directive of 8 June 2000.[25]

The issue was as follows: the *Conseil* had the choice of declaring or not whether the bill conforms to the Constitution. Declaring it non-conforming would have meant creating an obstacle to the transposition of the directive and therefore would have created a risk of state sanctions for non-transposition of the directive. Furthermore, it is certain that from a perspective of European law, the European Union Court of Justice (EUCJ), formerly European Court of Justice (ECJ), never allowed a state to hide behind the text of its Constitution to avoid transposing a directive, and this is precisely what censuring the bill would have meant.[26]

The basis of article 88-1 of the 1958 Constitution, at that time, was as follows:[27] 'The Republic shall participate in the European Communities and in the European Union constituted by States that have freely chosen, by virtue of the treaties that established them, to exercise some of their powers in common.' In accordance with this article, the *Conseil* decided that the transposition of a directive was a constitutional obligation. In paragraph 7 of the decision, it clearly stated that:

> The transposition in internal order of a communitarian directive is the result of a constitutional obligation that can only be contravened by an express disposition of the Constitution.[28]

As a result, it was not possible for the French Republic to avoid the transposition of a directive. However, this has never been an absolute obligation but rather a relative one. Indeed, if the Constitution prescribes something that appears to be contrary to a directive, then it has always been possible to block the mechanism of transposition of a directive. What is striking in this decision is mainly that the *Conseil* seemed to recognise the directive as transnational law. It also clarified the scope of the jurisdiction of the different courts. Paragraph 7 stated, 'If there is no such disposition, it belongs to the communitarian judge to control the adherence to a communitarian directive [...]'.[29]

We are facing, here, a standard method of operating: the Constitution considers EU law as different, by nature, from generic international law, without giving it a specific position in the hierarchy of norms. There is a clear balance in the text: EU law is recognised as having a special status, but if there is a clash with the Constitution, it will not become part of domestic law. If there is a possibility of conflict, the *Conseil* should consider it and give its opinion. If not, authority to control the validity of a directive in reference to a treaty does not belong to the domestic court, i.e. the *Conseil*, but to the European judge.

4.2.3 (False) harmony

Article 54 of the 1958 Constitution states the following:

> If, upon the demand of the President of the Republic, the Prime Minister or the President of one or other Assembly or sixty deputies or sixty senators, the Constitutional Council has ruled that an international agreement contains a clause contrary to the Constitution, the ratification or approval of this agreement shall not be authorized until the Constitution has been revised.

Following the signature of the Treaty of Maastricht on 7 February 1992, President Mitterrand, in accordance with this article, decided to submit the international agreement to the *Conseil constitutionel*, to clarify whether it was contrary to the Constitution or not. The *Conseil*, in its decision Maastricht I,[30] held that the authorisation to ratify the Treaty could only be taken after amending the Constitution. Therefore in 1992 the Constitution was modified to allow the ratification of the Treaty.[31] The decision Maastricht II confirmed that the amended Constitution now allowed the ratification.[32] This has now become the trend. If a piece of European legislation includes proposals, clauses or articles which appear to be contrary to the Constitution, then the Constitution has to be amended.[33] This way of applying this hierarchy of norms *de façade*, as a harmony that is only fictional, means that the order put in place in 1958 is still kept. International law, i.e. European norms, will still be considered supra-legislative and the Constitution, amended, remains the highest piece of legislation in the land. This is where the *Francovich* case and the latest European treaties meet the core of the French legal order:[34] this is the connection between the two orders. As discussed, European laws have placed new pressure on the French legal order. Article 55 of the 1958 Constitution was never clear enough to deal with the substance of the new international corpus of norms constituted by European laws.

The new article 88-1 of the 1958 Constitution gave a more formal recognition to the EC/EU, while France seems to fully 'accept' the system into its legal order. This article operates as the missing link – the element that clarifies and specifies the position of European law.

Under this new arrangement, each time a piece of legislation (from Brussels) arrives in France, assuming it conflicts with the Constitution of the Fifth Republic, the Constitution will have to be amended. In fact, the constitutional text will need to be amended each time it has to allow the move towards a more supranational integration, simply because it is a constitutional obligation to allow this. The situation differs from general international law but it does not confer precedence to international law (even EC/EU law) over the Constitution. Instead, in that move, the legislature provided a convenient escape for the French order. The position of the 1958 Constitution remains strong and permanently set as the highest law of the land. *De jure*, the Constitution of the French Fifth Republic is still the most important text. *De facto*, the edifice is of a rather different nature. This is a good way to avoid discussion about what the relationships might be between European law and the Constitution! The French domestic legal order under the 1958 Constitution is a formal, organised pyramid that recognises the coexistence of the 'foreign' European legal order, which, from time to time, permeates the domestic one.

These developments mirror the evolution of western European societies. The nation-state concept degenerates and makes space for a cosmopolitan society with new forms of law. This can also be witnessed in the conflict between EC/EU law and domestic law at a lower level – at the level 'under' the Constitution.

4.3 Position of EC/EU law in relation to French statute law

If we go back to article 55 of the 1958 Constitution, international norms are said to be supra-legal and infra-constitutional (as confirmed by a 1998 ruling of the *Conseil d'État*).[35] Both the *Conseil d'État* and the *Conseil constitutionnel* believed (then and now) that their mission was to control the application of the law, not to contest the application of the law. In the case of a conflict between statute law and a treaty, difficulties could be resolved by following the principle *lex posterior derogat priori*:[36] if a treaty was passed subsequent to a statute, then surely the statute law could be modified or abrogated. For example, in 1972, the *Conseil d'État* saw no difficulty in considering the precedence of a treaty over an earlier statute.[37] In this case the validity of the treaty was obvious. On the contrary, if the statute was adopted after a treaty, only good legislative practice could ensure that the treaty was respected. The *Conseil constitutionnel* decided not to be the instrument of control on the matter in its interpretation of article 55 of the 1958 Constitution, as upheld by the 1975 ruling on *IVG*.[38] The constitutional court did not feel concerned by a treaty taking precedence over a statute. As a consequence, it was left to the judicial and the administrative supreme courts to decide on that point of chronology of the legislation. Then again, if treaties were considered as part of the internal legal order, it was more complex for secondary legislations, because of the problem of timing or chronology. In fact, and more precisely, is that precedence universal? Can it be applied despite the chronology? Can the French Republic permanently give way to EU law over national/domestic legislation, even if the latter is more recent? The position of the two supreme courts differed and evolved in the same way as that outlined in the precedent section. The main concern here is similar and based on the substance of European law, and I need to address the issue in relation to both the judicial supreme court and the administrative supreme court.

4.3.1 *Cour de Cassation*

The judicial supreme court was the first supreme court to modify its case law in the 1975 landmark case, *Société Jacques Vabre*.[39] This case, which occurred a few months after *IVG*, was concerned with national customs and excise legislation and its compatibility with EC law. For instance, the Court mentioned that article 265 of the *Code des douanes* was incompatible with article 95 of the Treaty of Rome 'on the basis that article 55 of the Constitution gave it an authority superior to the one of internal law, even chronologically posterior'.[40] The question of time was considered. Article 265 of the Customs Code was adopted on 14 December 1966 while the treaty was adopted in 1957. The rest of the comment clearly states the position of the Court:

> But since the treaty of 25 March 1957, that, by virtue of the above-mentioned article of the Constitution, has an authority superior to that of the laws, institutes its own legal order integrated into that of the Member States, that because of this specificity, this own legal order that it has created is directly applicable to nationals of these States and imposed on their jurisdictions.[41]

The Court held that national customs legislation was incompatible with communitarian legislation. In doing this, the *Cour de Cassation* followed the *Conseil constitutionnel* and its 1975 *IVG* ruling. It was a clear message. One would have thought at the time that this decision was an invitation to modify and harmonise the case law of the two supreme courts in order to confirm the authority of the Treaty of Rome. The *Cour de Cassation* accepted the higher authority of communitarian legislation over domestic law but the *Conseil d'État* did not.[42]

4.3.2 *Conseil d'État*

The *Conseil d'État* recognised early its competence to judge the conformity of regulations to an international treaty. In the 1952 case *Dame Kirkwood*,[43] the *Conseil* used a convention between France and the USA in the matter of extradition as a legal basis to assess the legality of a regulation. However, in the matter of European law the administrative court remained opposed to the interpretation of the judicial court. The idea was that the *Conseil d'État* was using the so-called doctrine of 'screen-law', *loi écran*. Whenever the *Conseil d'État* had to examine the legality of a domestic regulation (which is its scope of judicial review in France), it could only do so by comparison with the nearest superior norm in the case of an autonomous regulation of article 37 of the 1958 Constitution. If the regulation was adopted as secondary legislation in the application of statute law, and if this law contradicted a treaty, then the regulation would be considered illegal only because of the failure of statute law and not because of the international instrument. The *Conseil d'État* has never considered itself to be a constitutional judge. The reasoning of the *Conseil* was that quashing a regulation in this particular case would cause a problem of enforcement of statute law; in other words, it would be construed as a court interfering with the work of the legislature and thus contrary to the separation of powers: this should not happen.[44]

However, the *Conseil d'État* abandoned this doctrine in a 1989 landmark case, *Nicolo*.[45] It accepted that it could scrutinise the compatibility of a French statute concerning the European parliamentary elections with the 1957 Treaty of Rome. This constituted a departure from more than ten years of the French equivalent to *stare decisis, jurisprudence constante*. The principle is, informally, that treaties are now 'superior' to domestic law, even in the case of a law enacted after a treaty. In *Nicolo*, of course, the *Conseil* only considered treaties. We know that regulations and directives are not only numerically and qualitatively important, they also have different implications to treaties. If looking at the position of treaties was necessary in this context, it was also necessary to consider transnational law. In the case of regulations, the *Conseil* in the 1990 *Boisdet* case[46] recognised a regulation as being superior to a national law, thereby increasing its scope of control.[47] Directives (which are, as we have mentioned, European laws that are not conceived to be compulsory, but for which the aims are considered compulsory, as upheld in the 1989 *Alitalia* case)[48] require that each member state implements the legislative or administrative rules necessary to reach the objectives of the directive. If the *Conseil* in *Alitalia* mentioned directives, these were not dealt with thoroughly until 1992. In the 1992 case *Rothmans et Philip Morris*,[49] which concerned the fixing of tobacco prices by the government, it was considered that the objectives of a directive were superior to domestic law.

It has become apparent that there are different ways of assessing European law in the context of its incorporation into the French legal order. The traditional separation between courts, which is found throughout the 'civil law' legal culture, finds here its clearest distinction. Delay between the recognition of European law in the judicial and the administrative courts can easily illustrate the degree of the defiance. The judicial supreme court quickly followed the lead of the constitutional court, while nearly fifteen years passed before the administrative supreme court made the same recognition.

This gradation is not without cause. Indeed, the judicial courts have (more or less) always been considered (at least in appearance) to be independent – referring to the executive or the legislature, that is where the sovereign, public power is vested. On the contrary, the *Conseil d'État*, with its many links to the executive, symbolises the less independent courts, populated with people trained in the famous National Administration School (ENA). This position of resistance or defiance from the administrative courts is an expression of the pathological 'hate' side of the Franco-European relationship.

4.4 Recent developments

By 1989, this process appeared to have successfully synchronised the way the French top courts were thinking about the relationship between European law and national law in France. In recent years, it seemed, politically, that the love–hate relationship between France and Europe was leaning towards the 'hate' (although a political change in the form of the Treaty of Lisbon slightly modified this). However, from a purely legal perspective, many changes occurred with regard to the relationship between European law and the French domestic legal order that may correct this perception.

In two 2006 decisions,[50] 2006-540 DC and 2006-543 DC,[51] the *Conseil constitutionnel* interpreted 'broadly' the participation of the French Republic in the European construction, as stated in article 88-1 of the 1958 Constitution. In both decisions, the *Conseil* concluded that the transposition of directives had constitutional value. In 2006-540 DC, paragraph 17, the *Conseil* went on to explain that the transposition of a directive was a constitutional obligation, emphasising that 'the transposition in internal law of a communitarian directive is a result of a constitutional requirement'.[52] In the same decision, paragraph 19, the *Conseil* considered that the transposition of a directive could not be contrary to a rule or a principle inherent to the constitutional identity of France, except, of course, if the constituents agreed so: 'considering ... that the transposition of a directive cannot go against a rule or a principle inherent to the constitutional identity of France, except if the constituents agree'.[53] These two points were reiterated in 2006-543 DC, paragraphs 4 and 6 respectively.

One new limit was set by the *Conseil* in these decisions: that no transposition could be contrary to a principle inherent to the constitutional identity of France. We sense here the dilemma faced by the French Republic. At the same time, we were told that France had to comply with EU law and allow a transposition (as an obligation) but (in terms of the hierarchy of norms) recognition of the supremacy of the Constitution. There is also a strong emphasis given to French republican ideas. Indeed, these are present under the principle inherent to the constitutional identity of France: the constitutional identity of France is republican.

More recently, the *Conseil d'État* held that looking at European legislation imposed an obligation on the administrative courts and, therefore, on the whole system of the administrative courts, to ensure that it conforms to the Constitution. However, this was deemed not to be an absolute ruling. In the landmark case *Arcelor* (8 February 2007),[54] the *Conseil d'État* ruled on the basis of an interpretation that corroborates the direction in which things are apparently moving. In this case, the steel company *Arcelor* demanded that the *Conseil*: (a) annul administrative decisions implicitly made by the silence kept by the President of the Republic (18 September 2005), the Prime Minister (15 September 2005), the minister of ecology (15 September 2005) and the minister delegated to deal with the industry (19 September 2005), when a demand was made to abrogate article 1 of the decree, dated 19 August 2004, in application of article L.229-5 to 19 of the *Code de l'environnement*, on the legal point that it extended the scope of government regulation to the industry sector; (b) force the administrative authorities to abrogate the same article in the standard time-scale of two months from the future *Conseil d'État* ruling (point (a)); (c) delay the implementation of the conclusion to allow the Tribunal of First Instance to give its interpretation on the validity of directive 2003/87/CE, and particularly on the issue of the scope of the directive (that is, to consider whether the directive includes the industry sector or not); (e) impute costs arising from the case to the state.

The ordinance of 15 April 2004 transposed directive 2003/87/CE creating article L.229-5 to 19 of the *Code de l'environnement*. On that basis (which has the normative value of statute law) was adopted a government regulation, the object of the case. This point was contested.

The sole function of the administrative courts is to control the legality of an administrative decision – of regulations. As mentioned previously, working on the hypothesis that an attempt is made to regard the Constitution as one of the texts that may be considered the legal basis in the control of legality, the *Conseil* always opposed the principle of *loi écran* (laws used as a screen between regulations and the Constitution) in order to respect the separation of controls: the *Conseil constitutionnel* controls the conformity of statute to the Constitution; the *Conseil d'État* controls the legality of regulation, i.e. the conformity of regulation to statute. In *Arcelor*, the contested regulation related to a directive.

In the reasoning of the administrative supreme court, the Constitution, its Preamble, articles 55 and 88-1, and the directives 96/61/CE and 2003/87/CE were the legal basis used as such for the ruling:

> Considering that if, according to article 55 of the Constitution, 'the treaties or agreements correctly ratified or approved have, from their publication, an authority superior to that of the laws, under reserve, for each agreement or treaty, of its application by the other party', the supremacy therefore conferred to international engagements should not be imposed, in the internal order, to the principles and measures of constitutional value.[55]

Indeed, article 55 of the 1958 Constitution considers international treaties, and whether they are correctly ratified or approved (and under the additional condition of reciprocity), in order to signify their position in the legal order as supra-legal. This article states the position of international instruments. They cannot be considered to have an equivalent status to the Constitution. Article 88-1, on the other hand, related specifically to the EC and EU and the obligation to transpose a directive. This meant that the constitutional control of regulations, taken in the context of a transposition, would be done though particular modalities. The *Conseil* was in a position to assess the constitutionality of a regulation, judging whether the transposed directive, transposed through a government regulation, conformed to a rule or principle of European law. The reasoning at that point was as follows: if there was a rule or a principle of European law, and there were no apparent difficulties in understanding that rule or principle, the administrative court would deal directly with the problem. If there was a difficulty, a preliminary ruling should be sought on the basis of the then article 234, TCE.[56] When there were no applicable rules or principles of European law, the administrative court might operate a constitutional control of the regulation.

The company Arcelor argued that property rights and freedom of commerce were breached. The *Conseil d'État* considered that these were in fact rules and principles of European law that effectively guarantee a respect of constitutional principles. As a result, the *Conseil* looked at the problem as a breach of a principle of European law and therefore asked for a preliminary ruling.

It is worth noting that the *Conseil d'État*, in the 2007 *Arcelor* case, chose a restrictive interpretation of the Constitution; that is, the Constitution in this case meant only the document including the Treaties that created the EC/EU.

4.5 Conclusion

Europe holds a particular place on the political agenda of all French presidents. As mentioned in his speech to commemorate the ratification of the Lisbon Treaty, President Sarkozy reminded us that:

> During the presidential campaign, I committed myself to do anything to convince our partners to turn the page of the European Constitution that could not enter into force while two countries, France and the Netherlands, had rejected it by referendum and that it was not questionable that none would ask the French people and the Dutch people to go back on their decision.[57]

And because President Sarkozy had strong support arising from what was regarded as the legitimacy of having won the election (under universal suffrage), he had no problem implementing its vision in law:

I said during the presidential campaign that this is what I would do if I was elected. This was part, my dear fellow countrymen, of the mandate you gave me when you elected me President of the Republic. This commitment I had taken solemnly before you; I did it.[58]

The Lisbon Treaty was ratified in France in February 2008.[59] He also pushed the negotiation of the Treaty on Stability, Coordination and Governance in the Economic and Monetary Union, subsequently ratified under the presidency of François Hollande.[60] This new phase of the love–hate story is interesting. Indeed, both the Treaty establishing a Constitution for Europe and the Lisbon Treaty require the French Constitution to be amended: this one was done in the parliamentary way (Congress),[61] while in 2005 a referendum was organised to ratify the treaty. Of course, the parliament was a newly elected one with 'full' legitimacy. As such, the French parliament was stronger than its counterpart of 2005, although this may be regarded as a somewhat weak justification. The Treaty on Stability did not require any change of the Constitution, but the decision of the *Conseil constitutionnel* left in the air the possibility of later changes under specific circumstance.[62] The Treaties of Lisbon and Stability could also have been ratified by referendum but this carried the risk of the same outcome as the 2005 referendum. Indeed, a new failure to win popular support would have blocked the 'European process', which would have diminished in the meantime the legitimacy of the President of the Republic. One needs to remember that even though the *gaullienne* reading of the Constitution was not used after 1969, the connection between a referendum and the legitimacy of the President is still very strong. The use of parliamentary ratification, rather than referendum, was therefore a safe bet. If there was no love–hate relationship between the French Republic and the European dimension, between French law and European law, there would be no need to 'trick' the people again. Sarkozy mentioned that:

> On the referendum, I said during the campaign that I will fight for the adoption of the simplified Treaty and that if I could convince our 26 partners that the simplified Treaty was the solution, I will use the parliament way. [...] So no, that is parliament, and furthermore, that is not a Constitution, that is not the treaty that came from the convention.[63]

If the President was right to assume he did not have to use the procedure of a referendum, he was wrong in his assessment of the justification. Article 11 of the Constitution states that:

> The President of the Republic may, on a proposal from the Government when Parliament is in session or on a joint motion of the two assemblies, published in either case in the official Journal, submit to a referendum any government bill which deals with the organization of the public authorities, or with reforms relating to the economic or social policy of

the Nation and to the public services contributing thereto, or which provides for authorization to ratify a treaty that, although not contrary to the Constitution, would affect the functioning of the institutions.

Therefore, the assumption President Sarkozy made that a treaty assimilated into a Constitution, or a Treaty coming from the work of a Convention, had to be ratified by referendum was erroneous. It could be ratified by referendum but there is no obligation and no necessity to do so. The sole justification is the risk of a negative vote damaging both the European myth and the position of the President.

One wonders if the implications of these changes during the last thirty years are not a sign of a change in the law, in a move towards a second modernity, as I have already mentioned. As argued by Giddens et al., the second modernity is linked to a transnational society. This is characterised by transnational institutions and transnational norms. Jean Monnet wrote, 'nothing is possible without men, nothing is durable without institutions'.[64] What are the signs of these changes? The *Conseil constitutionnel* did not take a position in 1975 on the European project, leaving the *Cour de Cassation* and the *Conseil d'État* with the entire responsibility for deciding whether transnational law could fully permeate in the domestic legal order. I say 'fully', as it was already possible for a transnational law to be recognised, in part, as domestic law in some circumstances. In the first instance, the *Cour de Cassation* decided to give full power to precedence and the doctrine of direct effect. However wide, the *Cour de Cassation*'s jurisdiction does not affect matters of public law. This means that the State (in a Marxian sense), or the society represented by the State (itself represented in that context by both *Conseil*s), in a socio-legal sense, resisted the move towards the cosmopolitan society. The nation-state concept can be said to remain present and strong after the ruling of the judicial supreme court. The *Conseil d'État* lifted the ruling in 1989 and the *Conseil constitutionnel* moved away from it in 2004. These could be considered as important signs of the transnationalisation of the French domestic legal order, contributing to the reduced authority of nation-state law. In summary, the second modernity thesis of Beck and the risk society finds a clear example in this battle between intergovernmental and supranational Europe, between the revolution of the transnational society and the reaction in support of the concept of the nation-state. In Beck's terms, 'Let us start to think of the EU not as an "unfinished nation" or an "incomplete federal state", but instead as a new type of cosmopolitan project.'[65] The French Republic has been under the pressure of the many tensions within and outside the Constitution. It has so far adapted and resisted, but its core, what it was supposed to be, has suffered and healed. Many more elements of that core have been under attack, such as the most revered indivisibility of the Republic that I will consider in the last two chapters.

5 Principle of indivisibility of the French Republic and the people's right to self-determination

The 'New Caledonia test'[1]

5.1 Introduction

France has been, for at least two centuries, a model of a unitary state. The structure of its vertical separation of powers is marked by a particular ideology. Primarily, this is the triumph of the *Montagnards* (Jacobins) over the *Girondins* (Girondists) during the Revolution. The opposition between the two historical parties, during the years 1789–93, was one of federalism against the unitary state. The *Girondins* were in favour of a federal state. The *Montagnards*, conducted by the triumvirate Robespierre, Danton and Marat, favoured a unitary state more because they feared federalism than because they loved a unitary state. The physical elimination of the *Girondins* in June 1793 marked the end of the possibility of a Republic organised as a federal state. The state became unitary. The French Republic became one and indivisible.[2] The people's sovereign legitimated the idea of a unitary state: one people, one nation, one Republic. This had developed, as a consequence, a centralised system of administration consecrated by the Imperial version of the Monarchy during the nineteenth century. Article 1 of the 1958 Constitution proclaims the indivisibility of the Republic as stated in the 'mythical' First Republic Constitution of 1793. That said, the 1958 Constitution has also been a text attempting to reconcile the *Montagnards* and the *Girondins*. Indeed, since 2003, the Constitution states that the organisation of the Republic is decentralised. Behind this statement and this amendment of the Constitution is hidden a stronger movement leading towards a 'more flexible unitary state'.[3] Indeed the administration of the state has evolved towards having more competence transferred to sub-national levels of administration.[4] Theoretically, this does not affect the roots of the Republic, but probably illustrates that France is now at a stage in its organisation somewhere between a unitary and a federal state. Indeed, France appears to (re)join other western European countries such as Spain and Italy in a category 'in between' unitary and federal – unitary with more or less decentralised organisation. However, there are major differences between these last two countries and France. Consideration of the organisation of the state does not affect Spain and Italy in the same way as France. They both need a specific way of organising their country, for political, historical, cultural and other reasons. But in the case of France it seems to reach another level as French Republicanism is based, as mentioned, on the fundamental idea of unity. In this chapter, I will analyse the relevance of this principle and will use an example the furthest away (in distance) that it is possible to be in French public law and public administration to demonstrate how the foundations of the French Republic are decaying. Undeniably, in analysing the relationship between the state and its remaining 'colonies', one can see the change in the way France understands itself. In fact, overseas territories are not only geographically a long way from the mainland, they also are a constraint to the French way of organising the state. French overseas territories are an attempt to bend a strong and very important dogmatic principle of indivisibility of the Republic. As mentioned, I will test this with the furthest geographical and legal case that can be found, that of New Caledonia. This small territory in the Pacific Ocean has been the field of development, in practice, of conflicting principles: the right to self-determination of the people versus the indivisibility of the Republic. To what extent are the roots of the French Republic attacked? How stale is the principle of indivisibility? I will first give a general overview of the way the state administration has been organised under the French Republic. I will then give a brief history of the organisation of the territory of New Caledonia during the period 1945–99. In a fourth section I will discuss the latest organisation of 1999 and finally I will comment on the road to independence and its particular elements.

5.2 General context

If the French Empire has long gone, remains of the past can still be found in many corners of today's world. Indeed 'until the end of World War II, France was the second-greatest colonial empire, with possessions in Southeast Asia, South America, the Caribbean, and North and West Africa'.[5] In the 1940s edition of *Le Plus Petit Atlas du Monde*,[6] the scale of the French empire shows how it stretched from one side of the planet to the other. In oceanic parts of the world, the French empire comprised miscellaneous establishments, the most important being the French territory nearest to New Zealand, named by Cook New Caledonia.[7] The territory became officially French in the name of Emperor Napoleon III on 24 September 1853, respecting, it was said, the international law of the time,[8] and for the last two centuries it has been under French administration for the best and sometimes for the worst.

The relationship between France and New Caledonia emphasises the vast problem of public administration, of how to administer a vast territory, and more precisely the relationship between the centre of power and its peripheries. As it stands, the administrative organisation of France is in appearance well structured but also complex. France has been a 'model' of unitary states where 'the centre was supposed to dominate the periphery'.[9] Even if this is not entirely true anymore in contemporary France, Paris as capital of the state, i.e. as the centre of political power of the French state, still appears to be the place where the decisions are taken for the entire country. That said, the Constitution of the Fifth French Republic was amended specifically on the matter.[10] The 2003 amendment demonstrates the move towards a decentralised system of government. The French Republic is indivisible but its organisation is decentralised.[11] It is then possible to analyse the different levels of decentralisation set up by the Constitution in the relationship between the centre and the periphery. Within the *métropole*, i.e. the French area known as *France métropolitaine*, are found, according to article 72 of the 1958 Constitution, from the largest to the lowest level of administration, the state, *l'État*, the *région*, the *département* and the *commune*.[12] The *régions* are, after the state, the largest territorial level of administration within the state, followed by the middle level, the *départements*, and finally the lowest level, the *communes*. Article 72 refers as well to the *collectivité à status particulier*, i.e. a local authority with a special framework, for example Corsica, then the *région* and *département d'outre mer* (ROM and DOM), i.e. overseas *régions* and *départements*, then the *collectivité d'outre mer* (COM), i.e. an overseas local authority, covered respectively by articles 73 and 74 of the 1958 Constitution. French Polynesia, for example, is a COM. Finally, we find New Caledonia under a specific section of the Constitution, *Titre XIII*.

To each level of administration is attached a certain degree of separation from the centre with increasing autonomy in the *métropole*, particularly with the case of Corsica, that reaches its strongest level in the overseas territories. Without a doubt, the *collectivité à status particulier*, ROM and DOM, COM and finally New Caledonia, is characterised by a decreasing influence of the French legal system linked both to a decreasing influence of the French culture and the increasing influence of the local one. Indeed, Corsica has a derogatory framework from the model-type of local government found in the *métropole*, i.e. ROM/DOM/COM.[13] On the one hand, ROM and DOM are ruled under the principle of *assimilation legislative* (legislative assimilation). In this design, the R/D/C model-type is applied to overseas territories but these have the possibility of softening the norms enacted from Paris in order to take into account their specificity.[14] On the other hand, COM is ruled under the principle of *subsidiarité legislative* (legislative subsidiarity) which is based on the idea that it is better for the territory to make its own norms on issues that are local than to leave them to Paris to decide. In that respect, the territory is allowed normative-making power on competences which are not covered by article 34 of the 1958 Constitution.[15] COM may enact locally on many local issues. Each COM has its own framework (*statut*), according to article 74 of the Constitution. They may also move towards autonomy if they so wish. The *statut* sets the conditions under which French statute laws and regulatory instruments are applicable in the COM. It also sets the competence, the institutional design and electoral rules of the COM. Only French Polynesia, so far, has used the provisions laid down by article 74. The *statut* came into force in 2004.[16] Finally, and as the furthest example of a loose relationship between centre and periphery, can be found the uniqueness of New Caledonia with the subjacent idea of self-determination of the territory. As mentioned, one chapter of the Constitution is reserved specifically and entirely to New Caledonia (*Titre XIII Dispositions transitoires relatives a la Nouvelle-Calédonie*). With this far-far-away legal relationship begins a blurred area where the nation-state law of the French Republic meets international public law, and particularly the principle of the right to self-determination. Indeed, the right of people to self-administer, namely 'the right of cohesive national groups ("peoples") to choose for themselves a form of political organisation and their relation to other groups', found its full explanation in the French context with the situation of New Caledonia.[17] Both paragraph 2 of the Preamble of the 1958 Constitution,[18] combined with article 53 of the Constitution,[19] refer to the right to self-determination. Essentially, an overseas COM may be able to secede without this being considered a contradiction of the principle of indivisibility of the Republic, as held by the *Conseil constitutionnel* on the territory of Mayotte.[20] It is this borderline, between the French public administration, the indivisibility of the Republic and the principle that pushed post-Second World War decolonisation and disintegration of the main colonial empires, that I intend to discuss further, showing the different attempts to promote the self-governance of the territory of New Caledonia, attempts that affect the indivisibility of the French Republic. This has found many expressions during the last sixty years through a constant reshaping of the administration of this French overseas territory.

5.3 Administration of New Caledonia before the statute of 1999

New Caledonia has been under French administration since the nineteenth century. Considered a colony, it was under direct administration until 1860 when it was declared a *colonie autonome*, an autonomous colony. I do not intend to give here an exhaustive overview of how the French Empire evolved and organised itself through the 'magnifier' of New Caledonia but rather to give a glimpse of what has happened in recent years. The numerous attempts and changes in the administration of New Caledonia characterise the difficulties of the French Republic in dealing with conflicting constitutional principles. The organisation of the relationship between the centre and its peripheries since 1945 shows a series of attraction and repulsion movements. It will be examined in two chronological periods closely related to the two post-1945 Constitutions of the Fourth and Fifth French Republics, the period 1945–58 and the period since 1958.

5.3.1 *The period 1945–58: postwar decolonisation and the Fourth French Republic*

The Fourth French Republic was established at the end of the Second World War. It took into account the French overseas territories within the scope of its constitutional norms, under what was then called a union. Indeed, article 17 of the Preamble of the 1946 Constitution mentions that the *Union Française*, the French union, is composed of nations and peoples that share and coordinate resources and efforts to develop their own civilisation, increase their well-being and create security.[21] This is further developed under *Titre VIII De l'Union française*. Indeed, New Caledonia, one of the French colonies, became under article 74 of the 1946 Constitution a *territoire d'outre-mer* (TOM).[22] This was supposed to bring a new development to the TOM, in respect of their own interests as part of the interests of the Republic. Mainly, the 1946 Constitution defined a new institutional design with a representative of the government in each TOM (article 76), a representative of the territory in the French parliament (article 79) and an elected assembly in each *département* (article 77). The *statut Deferre* in 1956[23] together with the decree of 21 July 1957[24] organised a new institutional setting with a *chef du territoire* (head of the overseas territory), a *conseil du gouvernement* (government council) and an *assemblée territoriale* (territory assembly). The *conseil du gouvernement*, presided over by the representative of the French state (*ministre*), was composed of six to eight members, all elected by the local assembly of the territory. Without a doubt, the Fourth French Republic was the one that had to face the greatest loss of territories. The movement initiated a new dynamic within the Republic. There was more autonomy granted to the overseas territories in general and New Caledonia in particular. The following Republic would not be as clear in this respect.

5.3.2 *The period 1958–99: constant evolution under the Fifth French Republic*

The establishment of the Fifth French Republic in 1958 gave an opportunity for a new settlement to the French colonies. Indeed, those colonies had to choose between their independence or remaining under the umbrella of France under the new Constitution. This conflicted with the definition given for the right to self-determination. By accepting to remain part of the French Republic, the people of New Caledonia chose to remain within the indivisible French Republic, a unitary state. This was a way of choosing their form of political organisation and their relation to other groups. However, New Caledonia chose to remain inside the French Republic, perhaps under the pressure of the French settlers present on the territory and not by the will of the different populations living on the territory. The right of cohesive national groups applied to New Caledonia in 1958 seems to have only taken into account the inhabitants of French origin and not the other 'peoples' such as the Kanak, for example. Thus the history of the colony was set to remain as it was under the previous Republic, a territory included within the French administrative organisation under the principle of indivisibility of the Republic. A certain equilibrium was finally reached under the pressure of the events of 1988 which seems to have put the territory definitely on the road to independence, probably due to the influence of the political emancipation of other territories over the years and also by the constant influence of public international law.[25]

In 1963, the *statut Jacquinot* was adopted by the French parliament.[26] It remained similar to the one of 1957 with a *chef du territoire*, a *conseil du gouvernement* and an *assemblée territoriale*. The *conseil du gouvernement*, presided over by the representative of the French state, the *gouverneur*, was composed of five members elected by the territory assembly. Overall, the powers of the *conseil du gouvernement* were reduced under this new *statut* and the movement towards a reduction in autonomy for New Caledonia was confirmed in 1969. The *statut Billotte* was then adopted to 're-centre' the power by reducing the attributions of the elected assembly and therefore by touching directly the core of the autonomy of the territory.[27]

There was a further development in 1976 when the *statut Stirn* was established.[28] The state was represented by a *Haut-Commissaire de la République en Nouvelle-Calédonie* (High Commissioner of the Republic in New Caledonia), assisted by a *conseil du gouvernement*. The council was granted specific competence by statute law and was mainly and most importantly in charge of the administration of the territory through its own regulations. In consequence, a certain level of norm-making power was transferred from the central state to the territory.[29] Without moving towards autonomy, as in the *statut Deferre*, this framework gave New Caledonia back the powers of the *conseil du gouvernement* taken by the 1969 *statut Billotte*.

In 1984, the *statut Lemoine*[30] once more increased the movement towards more autonomy. The council was replaced by a *gouvernement du territoire* (territorial government) with a *conseil de ministres* ('cabinet') as an executive elected by the assembly. Furthermore, a second chamber was created to represent only one of the local peoples, the Kanak, in particular to take care of their non-state norms and *coutumes* (customs).

Later, in 1985 the *statut Pisani* modified this organisation.[31] Four new local authorities were created within the territory, called *régions* to mimic the French local government organisation. The meeting of the four *conseils* of each *région* was named the *Congrès* and replaced the previous elected assembly. Every *conseil de région* was elected and chaired by a president, an executive of the *région*, to mimic again what was in place in France. A high commissioner became the executive of the territory with, as advisor, a *conseil exécutif* (executive council), i.e. *presidents du Congrès* and of the four *régions*, designed to be closer to the will of the territory. Finally, a *conseil consultatif coutumier* (customary consultative council) was also created to take into consideration the Kanak.

More importantly, it was decided that a local referendum would be held in order for the local peoples to decide whether or not they would consider becoming independent while remaining associated with France. This *statut* granted more autonomy to New Caledonia by using the schema of local administration laid down by the new 1982–3 decentralisation laws that would operate in France thereafter. In that respect, the *statut Pisani* was also an attempt to 'normalise' the situation in the territory by applying a structure similar to the one in place everywhere else except for the new executive council and the customary consultative council. The changes were therefore more the result of the increase in the pace of decentralisation reforms in France than the particular situation of New Caledonia.

In 1986, the *statut Pons I* removed some of the competence from the *régions* and centralise them in the *Congrès* again.[32] The high commissioner had to remain the executive of the territory. The referendum of 13 September 1987 confirmed the choice of the local peoples to stay within the French Republic while moving closer to independence. The following statute, the *statut Pons II*,[33] gave normative power to the territory, while giving the executive power to a wider *conseil exécutif* (executive council) of ten members (the *présidents du Congrès* and of the four *régions* plus five members elected by *Congrès*).

Following the riots of 1988 in the territory and the *accord de Matignon* on 26 June 1988, the *statut Blanc* presented the design of a new institutional framework. The new institutional setting was more logical in showing the local peoples the movement towards getting their territory managed locally. The 'distance' taken from the centre was organised by creating three *provinces* (provinces) to replace the *régions* of the *statuts Pisani, Pons I* and *Pons II*. This semantic approach was obviously interesting. The *provinces* in France are a rather different type of organisation than the *régions*. *Provinces* are related to geography, culture and local people and are more community based, whereas *régions* are the largest level of local administration often created in such a way as to destroy local community. The example of the *Provence-Alpes-Côte d'Azur* in the south of France is particularly relevant. The *départements* constituting this region have experienced a tumultuous past. The *Alpes Maritimes* was linked to *Alpes* but never to *Provence*. Ideologically, the belief of a French nation does not really allow for the recognition of communities, and this is one of the components of the indivisibility of the French Republic. *Province* is a non-legal term in the French Republic but during the *ancien régime*, i.e. before 1789, it was used in public administration. It is more an ethnological term nowadays. The use of *province* rather than *région* in the latest organisation of New Caledonia may be considered the recognition of the specificity of the territory. Three *provinces* were created (*Province Nord, Province Sud* and *Province des îles Loyauté*) and given general competence over their affairs (articles 6, 7 and 12, *statut Blanc*). The state remained competent for the external relations of the territory, immigration, police, justice and the army, for example, and civil law, except for what is ruled by local custom (article 8, *statut Blanc*), while the territory was given certain competence, such as raising taxes in the territory and administering the local civil service (article 10, *statut Blanc*). Each *province* was ruled by an *assemblée de province* (provincial assembly) chaired by a *président* (article 25, *statut Blanc*). The three *provinces* met through the *Congrès*, the ruling assembly on the affairs of the territory (articles 40, 56, *statut Blanc*), which was chaired by a *Président*. The high commissioner was still the executive of the territory (article 65, *statut Blanc*). Finally, a *conseil consultatif coutumier* (customary consultative council) was also (re)created to take into consideration the Kanak people.

The *statut Pons II* was used transitionally until a referendum brought the new *statut* into force, but the functions that were supposed to be taken care of by the *conseil exécutif* and its president were transferred to the high commissioner.[34]

On 6 November 1988,[35] a (national) referendum was held in France to approve the project of statute law establishing the new *statut* of New Caledonia and preparing the territory for independence. This was a definite departure from the idea of indivisibility of the French Republic. From perfect integration, New Caledonia was moving towards autonomy and was to be prepared for independence. A ten-year period was given to organise the independence of the territory.[36] This is now to be organised through a referendum that should take place between 2014 and 2018. Yet, independence is a final move from the indivisible Republic not only physically but also philosophically. After independence, the territory will be sovereign and outside the French Republic. In the meantime, a broader autonomy has been granted which provides the possibility of a weakening of the principle of indivisibility for at least two reasons. First, it is supposed to bring the territory to independence. This is a recognition of the possibility of division stretched to its limit, that is separation. If you can divide, then the Republic is not indivisible anymore. Second, it is supposed to organise the particular situation of the territory within the Republic. This is the recognition not only of the differences but also of the absence of unity, which is also telling us that the Republic is no longer indivisible. Thus the question is simple: is the French Republic still indivisible? In 1998, negotiations ended in a consensus on a new period for the referendum, with a new framework, and many changes have followed.

5.4 Administration of New Caledonia under the *statute* of 1999

New Caledonia has become what is qualified under French law as a *sui generis collectivité d'outre-mer*,[37] i.e. an overseas local authority with strong particularities that takes into account the local culture. These particularities are so pronounced that New Caledonia has, in fact, reached the furthest distance from the centre of all the local authorities in the French administrative organisation. The current organisation has been designed under the *accord de Nouméa* (Nouméa Agreement) of 5 May 1998,[38] legitimised by a local referendum on 8 November 1998[39] and legalised by *loi organique*, this is as mentioned previously, a special statute law completing the French Constitution.[40] An ordinary statute completed this special one. In consequence, the framework, *statut*, is now founded on the French Constitution (*Titre XIII*, i.e. articles 76 and 77 of the 1958 Constitution) and the two 1999 laws,[41] which organised the institutions at every level of administration, together with relevant attributions. This was meant to organise the administration of New Caledonia for the next 20 years.

From the start, this organisation departs from any other way of organising public administration in France. The territory is now divided into four levels of administration. From the centre to the most peripheral are found the state, then the territory, the provinces and finally the communes. On the one hand, nothing is really new: New Caledonia always had a peculiar institutional design. Indeed, the state and the communes pre-existed this new *statut* for a long time, the provinces and the territory being creations that are more recent. What is new is the substantial transfer of competence and more importantly the repartition of responsibility and norm-making power. I will analyse successively from the highest to the lowest level of administration the place of the state, of the territory, of the provinces and finally of the communes.

5.4.1 *The place of the state*

Everything stems from the state but there has been a balance and exchange between representation of the territory at state level and representation of the state at territory level, and above all a change in the jurisdiction of the state.

5.4.1.1 *Representation of the territory at state level*

Parliamentary representation of New Caledonia is organised by the presence of elected members of the parliament to both chambers of the French national parliament. There are two *députés* at the National Assembly and one *sénateur* in the Senate.[42] There are also representatives of New Caledonia within the members of the economic, social and environmental council.[43]

5.4.1.2 *Representation of the state at territory level*

The law 99-210 states that a *Haut-Commissaire de la République* (High Commissioner of the Republic) represents the state in the territory as it has been the case since 1958. In consequence, the new framework does not revert to the previous design, and in particular does not organise the representation of the state via a *préfet*, an agent of the state, as was found in the R/D/C design. New Caledonia remains different and the state once again acknowledges the difference. Article 1 L.99-210 also creates, in each province, a representation of the high commissioner through the *Commissaire délégué de la République pour la Province des Iles Loyauté*, the *Commissaire délégué de la République pour la Province Nord* and the *Commissaire délégué de la République pour la Province Sud* (delegated high commissioners for each *province*).

5.4.1.3 Changes in the jurisdiction of the state

The state remains competent within the limits listed in the statute.[44] It remains responsible for everything relating to nationality and civil liberties, policing, organising and providing justice and defence, controlling immigration, currency policy, and all matters of external relations, broadcasting, higher education and research.

The state will also remain competent in maritime transport and aviation, public and private secondary education, private primary education, civil laws and commercial laws, and the fire service until these are definitely transferred to the territory. This will occur during the period 2004–14.[45] That said, the *Congrès* is now allowed to rule on the possibility of transferring state competence concerning provincial and communal administration (norms, control including judicial review and public finances), higher education and broadcasting, although a *loi organique* will be needed. Substantial transfer will take place in matters that are included in the scope of action of the state. The state has the authority to decide so. Then again by doing so it shows a current tendency to give competence to a local authority, that are not the 'normal' competence given away to other types of local authority. Thus the state proves thereby that the justification for unity and the principle of indivisibility are weakening.

5.4.2 *The place of the territory*

The territory's institutions are the *Congrès*, the *gouvernement*, the *sénat* and *conseils coutumiers* and the *conseil économique et social*.[46]

5.4.2.1 *Congrès*

The *Congrès de la Nouvelle-Calédonie* is the elected assembly of the territory, which was inaugurated on 21 May 1999.

COMPOSITION OF THE CONGRÈS

The *Congrès* comprises 54 members (*Conseillers de la Nouvelle-Calédonie*)[47] elected for five years[48] from the members of the provincial assemblies and are subdivided as follows: 32 members from the *Province Sud*; 15 members from the *Province Nord*; 7 members from the *Province des îles Loyauté*.

It is interesting to note that the terminology used here for the *Congrès* shows a balance between the ideas of independence and French administration of the territory. The term *congrés*, of course, relates to vocabulary used in constitutional law to qualify state assemblies but *conseiller* is used within the French administrative organisation for local authority members.[49]

The *Congrès* holds meetings twice a year in ordinary sessions, the first from 1 to 30 June and the second from 1 to 30 November.[50] It may on a fixed order, on the demand of government, the majority of its members or the high commissioner be called into an extraordinary session.[51] It is striking here too to note the resemblance between this and the state institutional design.

The *Congrès* elects a board, comprising a president, vice presidents, secretaries and *questeur*.[52] There is an incompatibility between the function of the president of the *Congrès* and the president of one of the provincial assemblies at the same time.

THE NORM-MAKING FUNCTION OF THE CONGRÈS

The *Congrès* has normative power for the territory. It shares the initiative of norm-making, *délibération* and *loi du pay*[53] with the government.[54] The vocabulary used here in the nomenclature of norms highlights the balance between the idea of independence and the practice in local government administration. *Délibérations* are an administrative act adopted by a local authority assembly. *Loi du pays* refers to a new concept of local law.[55] These norms may be adopted within the scope of the competence transferred from the state to the territory. Within 12 listed areas of intervention by the *Congrès*,[56] the characteristic of the norms adopted is that of statute law, a characteristic reinforced by the use of the promulgation procedure of the *loi du pays* by the *Haut-commissaire de la République*.[57] Indeed, no other type of acts of local authorities requires a promulgation, which is normally the terminology in the French context (and also in one of the regional states) used for acts of the legislature. Norms adopted in other forms of decentralised assembly (the one of R/D/Cs for example) have the character of administrative acts, i.e. regulations or statutory instruments of local authorities. These norms are subject to control of their legality through judicial review before *tribunals administratifs*, the local administrative courts. The *loi du pays* have therefore another specificity: they are not controlled through judicial review but through constitutional review. Only the *Conseil constitutionnel* can know of these norms.[58] The question of the norm-making function of the *Congrès* is of extreme importance as the power of the *Congrès* within these 12 listed areas is the one of law-maker. Perhaps, in this respect, the decentralisation in the case of New Caledonia, with the subjacent idea of self-determination, is closer to the idea of devolution in the case of the UK constitution.[59] It is also a strong sign of the evolution of the principle founding the French Republic. Indeed, it is certainly very complicated to reconcile the principle of indivisibility with the plurality of law-makers. Although this is carefully framed, plurality contradicts the symbolic unity and therefore contributes to the decrease in the weight of indivisibility of the Republic.

Articles 83–98 L.99-209 list the attributions of the assembly. The *Congrès* votes the budget of the territory, it can enact in criminal matters but within the limit of the laws of the French Republic, i.e. it can only give complementary sentences and not create new ones. The *Congrès* acts as adviser for the centre of power (the French state) in national and European norms which are relevant to New Caledonia. It acts as adviser to the *Conseil d'État* for projects of statute law and statutory instruments concerning New Caledonia. The *Congrès* scrutinises the work of the government, which can be censured and dissolved by central government regulation. New Caledonia is still a local authority and its assembly is not that of a sovereign state. This last artefact operates more as a reminder than as a fundamental obstacle because it would be activated a posteriori. Furthermore, within the power of the state, the *Congrès* may intervene to complete, modify or abrogate national laws concerning New Caledonia. These are adaptations necessary for the good functioning of the territory. It also confirms again that its uniqueness affects the theoretical foundation of the French Republic.

5.4.2.2 Government

The *Gouvernement de la Nouvelle-Calédonie* is elected by the *Congrès* for five years as the executive of New Caledonia. It includes 5–11 members[60] elected by proportional representation from among the members of the *Congrès*.[61] The executive is accountable to the *Congrès*. The government prepares and executes the norms debated and adopted in the *Congrès*.[62]

The government elects its president and vice-president within five days after its election.[63] The president chairs the meetings of the government.[64] He or she also decides on the agenda of the meetings[65] and is the representative of New Caledonia. This 'executive' is very similar to a state executive in a parliamentary system of government.

5.4.2.3 Sénat and conseils coutumiers

The *sénat coutumier* is an assembly of 16 members representing the eight customary areas of New Caledonia (two representatives per area),[66] each being organised with *conseils coutumiers*.[67] The *sénateurs coutumiers* are nominated for five years (except for first-timers who are elected for six years).[68] It is chaired by a president with a yearly mandate.[69]

The *sénat coutumier* is the adviser of the president of the assembly, the president of the government and the president of one of the provinces on projects of norms concerning the Kanak identity revealing once more the place given to the local culture. It may be consulted on every other matter.[70] It is part of the norm-making process of New Caledonia and acts as the second chamber of the territory for questions concerning local civil laws, local property laws, leases between customary owners and persons exploiting land, the borderline of customary areas and finally the rules of elections to the *sénat coutumier* and *conseils coutumiers*.[71] It has to adopt *loi du pays* and *délibération* within two months otherwise they are adopted by the *sénat coutumier* by default. The texts then go to the *Congrès* for final approval. If the *Congrès* amends the texts, then the *sénat coutumier* has to approve them within one month otherwise these are approved by the *Congrès* again by default. This embryo of bicameralism is rather different to anything existing in matters of administrative organisation in France: under the R/D/C schema, only one assembly has the norm-making power. Here, the association of *sénat coutumier* in the norm-making process adds to the weakening impact on the territory. The *sénat coutumier* is designed as a guarantor of the Kanak people and the incidence on/of legislations and regulations relating to their well-being. This goes even deeper as the *sénat coutumier* could consult the *conseils coutumiers* when a draft regulation or a local 'bill' concerns one or more areas.[72] Finally, the *sénat coutumier* may propose a draft regulation or a local 'bill' on any issues relating to the Kanak identity.[73] It is there again a statement of the plurality recognised within the Republic.

5.4.2.4 *Conseil économique et social*

The *Conseil économique et social* (CES) is an advisory body to the other institutions. It represents the economic and social sides of the territory. It comprises 39 members elected for five years[74] and is composed as follows:[75] 28 representatives of professional organisations, unions and associations participating in the economic, social and cultural life of New Caledonia, four from the *Province des îles Loyauté*, eight from *Province Nord* and 16 from *Province Sud*; two members nominated by the *sénat coutumier*; and nine 'qualified personalities' representing the economic, social and cultural life of the territory nominated by government. It is consulted for draft *lois du pays* and *déliberations* of *Congrès* with economic or social implications on the advice of the president of either the *Congrès* or the government. Provincial assemblies, the *sénat coutumier* or the government may consult the CES on projects with economic, social or cultural implications.[76]

5.4.2.5 *The territory's competence*

Article 22 L.99-209 lists 32 areas of competence for the territory. These include competences such as the creation and collection of taxes relating to the territory, the provinces and the commune, employment and union laws, access to work for foreigners, welfare and health services including hospitals, customary civil rules, international trade, post and telecommunication, maritime, aviation and road transport for the territory (organisation and regulation) including road networks, airports and ports, regulation of everything relating to the economic exclusive zone, civil servants of the territory and communes, the regulation of professionals including lawyers, insurance laws, public services, procedural laws and land laws, the production and transport of electricity and finally primary education.

In 2009 New Caledonia became responsible for the entire competence that the state decided to transfer (competence listed above under the state section).

5.4.3 *The place of the provinces*

The *provinces* were created by statute on 9 November 1988, following the Matignon agreement (three provinces were created: *Province Sud, Province Nord, Province des îles Loyauté*).[77] Members of each *assemblée de province* (*Sud*: 40 members including 32 members of *Congrès*; *Nord*: 22 members including 15 members of *Congrès*; *îles Loyauté*, 14 members including seven members of *Congrès*) are elected by universal vote for five years as are *Congrès* members.[78]

Each provincial assembly is chaired by a president, the executive of the assembly.[79] The provinces have jurisdiction over matters that are outside the scope of the competence listed for the state, the territory or the communes.[80] Provinces have general jurisdiction in their own territory and, as the communes, are very powerful at their own administrative level.

5.4.4 *The place of the communes*

There are 33 communes in New Caledonia. Communes are defined under French law as having general competence in their own territory. The current statutes on New Caledonia do not affect these local authorities. The communes operate as their counter-parts in the *métropole*. That said, what applied to the *métropole* – the outcome of the decentralisation movement of 1982–3 – has only recently been introduced in New Caledonia.[81] In consequence, norms created by communes are now enforceable without prior control of the state.

The 1999 *statut* brought a clear and definite separation between state and local authority jurisdictions, which was largely influenced by the idea of adapting the general framework of French administrative organisation to the special situation of New Caledonia.

The new administrative organisation of New Caledonia was presented as a temporary framework, and is the most successful attempt at autonomy for the territory. But does this mean that the territory will evolve to independence, and how does this articulate with the principle of indivisibility?

5.5 Is New Caledonia closer than ever to independence?

What are the signs of increased independence? Do we have more signs of the proximity of independence? Perhaps we should look towards symbols such as the 'permission' to fly both the French and the New Caldeonian flags together: could this be one of the signs?[82] The *statut* of 1999 has probably given the territory a framework, which is the best expression of the distance taken from the centre of power, giving New Caledonia the greatest autonomy from the French central government ever. That said, it is still organised under the supervision of the French authorities but, more importantly, it is incorporated into the Constitution. The progress towards independence seems therefore definitive. There are signs that something is going beyond just a new institutional administrative design for the territory, that things are affecting the principle of indivisibility, such as the presence within the *statut* of the four 'elements': the organisation of the self-determination operation, the recognition of a civil status, the creation of a citizenship of New Caledonia and the widening of the external relations of the territory.

5.5.1 *The self-determination operation set out*

Clearly *Titre XI* of L.99-209 entitled *la consultation sur l'accession à la pleine souveraineté* (consultation towards the accession to full sovereignty) sets out the final aspects of the possibility of self-determination for New Caledonia. L.99-209 is a development of one particular point of article 77 of the 1958 Constitution stating that a law was to be adopted to determine the conditions and delays within which the concerned populations of New Caledonia would be consulted on the point of independence. This is the letter and the spirit of L.99-209. The consultation of populations as stated by the Constitution is therefore set out as follows.

5.5.1.1 *Timescale*

Article 217 L.99-209 states the different conditions of timescale and the outcome of the consultation. The referendum will have to be organised during the period between 2014 and six months before 2019. The final date will be fixed by the *Congrès* by a qualified majority of three-fifths of its members. If by 2018 the *Congrès* has not decided on a date, the French government will set up the date for the consultation instead. In the case of the *Congrès* being dissolved, no consultation will be organised within six months after the date of its dissolution.

5.5.1.2 *Outcome*

According to article 217, if the outcome of the referendum is positive, the territory will become independent. If the outcome is negative, a new consultation will be organised, on the advice of a third of the *Congrès*'s members to the high commissioner. A 'cooling off period' of at least six months after the previous referendum will need to be respected. The new consultation will then be organised within 18 months of the demand of the high commissioner but still taking into account that no consultation will take place within the period of six months before 2019.

5.5.1.3 *Electorate*

This crucial element has been thoroughly debated. Article 218 L.99-209 details who can be registered as potential voters for the referendum. According to L.99-209: as electors will be registered those who were electors for the referendum of the 8 November 1998, or who were not electors then but fulfilled the requested condition of domicile for the would-be electors for this referendum, or those who were not electors for the 1998 referendum and did not fulfil the condition of domicile requested for family, professional or medical reasons; also will be registered as elector individuals who are under customary civil status, or who have their centre of material and moral interests in New Caledonia and either were born in New Caledonia or have at least one parent born there, or could justify having continuously lived in New Caledonia for 20 years on the date of the consultation, 31 December 2014 at the latest; finally will be registered as electors those individuals who were born before 1 January 1989, who have lived in New Caledonia from 1988 to 1998, or who were born after 1 January 1989 and have at least one parent who was an elector in the 1998 referendum.

5.5.1.4 Campaign

Political parties and groups will have access to broadcasting with timing controlled by the French administrative independent authority in charge of the audio-visual, the *conseil supérieur de l'audiovisuel* (CSA). Each of the parties and groups will have at least the right to five minutes of broadcast.[83]

5.5.1.5 Control

A special commission will be set up to control the organisation and operation of the referendum.[84] This special commission will be composed of two judges from each court system (civil courts and administrative courts) and chaired by a *conseiller d'État*.

This final moment leading to self-determination of the territory of New Caledonia is now enshrined in a document giving us the precise details of what will happen and how it will happen. This is unique in French public administration. It shows that the French Republic recognises the possibility of division by recognising the right to self-determination of the populations of the territory. It is then possible to divide a part of the Republic. Based on the legal acknowledgment made in 1958 that New Caledonia was part of the Republic, and the possibilities opened to divide it, then the Republic is not indivisible anymore. This will be confirmed.

5.5.2 A local civil status, derogatory to the civil code

The derogatory civil rules are formalised as the document organising the life of the Caledonian. Articles 7 to 19 L.99-209 combined with article 75 of the 1958 Constitution designed the possibility of special civil rules for the citizens of the French Republic, i.e. in the case of New Caledonia the citizens of New Caledonia. The *statut civil coutumier* (customary civil rules) is a corpus of norms created by customary laws of the Kanak people. The inhabitants of the territory will be able to choose between the French common rules (under the *Code civil*) and the derogatory rules. The two sets of rules exist together in the territory and an individual will be allowed to move from one to another for his or her own benefit.

The *statut civil coutumier* differs from the *statut civil* laid down by the *Code civil* in many ways. Fundamentally, the basis of the derogatory civil rules reside in the primacy of masculinity and primacy of the group over individuals.[85] These are contradictory to the spirit of post Revolution French law and French republican ideas. The birth and recognition of a child by its parents is organised differently. The surname, for example, is given by the father in the *statut civil coutumier* while under the *Code civil* it is now highly variable and the name could be given by the mother as well or by the addition of the two surnames. Succession is ruled by *palabre* in the local customary rules and not by the *Code civil*. Marriage and divorce are ruled differently under the special status. Being under customary civil rules will bring a particular application of land law. Indeed, customary land law will apply there.[86] *Terres coutumières* (customary lands) coexist with lands under the *Code civil*.

The dimensions of the customary law are in many ways very important. Quantitatively, 80,443 persons are under *statut civil coutumier*, i.e. 40.86 per cent of the population of New Caledonia. Qualitatively, the customary civil rules will also take care of criminal affairs. Indeed, without prejudice on civil and land matters, it will be possible for the customary authorities to have a role in prevention and mediation.[87] The *sénat coutumier* and *conseils coutumiers* are in charge of the customary civil rules and the French civil courts are in charge of enforcing these customary civil rules.[88] *Assesseurs coutumiers* (guarantors of customary knowledge) assist the judge in his work.

Here again, the outcome is the recognition of plurality: if it is possible within the Republic to have different rules applied to different groups of people, then unity is gone and indivisibility as a principle with it.

5.5.3 A new citizenship of New Caledonia

The *loi organique* sets out the citizenship of New Caledonia.[89] Citizens are individuals of French nationality who fulfil one of the conditions listed under article 188 L.99-209 relating to the electorate to *Congrès* and provincial assembly that:

- fulfil the conditions to be listed on the register of electors and allowed to vote in the referendum of 8 November 1998;
- are on the annexed list and domiciled for at least ten years on the date of the elections to *Congrès* and provincial assemblies;
- have reached the age of majority which is 18 years old and either have been domiciled for at least ten years in New Caledonia or have at least one parent on the register of electors allowed to vote in the referendum

of 8 November 1998 or have at least one parent on the annexe list and domiciled for at least ten years on the date of the elections to *Congrès* and provincial assemblies.

This novelty of French constitutional law entrenches the recognition of specificity within the Republic with its idea of unity of nation through breaching the principles of equality and indivisibility of the Republic. Although it is neither indicated nor written anywhere that there is a nation of New Caledonia, it is recognised that the citizens of the territory have a vocation to be the only ones able to participate in elections to the institutions of the territory and moreover to the final consultation for self-determination. The citizenship of New Caledonia has been set out as a temporary solution between 'French citizenship-French nationality' (article 4 L.99-209 for instance states that only French nationals can be citizens of New Caledonia) and 'full citizenship-New Caledonia nationality'. This 'New Caledonia citizenship-French nationality' situation recognises that there are special rights for the population of the territory but not that individuals composing this population belong to a nation other than the French nation. That said it poses the question of what is a people? It is recognised that a Kanak people exists distinct from the French people. As mentioned in article 1 of the 1958 Constitution, France is an indivisible Republic. It is possible to imagine the presence of different cultures on the soil of the Republic as, for example, was held by the decision of the *Conseil constitutionnel* on Corsica, illustrated by the recognition of the teaching of Corsican language and culture.[90] On the other hand, it is contradictory to the fundamental principle of the Republic to imagine a *peuple corse, composante du peuple français*, a Corsican people as part of the French people.[91] The same logic does not seem to apply in the case of New Caledonia and the Kanak people. The Nouméa Agreement was a new step towards this idea for a Kanak people, within the framework and logic of the French Republican Constitution. It highlighted twice that there was within the French nation a French people and peoples of overseas territories.[92] In the agreement, the term Kanak people was found three times in the Preamble. It also recognised that the Kanak have an identity considered to be so special that a particular way of organising their territory within the French Republic is needed.[93] That said, this is also a crucial issue for self-determination. There is, strangely, no recognition of a separate people of New Caledonia, only of a Kanak people. The contradiction is entrenched in the set-up of a citizenship of New Caledonia, which appears only as a logical legal parade, a temporary solution that could bring full nationality status and full recognition of the Kanak people if self-determination is reached. On the other hand, it seems that the UN does not refer to Kanak but rather to New Caledonian. Indeed, the Committee for Decolonisation of the UN does not explicitly mention the Kanak people but rather uses the neutral word, the population of New Caledonia (AG/COL/176 of 10 July 2000 and 210 of 12 June 2003). Then again, what is meant by the population of New Caledonia seems to take into account everyone living on the territory, Kanak and others. This is closer to the idea of cohesive national groups that could have the right to decide on their destiny through self-determination rather than only one group alone. The questions of citizenship, nationality, people and population are crucial in the context of decolonisation. The use of each of these words by the UN, the French authorities and the Kanak people is not innocent. The notion of the French Republic composed of a plurality of people which are theoretically part of the same nation is undermining once again the dogmatic concept of the indivisibility of the Republic.

5.5.4 Regional cooperation and external relations

The 1999 *statut* sets out the external relations of New Caledonia. Within the competence of the state, the French authorities could empower the president of the government of the territory to negotiate and sign bilateral and multilateral agreements with states, territories or regional organisations in the Pacific area and with regional institutions of the UN.[94] Also within the jurisdiction of the territory, the *Congrès* could authorise the president of the government of the territory to negotiate and sign bilateral and multilateral agreements with states, territories or regional organisations in the Pacific area and with regional institutions of the UN.[95] Although it is a great power given to the territory, it is limited by many conditions. Primarily, the territory has to respect international agreements binding the French Republic when negotiating its own agreements. Then the French authorities have to be informed of the authorisation given by the *Congrès* to the president of the government and have to authorise the president to sign the international agreements. Finally, if the *Congrès* has to approve the agreement, only the procedure set out in articles 52 and 53 of the 1958 Constitution may be relied on to ratify it. The president of the government, within the same territorial competence, after authorisation given by *Congrès* and the president of a provincial assembly, within the competence of provinces, after authorisation given by his assembly may negotiate and sign agreements with French or foreign local authorities. *Congrès* and provincial assemblies have to approve the agreement after it has been signed.[96]

New Caledonia is a member and observer of several multilateral organisations. It is a member of the Pacific Community (France is also a member), the Pacific Regional Environment Programme (France is also a member), the Pacific Islands Development Programme, the Oceania Customs Organisation (although the competence of customs is shared between the state and the territory and the administration in charge is a state one, the *direction régionale des douanes de Nouvelle-Calédonie*), the World Organisation for Animal Health (France is also a member), the South Pacific Applied Geosciences Commission (associate member), the South Pacific Tourism Organisation (however, tourism is now within the competence of the province), United Nations Economic and Social Commission for Asia and the Pacific (associate member while France is a full member) and World Health Organisation (associate member as France is a member but the territory focuses on the Western Pacific area). Through its Pacific Territories, France is an associate member of the Pacific Economic Cooperation Council. New Caledonia is also an observer of the Forum Fisheries Agency and of the Pacific Forum.

New Caledonia has developed new cooperation with its closest neighbours. Bilateral agreements are now in place with Australia (framework of a Memorandum of Understanding 2002 for development of commercial exchanges and economic relations), Vanuatu (agreement 1993), New Zealand and Fiji, aimed at increasing economic development.

As expressed in article 3.2.1 of the Nouméa Agreement, New Caledonia will be able to become a member and associated member of the UN and its institutions, notably UNESCO. This was highlighted by the General Assembly of the UN Committee on Decolonisation (AG/COL/166 9 July 1999). This fourth element operates as a complement to the other three. The sum of these elements is the strongest statement of its kind in French public administration. It transcends constitutional law and brings an unquestionable assault against the principle of indivisibility.

5.6 Conclusion

In this chapter, I have tested one of the most important French republican principles using a remote island in the Pacific, far from France. The 'New Caledonia test' is after all a good way of investigating the conflict between two principles enshrined in the Fifth French Republic Constitution. Because of its long and resilient institutional history, New Caledonia is peculiar in French public administration. The greatest attraction is the element included in the general organisation of the territory, i.e. organisation of the self-determination, derogatory civil rules, citizenship and external relations and cooperation. It will be necessary to wait for the Polynesian organisation to test this 'New Caledonia test' itself. Perhaps some institutional particularities should be added to these conditions.

The decolonisation process has been long and painful. The postwar waves of accession to sovereignty brought with them a lot of suffering. In this postmodern era (or second modern era, in the words of Beck), supranational entities seem to be the fashionable development in world organisation and a cosmopolitan society is allegedly growing from the ashes of nation states. In that context, 'leftovers' from the large nineteenth- and twentieth-century empires act as permanent reminders of the past. In many ways, accession to sovereignty is outdated. Without entering the debate of what is sovereignty, the deal of European integration, for example, is based on the diminishing and the giving away of sovereignty to organise a larger political and legal entity. The defeat of the nation state concept shows how nationalism and egocentrism could be overturned by a kind of ideal peace and prosperity. It is unsure that the future independence of New Caledonia will mean peace and prosperity for either the Kanak people or the populations of New Caledonia. It is also unsure that this will be an instrument for peace and prosperity for the entire Pacific area itself. What is certain is that France has probably forgotten, for many reasons, to take into consideration the specificities, the identities and cultures of its overseas populations and is now trying, voluntarily or not, to prove that it could do better with a nice gesture, mainly towards New Caledonia. The dilemma of the foundation of the French Republic is that dogmatic concepts like indivisibility of the Republic have proved to be inflexible and have pushed the overseas situation to breaking point, reflectively operating as a direct attack against the legal principle itself. As expressed by Ulrich Beck, 'Postcolonial voices from the so-called periphery have to play a weightier role, not only for understanding the periphery, but also for understanding the so-called centre.'[97]

The French Revolution brought many benefits to individuals and in many ways to the organisation of society itself. However, a rather inflexible transcription of some of the revolutionary ideals and their exportation to overseas territories has a similar parallel in history, the conversion by the Christians of the indigenous populations in Latin America. Since the middle of the nineteenth century, as a result of the mission of the French Republics to export the ideals of the revolution, there remain peoples scattered around the world with their own identity, their own language, their own culture and beliefs and with their own ideas of their social structure. If the perspective of having new nationalities born through the sovereign recognition of minorities acts as a reminder of another century, in a world of globalisation and large-scale political and legal unions, it is ironically also a sign of great success for the French exportation of the revolution as it highlights for the conquered population a good understanding of the ideal of freedom. Under the veil of indivisibility, for many years the core of the French Republic, hides the best kept secret of French republican ideas – unity – that I will now consider through the issue of language.

6 The French Republic, its language and the paradigm of unity[1]

6.1 Introduction

According to a 2006 document released by the administrative body in charge of the French language, the *Délégation Générale de la Langue Française et aux Langues de France* (DGLFLF),[2] French is spoken by nearly 265 million people. This internal document had the appearance of a marketing tool, showing that French is not only spoken in France but has a larger impact. More interesting, perhaps, is the name of the central administration involved, which has prompted a certain amount of discussion,[3] the origins of which can be traced back to 1989 when the *Délégation Générale de la Langue Française* (DGLF) was created.[4] At that time, the scope of the DGLF was restricted to the national language spoken in France, that is of course the French language. In 2001, there was a change made that, prima facie, appeared to be straightforward but which, in fact, had important consequences. *Langues de France* (languages of France) was added to the name of the administration in charge of language, suggesting that the French Republic wanted to move from a monolithic understanding of language towards an acceptance of linguistic diversity in France.[5] On French soil, French and other languages 'officially' coexist and, of course, this name change was only recognising the reality of the situation on French territory.

When referring to the French Republic as a space, I mean the territory that resulted from the 'work' of the Kings of France over three dynasties (and mainly during the last, the dynasty of the Capetian). One aspect of the result was that different communities with different languages became connected by a process of amalgamation. I am including here all overseas territories, and am referring to the long history of aggregating first a coherent territory. The space 'France' that I want to consider is one where different regional languages were spoken and the French empire and its colonies, with their indigenous languages. As such, one may relate to 'internal' minorities and/or to 'external' minorities. For years, the French Republic has considered in its legal framework, at every level, the position of the French language and, particularly, the parochial notion of its 'protection'. The 'aggressor' has always been the language of others, and in recent times this has been, predominantly, the English language. The reaction has been to protect the French language against 'the invasion' of English by unifying the medium of communication, which, in turn, has negated the diversity of languages spoken on French territory. But the legal framework has only masked a deep, long-standing theoretical structure.

6.1.1 Preliminary remarks on the legal aspects

According to Professor Brunet, in an allusion to Humpty Dumpty, 'One can measure therefore how applying the law is exercising a power: the power of deciding on the meaning of words.'[6] One should keep in mind how important therefore language is for the law. We may look at the idea of the constitutionalisation of the language as a good example of freezing the meaning of words; it channels the worldview, the official meaning of things, and rejects, consequently, alterity. The 1958 Constitution was amended in 1992 to constitutionalise the French language as the language of the Republic.[7] Article 2 of the Constitution now states that 'the language of the Republic is French'.[8] In 1994, the statute the *Loi 'Toubon'*, so named after its initiator J. Toubon, imposed the French language in the public sphere;[9] the use of French was (en)forced in relation to legal persons of public law and private persons involved in operating a public service. Interestingly enough, the 1994 statute explicitly stated (in article 21) that the statute was not against the use of other languages (such as the regional languages qualified as *langues de France* in 2001). Indeed, this was reaffirmed in the *Conseil constitutionnel* ruling on the constitutionality of the *Loi 'Toubon'*.[10] The *Conseil* explained that article 2 of the 1958 Constitution had to be considered alongside the freedom of communication and expression proclaimed by article 11 of the 1789 Declaration of the Rights of Man and Citizens. According to the 1789 Declaration, everyone has the right to choose the best way to express their thoughts. Consequently, the use of the French language cannot be imposed in private communications. The issue of the French language is in fact important and topical because of the paradigm of unity that supports the myth of French republicanism. For many years, the idea has been to unify language and nation, as both interacting and self-reflecting. Therefore the change of the name of the authority in charge of the French language seems to be more than a simple renaming. The purpose of the DGLFLF is to preserve and validate the languages of France, including regional and indigenous languages spoken on the national territory, which are part of the national culture.[11] But beyond any effects on the French language, it is the paradigm of unity and the myth of French republicanism that are under pressure.

6.1.2 Preliminary remarks on the theoretical aspects

I mentioned earlier that changing the name of the agency in charge runs deeper than it appears at first sight. The action of naming is not neutral.

According to Lacan, '[n]aming constitutes a pact, by which two subjects agree at the same time to recognise the same object'.[12] The pact here refers to the official recognition of other languages on French territory: it has a social aspect. Language translates as cultural belonging, as identity, conceived through the inter-subjectivity of individuals associated in a group. In the words of Heidegger, '[l]anguage is as the Dasein is … it is historical'.[13] Through language, an individual is positioned in space and time. Through language, an individual is recognised in relation to others: members of a community communicate with each other. However, the problem of language should not be considered only from an individual perspective but must also be seen inter-subjectively. It relates to societal organisation, where individuals are linked by a 'closed circuit', as Saussure explained – a 'circuit' that is a 'speech circuit'. Language is not entirely, not only, a private experience: 'language is a social act'.[14] Saussure emphasised that point by dissociating *langue*/language and *parole*/speech. He explained that by doing so he was separating 'what is social from what is individual'.[15] He considered language to be a quasi-contract between the members of a community,[16] created through the dynamic of time around the relationships between individuals.[17] A group language, from the smallest (a family) to the largest (a country) – the 'human language' (the object of linguistic study) – exists because of social links that make it real.[18] Language is not merely an instrument of communication, or even a 'cultural form', but a trans-individual 'bond', an inter-subjective activity that produces its own forms of identification or counter-identification.[19] It is perhaps a cliché but we should remember that French structuralism is all about language, about the relation between language and the structuration of a community. In *Totemism*, Levi-Strauss connected the problems of the relationship 'human–other species' to the identification of social groups by means of symbolic objects, recognising that in primal society the organisation around a totem was linked to structural linguistics.[20] Individuals associate in groups through and by language and ultimately establish a society. In the case of France, the unity of language has been instrumental in unifying the country. This is perhaps a simplistic introduction but language can be seen as the cement of societal organisation: hence the relationship made in the title of this chapter between language and unity.

6.1.3   The paradigm of unity

What is at stake is the link between language and unity, but the paradigmatic aspect of the word unity is important here. Let us follow the contemporary meaning given to 'paradigm' as an object of scientific research, similar to the object of research referred to in the work of Althusser. The object is that which is scientifically observed and to which all the aspects of scientific observation relate. The object of my scientific observation here is the question of unity.[21] It will not be comprehended as a single entity but rather as the way unity interacts with language.

I would like to analyse this without relying exclusively on French structuralism. That is perhaps why I decided here not to refer to Althusser but rather to another pre-eminent European commentator of Marx, Gramsci. Gramsci considered the relationship between language and social or socio-political organisation.[22] He demonstrated a link between unified language and national unity, using Italy of course as illustration. As explained by Ives, '[Gramsci's] interests in a national, unified Italian language represent perhaps the strongest analogy to both his critique of the Italian Risorgimento as "a passive revolution" and his interest in Machiavelli as accurately diagnosing Italy's need for a strong and active unity.'[23] As mentioned by Gramsci, citing Dante's *De vulgari eloquentia*, 'the "question of the language" has always been an aspect of the political struggle':[24] throughout the history of France, the French language has been involved in the struggle to create the myth of the nation. Saussure too understood this relationship between language and the creation of a nation in political history in claiming that 'language makes the nation':[25]

> Some of the great historical facts, like the Roman conquest, have had an incalculable significance for a large number of linguistic facts. Colonisation, which is only a form of conquest, transports one idiom into different places, which brings changes to this idiom. We could, to support this, mention many facts: for example, Norway adopted Danish when politically unifying with Denmark; it is true the Norwegians tried to free themselves from this linguistic influence. The internal politics of states is not less important for the life of languages: certain governments, like Switzerland, admit the coexistence of many idioms; others, like France, aspire to linguistic unity.[26]

This quote from Saussure summarises how governments in a dynamic world context employ language. It also addresses the question of the French case brilliantly. Presented analytically, this dynamic can be expressed as follows: (a) imperial conquest exports language (the Roman Empire exported Latin, for example); (b) colonised countries encounter difficulties in dealing with linguistic colonisation (Danish was used in Norway, but the Norwegians wanted rid of it); (c) some states have chosen a pluri-lingual approach while others have chosen monolingual methods (Switzerland v. France). If this structure is applied to the French case, the following results: period (a), then (b), then (c), then (a) and finally (b) in the current context. France was part of Latin colonisation; then it became monolingual, and exported French during the period of Empire, continuing to do so at an institutionalised European level and beyond. Indeed, as noted by Oakes, 'Since the inception of what was then the EEC, promoting French as the preferred lingua franca for Europe has been an official French preoccupation,'[27] particularly because 'France has placed its trust in language planning as a means of generating a positive French identity.'[28] It is true that 'generating a positive French identity' has always been an important matter for the French Republic to the extent that the French Republic has become the French identity. According to Oakes's demonstration, it is possible to link the French Republic to the French language. In addition, it is possible to say that 'generating' ideas was a necessity imposed by violence.[29] The same comments may be made in the case of the former French colonies. Here too, the experience of the violence of a language imposed is apparent while the twisted ambivalence of the identity linked to language appears: the trauma of (the idea) of a monolinguistic Republic is clear. In reality, the inter-subjective relationship, which is supposed to create a community based on language, is an unequal inter-subjectivity. As stated by Žižek, citing Lacan and his notion of 'Master–Signifier' related to language, 'human communication in its most basic, constitutive dimension does not involve a space of egalitarian inter-subjectivity. It is not "balanced".'[30] This imbalance, or disequilibrium, means that languages have sometimes been violently and irrationally imposed on populations.

Looking once more at the time of the 'foundation' of 'France', there was a clear movement from a single small group to a more or less coherent aggregation of several groups: as such, it was obvious that serious challenges in terms of communication had to be faced. One can impose a language to allow communication between persons, populations, communities, societies, or one may organise means of communication that respect groups, diversity, identity and as a consequence the plurality of languages. Therefore the history of language is also the history of the struggles of world powers: civilisation by conquest; civilisation by communication; imposing one vision or respecting others.[31] This is also a matter of how a society can create unity through language by imposing one language on its communities – it needs to assert a single identity (either internally or externally, in the case of colonisation). France chose to declare that 'the others' (inside or outside) were different and chose to deny multiple languages as a way of organising society. In the words of Derrida, identification is a long and difficult process.[32] It implies recognising the absence of others, or signifying that the language (and culture) of the others does not bear the same value as 'our' (national?) language. In this intolerance of the others, typical for instance of colonisation, the dominant chooses to erase the dominated in order to affirm its existence. This type of reasoning underpins the way the French language was enforced as the single language of the French Republic: the other is conceptualised as inferior. If we analyse the French language and its relation to unity, we rapidly find that the language was initially imposed on the French territory as the sole means of communication. It was characterised by a dialectical relationship between identity and diversity. The 'French' evolved from a concept that first constructed 'France' and then constructed 'the Republic'; it developed into something that was imposed on 'the others', something that has always been present, but masked, until changes in attitude after the Second World War. I wish to show here that there has been a move away from a dogmatic vision of 'France' and its monolingual myth, to the implicit recognition of minorities, at least linguistically, as the recognition of the reality of pluralism.

6.2 Monolinguism as an aid to the construction of France and the Republic: the myth of one language unifying internal minorities

Through the symbolic mediation of language, the world is represented. This *mise en scène* allows the creation of a space that is perceived as real but is not. The operation is therefore similar to myth creation: something is created that is partially real and develops into something that is believed to be real. However, the efficiency of the myth owes much to the talent of the director conducting the *mise en scène*, to the actors, to the scenario, which in this case pre-dates the French Revolution. The myth began with the narration of the creation of 'France', based on one language; it went on to the development of the foundation of the Republic. From this perspective, language is employed as the means to organise the world through an ideological order; it is a theatrical representation of a society that believes it is what is represented: a society formed by language into a country (France), then into a Republic.

6.2.1 *The problem of language and the unitary form of the state*

Let us begin with the problem of unitary states, best examples of which are, in my opinion, France and the UK. Both are former centres of empires, which enable us to examine the amalgamation of territories and the problems of internal and external minorities. Let us compare the two countries on the question of language and their 'internal' minorities.

In the UK, the question of language was dealt with by the devolution legislation of the late 1990s. The situation was addressed in Wales by the Welsh Language Act 1993,[33] which established that Welsh and English were to be treated 'on the basis of equality', when reasonably practical and appropriate to the circumstances. The UK is often classified as a unitary state; it has different languages coexisting on its territory, and encompasses the English language – one of the main languages spoken throughout the world (and for many the new *lingua franca*). Wales has been particularly involved in this process. It is interesting, therefore, to look at the preamble of the Welsh Language Act 1993:

> An Act to establish a Board having the function of promoting and facilitating the use of the Welsh language, to provide for the preparation by public bodies of schemes giving effect to the principle that in the conduct of public business and the administration of justice in Wales the English and Welsh languages should be treated on a basis of equality, to

make further provision relating to the Welsh language, to repeal certain spent enactments relating to Wales, and for connected purposes.

The recognition of the two languages to be used in Wales is an important matter. Indeed, 'public business and the administration of justice' can be conducted in either language – hence the idea of equality between the two. Since 2005, this has also been the case in Scotland.[34] The preamble to the Gaelic Language (Scotland) Act 2005 states that it is:

> An Act of the Scottish Parliament to establish a body having functions exercisable with a view to securing the status of the Gaelic language as an official language of Scotland commanding equal respect to the English language, including the functions of preparing a national Gaelic language plan, of requiring certain public authorities to prepare and publish Gaelic language plans in connection with the exercise of their functions and to maintain and implement such plans, and of issuing guidance in relation to Gaelic education.

This act replaces the wording found in the Welsh Language Act, which states that both languages 'should be treated on a basis of equality' with the statement that the two languages should command 'equal respect'. This act was passed later than the Welsh one; the attitude towards the Gaelic language does not appear to be similar to the one towards the Welsh language, and this may confirm, prima facie, the asymmetrical aspect of devolution.[35]

In Northern Ireland, '[u]llans was not neglected in the negotiations between the governments of the United Kingdom and the Republic of Ireland in 1998.'[36] The Belfast Agreement (also known as the Good Friday Agreement) of 1998 was primarily an agreement between the UK and Ireland with regard to Northern Ireland. The linguistic question, because of the evident imbalance of power between the languages and between the two territorial entities, concerned the protection of the Irish language. This was specifically organised in the text, together with reference to the European Charter for Regional or Minority Languages (EChRML). However, the bilingual reference does not give a full picture of the situation in Northern Ireland. The Agreement refers to the Ulster-Scots and other languages:

> 3. All participants recognise the importance of respect, understanding and tolerance in relation to linguistic diversity, including in Northern Ireland, the Irish language, Ulster-Scots and the languages of the various ethnic communities, all of which are part of the cultural wealth of the island of Ireland.

This chapter is not about the multilingual or bilingual situation of a country as such, but about how language relates to unity in the French republican context, and the ways in which it may foster peculiar situations for minority cultures. That said, the situation of the UK is intriguing, as is the case of Ireland, because they are specific cases of unitary states. In France, the UK and Ireland, there is no federal link to linguistic matters, as there is in Belgium and Switzerland, for example. A unitary state seems normally able to 'survive' a bilingual approach hence it is often a constitutional matter. For instance, Ireland recognised in its 1937 Constitution both English and Irish as official languages.[37] Even Saussure specifically referred to Ireland in the chapter of the *cours* focusing on the coexistence of different languages, stating that 'in Ireland are spoken Celtic and English'.[38] Both languages relate to minorities. They also relate to cultural differences and separate ethnic identities. They are strongly related because of the colonial history.[39]

The UK appears to recognise that the devolution process has reinforced a certain amount of bilingualism. If we return to the logical approach of Saussure applied to the specific case of the UK, it has moved from (a) imperial conquest exports language to (c) some states have chosen a pluri-lingual approach while others have chosen a monolingual one (Switzerland v. France, for example). In the meantime, in contrast, France remains rooted in the idea of the uniqueness of language as it relates to the unity of (the idea of) France, and also to (the idea of) the Republic.

6.2.2 *Unicity of language as structuring (the idea of) France*

During the sixteenth century, the royal ordinance of Villers-Cotterêts (*Ordonnance du Roy sur le faict de justice*, 1539) transposed the ideological dimension of language (in this particular case, the French language) into law. The royal ordinance concerned not only the administration of the state and the political use of the language but also the cohesion of the nation and its historicity.

Like almost all the countries of Europe, France used to be a bilingual state where Latin coexisted with the local, or common, language. French became the official language under the royal ordinance of François I. It imposed French as the language of administration instead of Latin, which was highly criticised in the text because it lacked 'precision'.[40] As a consequence, article 111 of the ordinance proclaimed French as the language to be used:

> we now want every decisions, together with every procedures, either of our sovereign courts or subordinated and inferiors, registers, investigations, contracts, commissions, sentences, wills and every other acts, or others, of justice or annexes, to be pronounced, registered and delivered to parties in maternal French language and not differently.[41]

The royal ordinance was a statute organising the administration of justice in France. It was designed to reduce the power of the Church while increasing the authority of the King. Thus, a change in the medium of communication was supposed to change the 'master'. The French language at the time was not widely spoken and was called *françoys*, or the vulgar mother tongue (*langage maternel vulgaire*). In Heidegger's terms, it would be considered as the ordinary language as opposed to the originary language. This move from Latin, the originary language, to French, the ordinary language (the change described in Saussure's logical demonstration above), was not aimed at local languages – the dialects spoken by the 'internal' minorities of the time – but at Latin and the power of the Catholic Church behind it. Attacking the status of Latin, 'the language of the educated people',[42] was indeed a political manoeuvre against the influence of the Church. In doing so, the King asserted his political leadership and his sovereignty through language. From this moment, it was obvious that language had power. The French language changed value from ordinary status to originary status. However, the 'real' process of imposing the (French) language was violent and was exacerbated during the revolution, the foundation of the Republic.

6.2.3 Unicity of language as structuring (the idea of) the Republic

Throughout the eighteenth century, the French Revolution and the French language were closely interrelated. To unify the Republic, under the paradigm of unity, it became important to impose one language on the French people, unified as the French nation. At this stage, 'violence' was exercised on local minority languages rather than on Latin.

At the beginning of the 1792–3 Convention, a commission was established that allowed people to believe the Republic would become multilingual, as all legal documents were (supposed to be) translated into local languages. This did not last, as the *Girondins* were politically (and physically) eliminated by the *Montagnards*. This was the triumph of the Jacobins (*Montagnards*) over the Girondists (*Girondins*).[43] With the Jacobin triumph came the end of aspirations for a federal Republic more or less based on identity and linguistic plurality. The idea of a multilingual society rapidly became a political oddity and legally unrealistic. Indeed, one of the most famous French revolutionaries, the abbot Henri-Baptiste Grégoire, declared a war against local languages. After a lengthy period of research, he prepared and delivered the Report on the necessity and means to annihilate provincial dialects and to universalise the use of French (*Rapport sur la nécessité et les moyens d'anéantir les patois et d'universaliser l'usage de la langue française*), in which he used the term Babel to describe the situation in France.[44] Naturally, this was not a neutral term for a priest to use and it had two correlative significations: (a) France was at the time of the revolution a multilingual territory and (b) this was a bad situation. It was indeed a bad situation because it *was* like Babel, and as a man of God, Grégoire knew that Babel was the place and the proof of God's punishment. According to Ost, 'At the basis of the "common linguistic sense", the idea of language is essentially, and at least ideally, an immense lexicon that would be nothing other than the heritage of the one existing in the Garden of Eden where God had named everything according to their nature, without ambiguity, lacuna, or redundancy.'[45]

The building of Babel was a mistake followed by an exemplary punishment. Grégoire wrote about *la nécessité d'anéantir*, the necessity (or the urge) to annihilate other languages. The messianic work of the French Revolution was to overcome Babel. This continued when Robespierre seized power and imposed the French language throughout the territory through governmental regulations intended to terrorise: the 'linguistic terror' was legalised by government regulation.[46]

According to this 1794 regulation, every act emanating from a public authority, anywhere on the territory of the French Republic, had to be written in French.[47] One month after the publication of this regulation, its scope was extended to private documents.[48] It became a crime (carrying a punishment of six months' imprisonment) to deal with documents written in dialects or other languages; this was aimed at civil servants, agents of the government and, later, civil servants involved in tax collection.[49]

Another, perhaps less evident, authoritarian way in which the French language was forced on the population was through education. In fact, the revolution considered education as a major public policy. Article 1 of the 1792 Report and project of regulation on the organisation of primary schools presented to the National Convention, in the name of the committee of public instruction, expressed the connection to be made between education and the official language: 'Public teaching will be everywhere conducted in a way that its first benefit will be the French language becoming, in a very short period, the familiar language of all parts of the Republic.'[50]

From that point onwards, the French language was not only employed as a mean of combat within France, but also it became a means of organising the mythical army – the citizens in arms – of the French people, which aimed to export the ideas of the French Revolution throughout the world, imposing the language on 'external' minorities. But it should be remembered that the language that became then glorified (the French language) was the language of the Parisian bourgeoisie. The national language was in fact the language of the capital's wealthy citizens. There was therefore no difference between the republican idea of having a unique language and the linguistic logic of the monarchy. It was from a dominant position that French was imposed on others; other languages were considered to be inferior. One can here find the obvious 'real' reason behind the use of certain languages rather than others: 'the other' is always considered to be inferior. The social origin of French highlighted the division between the cities and the countryside: the Parisian language was enforced and became the national language, rather than one of the languages of the 'others'.

The French language and the paradigm of unity merged with the help of the Jacobin method, which linked the 'national' with the 'popular' – the concept of political hegemony, that is 'the alliance between the bourgeoisie-intellectuals (*ingegno*) and the people'.[51] This theoretical construction of the people-nation, 'the protagonist of French history', became the important issue.[52] During the nineteenth century French became the media of communication in France.

In some parts of the territory, a certain (official or quasi-official) bilingual approach operated, as with the use of Germanic idioms in Alsace and Lorraine, and Italian idioms in Savoy and Nice.[53] It was during the Third Republic that this ideology won and a myth was created using unity as the key element. It imposed the idea of a united Republic, cemented by language in the conceptualisation of the republican state. As mentioned by Jones, 'students of French history must learn the language of the state tradition in order to appreciate the force exerted by the concept of the state in public argument, and not dismiss it as mystical verbosity.'[54] In fact, the fascination with unity has always masked the reality of internal and external minorities in France. The Third Republic, and in a way those that followed, relied on this fiction of unity to sustain the system. But in recent years there have been many changes toward the recognition of pluralism.

6.3 From the affirmation of monolinguism to the recognition of pluri-linguism: the reality of pluri-linguistic (internal and external) minorities

The French language is a witness to a cultural mediation. Every letter, every word, every sentence, links back to references and to the myth defined by the great narratives of French republicanism. As stressed by Derrida in *Force de Loi*, 'one of the violences of the founding Law or the imposition of state Law consists of imposing another language onto national or ethnic minorities grouped by the state'.[55] Derrida defined two 'violent' moments in France. The first occurred when the French language was set in opposition to Latin in order to consolidate the monarchic state, to permit every inhabitant of the Kingdom of France to have a common language, or even to have the possibility to be 'represented' in a common language. The second moment was the Revolution, when linguistic unification became authoritarian and repressive.[56]

The primary violence, that of one against another, understood as a group against another group, is the violence expressed through forcing or imposing the language of one upon another. It is true that the issue of language is a major issue in separatist actions within the state, whether it is a unitary state (like the claims of the Basques, or of the Corsicans in France) or federal. One can reflect here on Belgium after the 2007 general election,[57] or in the case of quasi-federal states, on the Spanish situation with Catalonia. As previously stated, it is also certain that language is an important element in the foundation of some federal states (Switzerland and Belgium in Europe, or Canada on the American continent).

Devolution, decentralisation and the federal organisation of states may therefore depend on how the language of the other is understood, at least in a legal sense. The issue goes to the heart of how the central power wants to view the culture of others. But in any case, the hegemonic position of one group in relation to another relates to the hegemony of its language. As stated by Wilmer, 'two means were used to persuade people to identify themselves as citizen-subjects of states – violence and coercion on the one hand, and the appropriation of symbolic power through language and narrative (historical, ethnic and religious) on the other.'[58] The narrative enforced by the Parisian bourgeoisie, in this case, refers to the hegemonic majority that creates 'other' minorities – linguistic ones.[59]

6.3.1 *The reality of external minorities: populations of overseas territories v. the French Constitution*

The issue of language in the unitary French state does not solely concern the internal former provinces. The minorities affected are both 'internal' and 'external', as we have seen. The *langues de France* are not only the former regional languages of the French provinces, but also, and more problematically in contemporary France, the languages of colonised populations. The issue necessarily has another dimension when linked to these overseas territories. It is a problem of a (post-) colonial world merging with that of public administration. I mentioned that the principle of indivisibility of the French Republic, which is an expression of the paradigm of unity, relates to the territorial position from the centre of power.[60] In that respect, and within this logic, the furthest territories from the centre remain New Caledonia and French Polynesia. In the spirit of reparation that underlies the changes in terminology (moving here from considering only the *langue française* to considering the *langue française et les langues de France*), the 2000 statute concerning overseas territories recognised the specificity, and the importance, of the languages of the overseas territories.[61] Article 34 of the statute considered these languages as 'the nation's linguistic patrimony' (*patrimoine linguistique de la Nation*).

In the case of New Caledonia, the Nouméa Agreement aimed at respect for the Kanak identity and culture and for the languages of the Kanak people.[62] These languages have been considered as significant as French, notably in education. The Nouméa Agreement, being part of a type of peace process, needed to reflect a balance between the centre and the periphery: language played a central part here.

With regard to French Polynesia, article 115 of the 1996 statute on the territory reaffirmed the position of French as the official language but left open the opportunity to use other languages, such as Tahitian and other Polynesian languages.[63] The constitutional council upheld the interpretation of 'official language' in the 1996 statute as having similar meaning to what was meant by the *Loi 'Toubon'*.[64] Article 57 of the 2004 statute on the territory reaffirmed the position of French as the official language, specified what was meant by 'official language' and listed what were the 'other languages':[65] 'French, Tahitian, Marquisian, Paumotu and Mangerivian are the languages of French Polynesia'.[66] The state recognised its role in the protection of the 'other languages' while insisting on the true nature of the dialectic French language/languages of France. The use of French was 'imposed to legal persons of public law and to private persons involved in a mission of public service and to anybody interacting with the administrations and the public services.'[67] For the other languages, '[t]he natural persons and private persons use it freely in their acts and conventions; these will not carry nullity on the grounds that they are not written in the official language.'[68]

The constitutional council ruled that while the legislator 'generously' acknowledged that there were different languages spoken on the territory of French Polynesia, French included, the French language had to be considered as the 'superior one' in the public sphere: 'the use of French is necessary in the public sphere'.[69] The dialectic 'French language'/'languages of France' appears to be resolved because of the repartition of 'tasks' through specialisation: the French language must be used in the public sphere; the languages of France are used in the private sphere.

The *Conseil d'État* had to consider in a case concerning the territory an internal regulation made by the territorial assembly of French Polynesia.[70] Article 15 of the internal regulation (May 2006) holds that the assembly debates have to be conducted in French, Tahitian or in one of the Polynesian languages. The *Conseil d'État* considered that the official language of Polynesia was French and therefore that a local law (*loi de pays*) could only be rightfully adopted if the proper procedure was followed. The procedure, it was expressly stated, had to be conducted in French. In addition, it was implied that the use of French (the language of the Republic) was part of that procedure. The *Conseil d'État* reiterated the idea that a local law adopted after a debate in a language other than French would be considered illegal because it would have been adopted following an irregular procedure. The administrative decision of the local assembly was, as a consequence, found illegal because it was in violation of the statute *loi organique* of 27 February 2004, which completes the Constitution and made French the official language of the territory.[71]

Article 57 of the 2004 *loi organique*, which mirrors the text of the 1958 Constitution, stated that 'French is the official language of French Polynesia. Its use is imposed on legal persons of public law and on private persons involved in a mission of public service, together with anyone interacting with administrations and public services.'[72] However, plurality of language was not excluded. In fact, other languages were considered, although not as official languages. The architecture of this article is striking. It starts with the positioning of the French language as the official language; then the second paragraph mentions Tahitian. We end up with an order of precedence that confers value through a simple binary classification first/second: first French, second Tahitian. Tahitian is allowed in the private sphere but, as is the case for regional languages on French territory, the French language has to be used in every communication in the public sphere:

> The Tahitian language is a fundamental element of the cultural identity:
> it is the cement of social cohesion, the means of daily communication, it

is recognised and has to be preserved, as other Polynesian languages have to be, together with the language of the Republic, in order to act as guarantor of cultural diversity that has created the richness of French Polynesia.[73]

The conferring of value through the positioning of first/second is a statement of supremacy and superiority and takes a hegemonic position. Tahitian is, however, recognised as an important element of the cultural identity of the territory. But in the public sphere, all communication has to be made through the French language. There is therefore a division between the political, or legal, culture and the general culture. The political and legal cultures are French; the culture itself is Tahitian. In a text that created the autonomy of a French overseas territory, the violence of the language expresses a perfect opposition to this autonomy. It sends a mixed signal. If you are Tahitian, your territory is autonomous and you may have certain rights that are particular to your population, and to your territory, but you cannot, in legal or political matters, use your language. We are confronted at the same time with a superposition of languages while the overarching principle is the paradigm of unity. Only the French language is the language of the French Republic. No other languages can and will be used in public matters. To summarise, we have the following: one Republic, one people, one language. A few populations with different languages are recognised, as particular cultural identities but also as subordinate ethnicities. In Heideggerian terms, the French language (of the Parisian bourgeoisie of the nineteenth century) has become the originary language of the state. If it is so, then every other languages must 'only' or 'simply' be ordinary.

Although the *Conseil d'État* cannot directly control the constitutionality of an administrative act, in the 2006 case concerning French Polynesia, the ruling had to be considered in relation to the 1958 Constitution and specifically its article 2, paragraph 1: 'The language of the Republic is French.'[74] The language relates then to the idea of the French nation, its people and components and a number of interesting cases involving the *Conseil constitutionnel* need to be considered accordingly[75] In the landmark decision, *Status de la Corse*,[76] the *Conseil* ruled that there was 'only one people', and that therefore there was no legal possibility for a 'Corsican people' to exist as a sub-section or component of the 'French people'. This was compared to overseas territories that were allowed to have 'peoples' (later considered to be 'populations' in a 2000 decision[77]) that (co-)existed with the French. The issue here involved the teaching of Corsican. It was considered that the promotion of the Corsican language could not be considered contrary to the Constitution (but this was prior to the recognition of the French language in the 1992 constitutional amendment). However, the two issues of unity and language were linked again, as they were explicitly in 1999, when the *Conseil constitutionnel* linked language and unicity in a landmark decision on the EChRML which rejected and blocked the ratification.[78] But it seems that the monolingual approach, developed during the French Revolution and beyond, suited the ideal of unity and its legal appendix, the indivisibility of the Republic. In effect, the *Conseil constitutionnel* illuminated the normative framework for language. Article 1 of the 1958 Constitution was considered to provide the initial legal basis of this framework, in stating 'France is a Republic, indivisible, secular, democratic and social. It guarantees equality before the law of all citizens without distinction of origin, of race or of religion. It respects all beliefs.'[79] As a kind of next stage, the *Conseil constitutionnel* reaffirmed the paradigm of unity and its constitutional value: 'the principle of unicity of the French people, of which no section can attribute to itself the exercise of national sovereignty, has also constitutional value.'[80] And because this paradigm of unity was recognised as having constitutional value, everything that created rights for a specific group – defined as a community of origin, culture or belief – was not to be tolerated. Of course, behind these considerations was hiding the spectre of language, as stated later in the decision, which considered that 'these fundamental principles are opposed to the recognition of collectives rights to any groups, defined as a community of origin, culture, language or beliefs'.[81] Interestingly enough, the *Conseil* explained that article 11 of the 1789 Declaration, on freedom of communication and opinion, did not recognise a right that was absolute, and therefore, in the case of conflict with the constitutional text, narrowly defined (the articles of the Constitution), the constitutional text would take precedence:

> The free communication of thoughts and opinions is one of the most cherished rights of man: every citizen can speak, write, print freely, except if he has to answer an abuse of this freedom in a case specified by the law, that has to be correlated with paragraph 1 of article 2 of the Constitution, under which 'the language of the Republic is French'.[82]

The *Conseil constitutionnel* interpreted this as an obligation to use French in the public sphere – while in the private sphere, it was (always and without restriction) possible to use another language. But the relationship between the people and the administration belongs to the public sphere and, as such, has to be conducted solely in French. It specifically referred to the compulsory use of French by legal persons of public law, and by private persons involved in a public service mission. Individuals in their relations with the administration and the public services must use the French language only. Consequently, there is no right to use a language other than French and no one can be forced to use a language other than French. That said, the *Conseil constitutionnel* reiterated the point that article 2 of the 1958 Constitution did not consider as contrary to the Constitution the use of translations, the importance of other languages in education or research, audiovisual communication, or freedom of expression and communication.

The bottom line was that the *Conseil constitutionnel* could not allow the ratification of the EChRML because the EChRML was creating specific rights for communities. Indeed, by doing so, it was in breach of the Constitution because it conflicts with the paradigm of unity. The Charter was conferring specific rights to groups of speakers of regional or minority dialects within 'territories' where those dialects were used. The *Conseil* felt that the Charter was therefore contrary to the Constitution and particularly 'to the constitutional principle of indivisibility of the Republic, equality before the law and unicity of the French people'.[83] It also ruled that it was contrary to 'the first paragraph of article 2 of the Constitution, which recognises a right to practise a language other than French not only in "private life" but also in "public life".'[84] (The Charter definition encompasses both justice and public administration in this context.)

Interestingly, in both the French and British cases, the control of the central state (of the unitarian state) is waning over time. France has increased the freedoms and rights of its local authorities, and since 1997 the UK has given similar rights and freedoms to Wales, Scotland and Northern Ireland. However, the 'cement' of the language does not appear to be similarly binding in all instances. No bilingual arrangements have been constitutionally organised in France, although regional languages have been considered as cultural interests. In the 2006 case on the Tahitian language issue, indigenous languages were found to be fundamental to French Polynesian cultural identity (including issues of social cohesion and the daily means of communication), and in that respect it needed to be protected, like the other Polynesian languages.

The logic of the conflicting constitutional principles in the 1958 Constitution pushed New Caledonia, the most decentralised and *sui generis* type of French local authority, to be recognised as having a separate citizenship from the French. In French Polynesia, the antepenultimate level of administration, the position was considered differently. Therefore, while the UK considered language to be an important matter that concerns the respect of the rights of 'the other', France still strongly rejected, even at the most decentralised level, the possibility of accepting the reality behind the legal issues. Members of the French Polynesian Assembly naturally favoured a multilingual approach for their debates, as did at some point the representative of the state in French Polynesia. In 1980, the act of a local authority (*délibération* n° 2036, 28 November, signed by the *vice-président du conseil du gouvernement*, F. A Sanford, and the *Haut-commissaire*, P. Cousseran) stated that the local assembly (*Assemblée territoriale de la Polynésie française*) elevated Tahitian to the status of official language of the territory conjointly with French. This position was unique and never encountered again.

So what might happen now? Could Tahitian be recognised as an official language? This would require a modification of the Constitution, notably its article 2, or ultimately the accession of the overseas territory to full independence and a recognised sovereignty. Until or unless this occurs, this remains the case for Polynesia and many other territories. But it is a symbolic operation; no Tahitian will use in his or her day-to-day communication a language other than their own. In the same way, a Corsican raised speaking Corsican will only communicate in Corsican and not decide suddenly to communicate in a language other than Corsican.[85] Then again, this is something an individual will do in the private sphere. This has never been a legal problem (it is even protected, on the whole), no one will ever prevent someone from communicating in Corsican, for example, within the local assembly building (*Assemblée territoriale*) in the public sphere (but not during the debates). In Wallis and Futuna, far less distant from the central government than Polynesia, both Wallisien and Futunien are used for communication (alongside French) during the work of the local assembly (*Assemblée locale*). Councillors communicate in their 'mother tongue' then translate their contributions; in plenary sessions their debates are frequently conducted in a language other than French, in front of the representative of the state, the *préfet*, before announcing the decision in French. This illustrates practical variations of the general constitutional principle. Then again, the best summary of 'what can be done' or 'what is allowed' is probably what the administrative judge ruled in a 2007 case.[86] The *Conseil d'État* decided that French had to be spoken 'substantially' during debates, thus contradicting the practice outlined here; this left open a certain level of flexibility in the interpretation. It logically reiterated that French was the cement of the indivisibility of the French Republic, unicity of the French people and one language. This is a reminder of the violent characteristic of French. It has to be enforced. If the power (language) is undermined, the edifice may collapse. As a result, and because of the violent use of language, the position of the state in this matter contributes to the fuelling of relationships that are far from harmonious between the metropolis and the peripheries. Recent developments have seen the issue arising again in relation to internal minorities, and as a consequence both types of minority populations have contributed to unearthing the reality beneath the myth: pluralism.

6.3.2 *The constitutional recognition of linguistic plurality*

As stated, there has been in recent years a movement at the legislative level from sole consideration of the French language (*langue française*) towards considering the French language and languages of France (*la langue française et les langues de France*) as linguistic patrimony of the Nation (*patrimoine linguistique de la Nation*). This has been evident in laws involving the statutes of autonomy of certain overseas territories like New Caledonia and French Polynesia, as we have seen. However, there has never been any attempt to recognise these languages at constitutional level. The French language is presently encapsulated in the Constitution and it may well be the case that that statement prevents other situations from occurring. Again, the principal matter here is the paradigm of unity underpinning the foundation of the French Republic: the unity of the people, the unity of the language of the people and the indivisibility of the Republic. This has a strong theoretical foundation in the long history of France that, for Derrida, has to do with the unity of the kingdom of France. The revolution appropriated this idea and transformed it through Jacobinism with the help of education and language. This is what transpired from the 1999 decision of the *Conseil constitutionnel* on the EChRML. In this landmark case, the non-conformity of the Charter to the Constitution was based on 'the constitutional principle of indivisibility of the Republic, equality before the law and unicity of the French people'.[87] It is, *de jure*, possible to speak one of the regional languages or to speak a regional language, but not in the 'public sphere'.

We have seen that the 2008 constitutional amendment modified many areas of the Constitution. Although it had not been planned in the project presented by the government, article 40 of the adopted text added an article 75-1 to the text of the Constitution, under a title referring to the local decentralised authorities (*collectivités territoriales*):[88]

> After article 75 of the Constitution is inserted an article 75-1 drafted as followed: 'Art. 75-1. Regional languages belonging to the patrimony of France'.[89]

Through this article, regional languages have been recognised and enshrined in the 1958 Constitution. That said, the recognition is slightly peculiar. Indeed, we have here their recognition as patrimony of France, a sort of cultural recognition in a legal document rather than a proper 'constitutionalisation' of these languages. In addition, only a substantial modification of article 2 of the Constitution could have permitted a complete recognition of regional languages at constitutional level, and there was no plan to constitutionally recognise the *langues régionales*.

The draft constitutional amendment presented to the French MPs by the government, text 820,[90] initiated by President Sarkozy, did not refer at all to the language issue. During the legislative debate, the government bill was supposed to be adopted by both chambers of the French parliament before its adoption by the congress with a qualifying majority (three-fifths). In May 2008, there was a change apparently brought about as the result of pressure from the lower chamber Chair of the Law Commission, when an amendment 605[91] was adopted by the National Assembly during the first reading. This text intended to add to article 1 of the 1958 Constitution: 'Regional languages belong to its patrimony.'[92] This was not a simple task.[93] In fact, the text sent to the Senate for the first reading, text TA 150,[94] *projet* 365,[95] was rejected. The upper chamber, which is also where the local authorities are represented, considered that the reference to regional languages had to be removed from the text before it could be adopted (text TA 116[96], *projet* 993[97]). Comments were made on the tautological aspect of the last two sentences of article 1 if it were to be modified as suggested. It would read as follows: 'The organisation of the Republic is decentralised. The regional languages belong to its patrimony.'[98] It was clear that the recognition of regional languages is implicitly done through the use of the term 'decentralisation'. The *Conseil constitutionnel* might, of course, have given its own interpretation of the new article 1, and might have decided that, contrary to what the government thought, regional languages may well be protected as a component of the patrimony. Then again, there may have been a conflict between articles 1 and 2, which may have been resolved by the well known mechanism in linguistic matters: in the public sphere, we speak French; in private, we can use regional languages. The result would have been a situation similar to the current one, with the protection of the freedom of expression under article 2 of the 1789 Declaration. Only in the private sphere is the use of regional languages allowed.

The National Assembly, during the second reading, modified the text once more by using a different strategy, that is by proposing an insertion not in article 1 (or article 2) but in a new article, article 75-1. The deputies added article 30 sexties to the project (TA 172,[99] *projet* 459[100]), which was finally adopted by both chambers and became the final draft.[101] The conclusion of the National Assembly was thus concerned with both change and stagnation. Indeed, there was no will to modify the Constitution, either in order to add regional languages as an element of sovereignty or to allow the ratification of the EChRML. That said, the government had been lenient over amendment 605 during negotiations with the National Assembly, because it was considered by some ministers not as an attempt to modify the spirit of the 1958 Constitution or allow the ratification of the Charter but (apparently) just a symbolic gesture.

What changed between the different amendments 605, 38, 117 and 86 (texte 993)[102] was not the substantial idea of regional languages as part of the patrimony of France but the position of regional languages in the articles of the 1958 Constitution. In amendments 38, 117 and 86, MPs argued that the move from article 1 to article 75-1 lifted all doubts about the primacy of the French language. Insertion of a reference to regional languages in article 1, above the reference to the French language in article 2, could not have been considered logical. In the summary justifications given by the MPs who introduced the amendment were mentioned the Assembly's attempt to introduce in amendment 605 a mention in article 1 of the 1958 Constitution. The primary concern was the respect of the primacy of the French language in article 2 of the 1958 Constitution. Therefore the MPs proposed to reintroduce further in the constitutional text the idea adopted by the Assembly and suppressed by the Senate. It was under the *Titre de la Constitution relatif aux collectivités territoriales*, the section of the 1958 Constitution concerning local decentralised authorities, that it was done. The summary justifications under amendment 86 were further developed. The MPs considered that the debate that took place at the National Assembly on 7 May 2008 was to consider the position of the 79 languages of France used by 10 million people and taught to 400,000 pupils by 9,000 teachers. The MPs formally took note of the will of the President and the ministerial department of culture to draft a new framework that should allow more concrete rights in education, in the creation and dissemination of cultural broadcasts and in road traffic signs. They noted that such a statute could be considered as not conforming to the Constitution by the *Conseil constitutionnel*, in the case of a constitutional review, if there was no proper constitutional basis. They then went on to use similar explanations and justifications to those found in previous amendments.

The logic of the constitutional architecture has been fully respected: (a) the French language remains above other languages; (b) the French language remains an issue of sovereignty and no reference to other languages is made here; (c) other languages have been recognised as part of French civilisation and as appendices to the decentralised local authorities. At the same time, the justice minister rejected the ratification of the Charter, although two interesting propositions were debated and adopted at this time, both touching on the issue of language.[103] Article 42 of the 2008 constitutional amendment inserted the constitutional recognition of the francophone area and community:

> I. – In Section XIV of the Constitution is re-established article 87 drafted as follows: 'Art.87. – The Republic participates in the development of solidarity and the cooperation between states and peoples that share French';
> II. – Title XIV of the Constitution is now drafted as follows: 'Of the francophony and of the cooperation agreements'.[104]

Furthermore, MPs prepared the way for recognition of other languages and consideration of other cultures through the adoption (via the minister for cultural affairs) of a proposal for a framework statute on regional languages (which is a separate issue from the modification of the Constitution). One of the sixty campaign promises of President Hollande was to ratify the Charter. The French parliament at the end of 2012 started studying the feasibility of such a ratification and the implications for the Constitution.[105]

6.4 Conclusion

In this chapter I have tried to highlight the importance of the linguistic issue throughout France's long history. The country has developed on the basis of unification not only of a territory but also of a language. The language, and the ways in which the paradigm of unity operates, appear to play a fundamental role in the French state, regardless of the system of government, except perhaps in the scale of the violence used in its enforcement. It is a matter that transcends the Monarchy and the Republic. More importantly, because of this paradigm, language has been used to violently repress the cultural identity of others, both internally and externally. The myth of unity that has been instrumental in the development of France as we know it seems now to fade and leaves space for the reality of pluralism.

Perhaps, like Sacco, we should praise diversity: many cultures exist here, but rather than comparing our culture to others, perhaps we should select elements offered by other cultures, and ensure that in important ways these languages and cultures support each other. For what is at stake here is the perception of the survival of one culture or, worse still, a clash between apparent rivals. It is, in fact, the dialectic of identity v. alterity that is the essence of the matter in hand. And finally, what we can learn from the French experience is that the sense of superiority of one culture over another interacts, in a complex relationship, with a sense of the inferiority in ourselves, which generates fears that contribute, in turn, to the aggression of one culture towards the other.[106]

Conclusion

Until at least the middle of the 1980s, in French law faculties, it was evident that professors were repeating what was taught to them by previous generations. To state the obvious, higher education, like every other level of education, is about transmitting knowledge from one generation to another. Education, whether at school or at university, is a process similar to parenting: it helps human development and establishes belonging to a specific social structure. That said, education in France goes further than simply educating individuals. It follows a French tradition of repeating and reliving republican ideas to help them to become permanent. Sometimes, the term re-education seems more appropriate to characterise what is really happening. Ultimately, the aim of education has been to affirm and reaffirm the 'new' republican system of government, simply, perhaps, to stabilise the post-1789 (new) era. The French Revolution was in some respects a revolution of the mind. Since the (first) post-Revolution Constitution of 1791, which was not a republican one, education has been a cornerstone of the design of the republican future. It was at school that the ideas and ideals of the Republic were taught through an official curriculum, 'preached' by primary school teachers, *les instituteurs*, who were nicknamed by Péguy the *hussards noirs* (black hussars) of the Republic.[1] By analogy, it must have seemed logical to teach constitutional law in a way that would perpetuate the system rather than change it.

It was therefore rare in French law faculties to look critically at the Constitution of the Fifth Republic. On the contrary, everything was done to make students feel that this Constitution was the most celebrated landmark of the French legal environment. Often, the Constitution was represented as being something similar to a block of concrete, something stable and solid – something monolithic. In fact, this metaphor has a further parallel. The drafting and implementation of the Constitution took place at the end of the 1950s and the beginning of the 1960s, and those who drafted the text considered the Constitution to be 'of' the modern era. Indeed, this time was still the modern era, perhaps especially in architectural terms. Contemporary events in Paris and its suburbs illustrate this idea or metaphor of the block of concrete: miles of tower blocks were built, and new towns – illustrations of modernism – somehow represented a vile implementation of Le Corbusier's ideas. To go back to the Constitution, it was no coincidence that years after its promulgation, the *Conseil constitutionnel* referred, in its work of constitutional control, not simply to the text of the Constitution itself, comprising solely its articles, but to something broader, to the entire set of constitutional norms. Interestingly, this ensemble of constitutional norms was nicknamed as we have seen, the *bloc de constitutionnalité*, or the 'block of constitutionality'. The constitutional counsellors and many legal academics acknowledged that the Constitution was something of a (concrete) block.[2]

The main problem with a concrete block is that while it is comforting because of the feeling of solidity, it lacks flexibility. In the suburbs of many cities, the concrete decayed, and the ideal of tower blocks and new towns collapsed. My main point in this study was to show that like the blocks of concrete in the Paris suburbs, the 1958 Constitution, in its resolutely modern form, has been decaying over time. This is why the constitutional amendment brought forward by President Sarkozy in 2008 was a qualified 'modernisation' of the institutions. Using my metaphorical assumption about the block of concrete, the amendment was equivalent to a renovation of the institutions – a 're-plastering' of the monolith.[3]

This idea of the monolith has a long history. If we refer to Kelly, centralisation of power has been a characteristic of the State since the Middle Ages.[4] In this context, the degree of centralisation increased over the years, resulting in the large centralised (empire) states, such as France, Britain and Austro-Hungary. This is perhaps the reason why this Constitution may be perceived in terms of the metaphor of the concrete block. The centralisation of power permeated new republican ideas and the legal documents supporting them. That said, recent changes have been witnessed, as hopefully I have demonstrated.

For instance, if we consider the work of German sociologist Ulrich Beck and his concept of the Risk Society, we realise that western European societies have left the modern era. For Beck, risks 'reinforce the State but cancel its central form, the Nation-State'.[5] In this sense, the main charter of the nation state can no longer be considered to be monolithic. This can be seen in the problematic relationship between France and European law. It is, in addition, seen in the emerging linguistic pluralism that seems to make its way through the notional 'block' that is the Constitution. For Beck, risks are mainly environmental. In that respect, the 'greening' of the French Constitution is probably one of the most important developments, as shown in the chapters relating to the Charter for the Environment.

According to Beck, furthermore, the period of first modernity (around the time of the Industrial Revolution) witnessed the formation of the Nation State, maintained by its key legal concept, sovereignty. The state had a monopoly over conflict resolution and the modern state developed at a national level, the optimal dimension for its fostering. French Republicanism grew over this time supported by the paradigm of unity. But as stated by

Beck, 'The cosmopolitan project contradicts and replaces the nation-state project.'[6] In the phase of second modernity, the concept of the nation state declined. A cosmopolitan society emerged and the state had to face 'risks'. This was a time when nation-state-centred society, politics, sociology and political science 'opened up'.[7] In the period of second modernity, the Risk Society radically affected the nation state: 'a legally binding world society of individuals' developed with the 'status of world citizenship'.[8]

Because of this new type of relation between individuals and society, the law was consequently modified.[9] Primarily, the creation of new laws was no longer attached to the nation state: legal pluralism emerged. The move from a nation state to a cosmopolitan state diminished the now outdated concepts Beck named 'zombie notions' such as sovereignty and the 'international'. The transnational level of law developed while human rights became central, as I have attempted to show in the chapters on the generation of rights. Secondly, the state as a 'framework' did not disappear but the nation seemed to 'melt' into a larger, trans-border society. The territoriality of the application and the sanction of the law did not seem to be affected by this move. Risks 'reinforce the State but cancel its central form, the nation-state'.[10]

The French Fifth Republic, born at the end of the modern era, has developed into a society that has become a Risk Society as Beck outlines. Many tensions within the Constitution have been revealed over the years, showing that the (modern) edifice has been crumbling. From this monolith of a Constitution designed at the end of the 1950s, many notions and ideas have now emerged. The most recent developments reflect the changes that have occurred in the dismantling of the concrete block that is the Constitution. There was, in my opinion, no surprise in the Constitution's 2008 amendment.

Prior to his election, candidate Sarkozy set out in his political manifesto the need to modernise both the French economy and institutions. After his election, he gave the task of preparing to modernise the fifty-year-old Constitution to a committee, chaired by former Prime Minister Balladur.[11] François Hollande continued the trend with a report delivered by a commission in charge of modernising the political life, although much of what has been proposed concerned the Constitution, chaired by former Prime Minister Jospin.[12]

The French Republic Constitution has now grown up to become adult. It is positioned, with the blessing of the constitutional council, at the apex of the legal order. That is perhaps the epitaph to old republican ideas, yet at the same time it proves of how dynamic this Constitution has been and can be. We need to remember that the French parliament was throughout republican history the body where the sovereignty of the people/nation was expressed. In 1958, a Constitution was created limiting the exercise of sovereignty through parliament, a point that was finally acknowledged in the 2008 developments. This was a new turn that takes its place alongside the other major changes reviewed in this book: the increasing impact of EU integration, the 'greening' of the Constitution, the addition of new rights, the reduction of the influence of the principle of indivisibility on the French territory and the increasing recognition of pluralism in the Constitution.

These points clarify the real aim of this Constitution: to secure republican government. As stated during the 2008 constitutional amendment debate, the dynamics in the French Constitution are also 'the best guarantee of a sustainable link between the French and the Fifth Republic'.[13] This is a statement of the contemporaneity of French republican ideas. The birth of the new Republic was announced on 4 September 1958, the day of the commemoration of the Constitution of the Third Republic, the mythical long-lasting Republic. De Gaulle's speech that day was a clear statement of this real aim. In order to reach it, the Constitution of the Fifth Republic had to produce a text that would stand the test of time. This is a republican manifesto that has been clear when needed and opaque when needed, very stable and able to adapt to time and space. But what appears to have contributed most to the real aim of the Constitution of the Fifth Republic is a historical consensus that incorporated not only the brief republican history of France, but also the longest-lasting system of government in France – the monarchy.

Notes

Introduction

1. I will refer from time to time to the Constitution of the Fifth French Republic or to the 1958 Constitution, the Declaration of the Rights of Man and of the Citizen or the 1789 Declaration, the 1946 Constitution preamble and the 2004 Charter for the Environment Official Text available at http://www.legifrance.gouv.fr/Droit-francais/Constitution/Constitution-du-4-octobre-1958 (last accessed 10 January 2013). The constitutional council (*Conseil constitutionnel*) recognises as part of the constitutional norms (*bloc de constitutionnalité*), the Preamble of the 1958 Constitution, itself referring to the former and new declaration of rights and public and civil liberties: the Declaration of the Rights of Man and Citizens, 26 August 1789, the 1946 Constitution Preamble and since 2005 the Charter for the Environment of 2004. The 1946 Constitution Preamble refers also to the 1789 Declaration and to the *Principes fondamentaux reconnus par les Lois de la République* (the Rights and Civil Liberties Recognised by the Statute Laws of the Third French Republic), while listing the *Principes économiques et sociaux particulièrement nécessaire à notre temps* (the 'socio-economic' rights and civil liberties particularly useful to our time).
2. http://www.lemonde.fr/societe/article/2007/07/12/m-sarkozy-inscrit-ses-projets-dans-la-tradition-gaulliste_934993_3224.html (last accessed 10 January 2013).
3. From approximately 496 (Clovis) / 987 (Hugues Capet) to 1791. See J.-J. Sueur, *Histoire du Droit Public Français, XVe-XVIIIe siècle, Tome 1 La Constitution Monarchique*, 4th edn. Paris: Thémis Puf, 1989.
4. From 1870 (the end of the Second Republic) / 1875 (the promulgation of the three constitutional laws) to 1940 (the beginning of the 'French State' of Marshall Petain) / 1946 (the promulgation of the Constitution of the Fourth Republic). See a very good study by H. S. Jones, *The French State in Question: Public Law and Political Argument in the Third Republic*, Cambridge: Cambridge University Press, 1993.
5. *Loi constitutionnelle n° 2008-724 du 23 juillet 2008 de modernisation des institutions de la Ve République* (1). See: http://www.legifrance.gouv.fr/affichTexte.do?cidTexte=JORFTEXT000019237256&dateTexte= (last accessed 10 January 2013).
6. Plato, *The Republic*, New York: Plain Label Books, 1946, p. 250.
7. Aristotle, *The Politics*, London: Penguin Classics, 1981, p. 102.
8. Ibid., p. 310.
9. Cicero, *The Republic* and *The Laws*, Oxford: Oxford University Press, 1998, p. 18.

10. Montesquieu, *The Spirit of the Laws*, Cambridge: Cambridge University Press, 1989, p. 42.

11. M. N. S. Sellers, *Republican Legal Theory: The History, Constitution and Purposes of Law in a Free State*, London: Palgrave, 2003, p. 18.

12. Ibid., p. 22.

13. Henri Grégoire (1750–1831) was 'constitutional' bishop of Blois. He was the first to take the oath of the civil Constitution of the clergy in 1791 and became MP of its diocese.

14. *Décret qui abolit la royauté en France, 21–22 septembre 1792, Journal officiel de la Convention Nationale – La Convention Nationale (1792–1793), Procès-verbaux officiels des séances depuis le 21 septembre 1792, Constitution de la grande assemblée révolutionnaire, jusqu'au 21 janvier 1793, exécution du roi Louis XVI, seule édition authentique et inaltérée contenant les portraits des principaux conventionnels et des autres personnages connus de cette sublime époque*, auteur non mentionné, Librairie B. Simon & Cie, Paris, sans date, pages 10 à 11.

15. *Collot-d'Herbois*: 'Vous venez de prendre une délibération sage; mais il en est une que vous ne pouvez remettre à demain, que vous ne pouvez remettre à ce soir, que vous ne pouvez différer un seul instant sans être infidèles au voeu de la nation, c'est l'abolition de la royauté.' (*Applaudissements unanimes.*)

Quinette: 'Ce n'est pas nous qui sommes juges de la royauté: c'est le peuple; nous n'avons la mission que de faire un gouvernement positif, et le peuple optera ensuite entre l'ancien où se trouvait une royauté, et celui que nous lui présenterons. Quant à moi, comme représentant du peuple français, je ne songe ni au roi ni à la royauté; je m'occupe tout entier de ma mission, sans songer qu'une pareille institution ait jamais pu exister. Je pense donc qu'il est inutile de s'occuper en ce moment de la proposition du préopinant.'

Grégoire: 'Certes, personne de nous ne proposera jamais de conserver en France la race funeste des rois; nous savons trop bien que toutes les dynasties n'ont jamais été que des races dévorantes qui ne vivaient que de chair humaine. Mais il faut pleinement rassurer les mais de la liberté. Il faut détruire ce talisman magique dont la force serait propre à stupéfier encore bien des hommes. Je demande donc que, par une loi solennelle, vous consacriez l'abolition de la royauté.'

(*L'assemblée entière se lève par un mouvement spontané et décrète par acclamation la proposition de l'abbé Grégoire, évêque de Blois.*)

Bazire: 'Je demande à faire une motion d'ordre. L'assemblée vient de manifester par l'unanimité de ses acclamations sa haine profonde pour les rois. On ne peut qu'applaudir à ce sentiment si concordant avec celui de l'universalité du peuple français. Mais il serait d'un exemple effrayant pour le peuple de voir une Assemblée, chargée de ses plus chers intérêts, délibérer dans un moment d'enthousiasme. Je demande que la question soit discutée.'

Grégoire: 'Eh! Qu'est-il besoin de discuter quand tout le monde est d'accord? Les rois sont dans l'ordre moral ce que les monstres sont dans l'ordre physique. Les cours sont l'atelier des crimes et la tanière des tyrans. L'histoire des rois est le martyrologue des nations. Dès que nous sommes tous également pénétrés de cette vérité, qu'est-il besoin de discuter? Je demande que ma proposition soit mise aux voix, sauf à la rédiger ensuite avec un considérant digne de la solennité de ce décret.'

Ducos: 'Le considérant de votre décret, ce sera l'histoire des crimes de Louis XVI, histoire déjà trop bien connue du peuple français. Je demande donc qu'il soit rédigé dans les termes les plus simples; il n'a pas besoin d'explication après les lumières qu'a répandues la journée du 10 août.'

(*La discussion est fermée.*)

(*Il se fait un profond silence.*)

(*La proposition de Grégoire, mise aux voix, est adoptée au bruit des plus vifs applaudissements.*)

'La Convention nationale décrète que la royauté est abolie en France.'

(*Les acclamations de joie, les cris de: "Vive la nation!" répétés par tous les spectateurs, se prolongent pendant plusieurs instants.*)

'Journal officiel de la Convention Nationale – La Convention Nationale (1792–1793), Procès-verbaux officiels des séances depuis le 21 septembre 1792, Constitution de la grande assemblée révolutionnaire, jusqu'au 21 janvier 1793, exécution du roi Louis XVI, seule édition authentique et inaltérée contenant les portraits des principaux conventionnels et des autres personnages connus de cette sublime époque', auteur non mentionné, Librairie B. Simon & Cie, Paris, sans date, pages 10 à 11. See: http://www.fordham.edu/halsall/french/royaute.htm (last accessed 10 January 2013).

16. For a detailed and challenging study on emancipation, see E. Laclau, 'Beyond Emancipation', in *Emancipation(s)*, London: Verso, 2007, pp. 1–19. It seems that proclaiming a Republic is still something that people use to signify liberation from an oppressor. Recently, a Republic was proclaimed in Nepal. The local MPs declared that the King had fifteen days to leave, from 28 May 2008. The constituent assembly declared the end of the monarchy and then proclaimed a Republic. In the same way, on 24 April 1916, Padraic Pearse proclaimed the Republic of Ireland: 'Standing on that fundamental right and again asserting it in arms in the face of the world, we hereby proclaim the Irish Republic as a Sovereign Independent State, and we pledge our lives and the lives of our comrades-in-arms to the cause of its freedom, of its welfare, and of its exaltation among the nations.' See: http://archive-ie.com/page/11755/2012-05-17/http://www.taoiseach.ie/eng/Taoiseach_and_Government/History_of_Government/1916_Commemorations/Proclamation_of_Independence.html (last accessed 10 January 2013).

17. It is a major issue still discussed nowadays with the idea of the VIth Republic. http://www.vie-publique.fr/decouverte-institutions/institutions/veme-republique/transformations/evolution-institutions-vers-vie-republic.html (last accessed 15 May 2013).

18. S. Freud, *Totem and Taboo*, London: Ark, 1983, p. 141. One may consider that election of a head of state institutionalises the quasi permanent killing of the Father.

19. S. Freud, 'Moses and monotheism: three essays', *SE*, 23, London: Hogarth, 1939, pp. 1–138, esp. p. 81.

20. See M. Foucault, *Surveiller et Punir*, Paris: Tel Gallimard, 1975.

21. Sellers, *Republican Legal Theory*, p. 2.

22. M. Delpech, *Que Marianne était jolie* [song], 1973. Marianne symbolises the Republic. Delpech sings that she has five children, four dead and one that she does not recognise anymore, as a critic of the Fifth Republic.

23. The Fourth Republic followed the collapse of the institutions of the Third Republic after the German invasion of 1939–40. It ended when Marshall Pétain was given full powers.

24. Guy Mollet (Section Française de l'Internationale Ouvrière (SFIO)), Pierre Pflimlin (Mouvement pour un Rassemblement Populaire (MRP)), Louis Jacquinot

(Indépendant), Félix Houphouët-Boigny (Rassemblement Démocratique Africain, (RDA) apparenté à l'Union Démocratique et Socialiste de la résistance (UDSR)). No communist representatives were invited.

25. In fact, a third statute was voted for that day, which concerned exceptional powers in Algeria.

26. *Loi n° 58-520 du 3 juin 1958 relative aux pleins pouvoirs accordés au gouvernement du Général de Gaulle (durée six mois)*, JORF 4 June 1958, p. 5327.

27. *Loi du 3 juin 1958 constitutionnelle portant derogation transitoire aux dispositions de l'art. 90 de la Constitution et prévoyant un referendum*, JORF, 4 June 1958, p. 5326.

28. The current text comprises a preamble (with reference to the 1789 Declaration, the Preamble of the 1946 Constitution and the new Charter for the Environment of 2004) and 89 articles.

29. De Gaulle positioned himself in the Republican history. He gave a speech at the *Place de la République* in Paris on 4 September 1958, the date commemorating the proclamation of the Third Republic (4 September 1870) by Gambetta after the end of the Second Empire. Extract from the speech of De Gaulle: *Discours prononcé place de la République, 4 September 1958*: 'Certes la République a revêtu des formes diverses au cours de ses règnes successifs. En 1792 on la vit, révolutionnaire et guerrière, renverser trônes et privilèges, pour succomber, huit ans plus tard dans les abus et les troubles qu'elle n'avait pu maîtriser. En 1848, on la vit s'élever au-dessus des barricades, se refuser à l'anarchie, se montrer sociale au-dedans et fraternelle au-dehors, mais bientôt s'effacer encore, faute d'avoir accordé l'ordre avec l'élan du renouveau. Le 4 septembre 1870, au lendemain de Sedan, on la vit s'offrir au pays pour réparer le désastre. De fait, la République sut relever la France, reconstituer les armées, recréer un vaste empire renouer des alliances solides, faire de bonnes lois sociales, développer l'instruction. Si bien qu'elle eut la gloire d'assurer pendant la Première Guerre mondiale notre salut et notre victoire. Le 11 novembre, quand le peuple s'assemble et que les drapeaux s'inclinent pour la commémoration, l'hommage, que la patrie décerne à ceux qui l'ont bien servie, s'adresse aussi à la République. Cependant, le régime comportait des vices de fonctionnement qui avaient pu sembler supportables à une époque assez statique, mais qui n'étaient plus compatibles avec les mouvements humains, les changements économiques, les périls extérieurs qui précédaient la Deuxième Guerre mondiale. Faute qu'on y eût remédié, les événements terribles de 1940 emportèrent tout. Mais quand, le 18 juin, commença le combat pour la libération de la France, il fut aussitôt proclamé que la République à refaire serait une République nouvelle. La Résistance tout entière ne cessa pas de l'affirmer.' See: http://www.charles-de-gaulle.org/pages/l-homme/accueil/discours/le-president-de-la-cinquieme-republique-1958-1969/discours-prononce-place-de-la-republique-a-paris-4-septembre-1958.php (last accessed 10 January 2013).

30. F. Joset and D. Muzet, *Le Téléprésident: Essai sur un pouvoir médiatique*, Paris: L'aude, 2008.

31. G. Debord, *La Société du Spectacle*, Paris: Folio Gallimard, 1992, p. 20, Thesis 11.

32. J. Lacan, 'Le stade du miroir comme formateur de la fonction du je', *Ecrit 1*, Paris: Points, Seuil, 1999, pp. 92–100.

33. R. Feldstein, 'The mirror of manufactured cultural relations', in R. Feldstein, B. Fink and M. Jaanus, *Reading Seminars I and II: Lacan's Return to Freud*, New York: SUNY Press, 1996, p. 136.

34. President Sarkozy, who was supposed to be the first to be re-elected for a maximum of two consecutive mandates, lost the presidential elections of 2012.

It worth noting that nothing is mentioned about the possibility offered or not to the President to come back after one term – a 'cooling-off period'.

35. The 1848 Constitution did not allow the elected President to stand for more than one mandate of four years without a 'cooling-off period'. This did not satisfy Louis Napoleon Bonaparte who, after a coup, started the Second Empire. Note also that I am using he and not she. This not only shows that no female has been elected President to date, but it also recalls the succession law in the French monarchy (Salic Law).

36. Debord, *Société du Spectacle*, p. 160, Thesis 164.

1 Nature and evolution of the Constitution of the French Fifth Republic

1. The present chapter is a revised, amended and updated version of a lecture delivered to the Law School of the International University of Audentes, Tallinn, Estonia in May 2007. A revised version was presented at the Public Law section at the 2007 SLS Conference in Durham. A shorter version was published as 'Semi-presidentialism à la française: recent evolutions of the "two headed" executive', *Constitutional Forum*, 18 (2), 2009, pp. 69–79.

2. M. Sembat is supposed to have declared 'La république est la femme sans tête et le régime est caraterisé par *le trou d'en haut*, l' "absence de chef"', cited in M. Weyembergh, *Charles Maurras et la Révolution française*, Paris: VRIN, 1992, p. 71. Also 'la république est une femme sans tête', M. Duverger, *Échec au Roi*, Paris: Albin Michel, 1978, p. 21.

3. 'Le vrai père de la Constitution française est Charles Maurras, qui est le vrai père intellectuel de Charles de Gaulle, c'est-à-dire que la France a besoin d'une tête.' Actes du Colloque, 'Aux Racines du Mal Français', Maison des Polytechniciens 19 et 20 octobre 2005, Table Ronde 1: Le Déficit Démocratique.

4. F. Mitterrand, *Le Coup d'État Permanent*, Paris: Plon, 1964.

5. Première conférence de presse à l'Élysée, *Le Monde*, 26 September 1981. "Ces institutions étaient dangereuses avant moi, elles le seront après moi. Pour le moment, je m'en accommode".

6. *Loi* 62-1292, 6 November 1962, *relative à l'élection du Président de la République au suffrage universel*, JORF, 7 November 1962; *Loi constitutionnelle* 2000-964, 2 October 2000 *relative à la durée du mandat du Président de la République*, JORF 229, 3 October 2000, 15582; *Loi constitutionnelle* 2008-724, 23 July 2008, *de modernisation des institutions de la Ve République*, JORF, 24 July 2008, 11890.

7. G. Sartori, *Comparative Constitutional Engineering: An Inquiry into Structures, Incentives and Outcomes*, 2nd edn, New York: New York University Press, 1997.

8. P. Leyland, *The Constitution of the United Kingdom A Contextual Analysis*, Oxford: Hart Publishing, 2007, p. 28.

9. Duverger, *Échec au Roi*, pp. 31–56.

10. According to Jones, the Orleanist system 'combine[s] parliamentary government with a very limited franchise'. H. S. Jones, *The French State in Question: Public Law and Political Argument in the Third Republic*, Cambridge: Cambridge University Press, 1993, p. 15. This is a transitory system between monarchy and Republic and relates to the reign of Louis Philippe I, Philippe d'Orléans.

11. R. Elgie, *Semi-presidentialism in Europe*, New York: Oxford University Press, 1999.

12. http://www.charles-de-gaulle.org/pages/l-homme/accueil/discours/de-gaulle-et-la-quatrieme-republique-1946-1958/discours-de-bayeux-16-juin-1946.php (last accessed 10 January 2013).

13. Weyembergh, *Charles Maurras et la Révolution*, p. 71.

14. *Loi du 3 juin* 1958 *constitutionnelle portant derogation transitoire aux dispositions de l'art. 90 de la Constitution et prévoyant un referendum*, JORF, 4 June 1958, p. 5326.

15. According to article 6 and 7 of the original 1958 Constitution, the President would be elected for seven years by an enlarged electoral college comprising the members of parliament, the departmental councils, overseas territory assemblies and representatives of communal councils; these would total approximately 80,000 electors.

16. J. Bell, *Principles of French Law*, Oxford: Oxford University Press, 1998, p. 141.

17. In 1985 a landmark decision exposed the mission of the Constitutional Council: to scrutinise the work of the French parliament. Particularly, statute law was said to be, in para. 27, the expression of the general will in conformity to the constitution: *La loi votée n'exprime la volonté generale 'que dans le respect de la constitution'*. (*Cons. const.*, *Décision* 85–197 DC, 23 August 1985, *Loi sur l'évolution de la Nouvelle-Calédonie*, JORF, 24 August 1958, p. 9814. Online at: http://www.conseil-constitutionnel.fr/conseil-constitutionnel/francais/les-decisions/acces-par-date/decisions-depuis-1959/1985/85-197-dc/decision-n-85-197-dc-du-23-aout-1985.8176.html (last accessed 10 January 2013).)

18. See the changes in *Loi constitutionnelle n° 2008-724 du 23 juillet* 2008 *de modernisation des institutions de la Ve République* (1). Online at: http://www.legifrance.gouv.fr/affichTexte.do?cidTexte=JORFTEXT000019237256&dateTexte= (last accessed 10 January 2013).

19. Ibid. See part of the address of President Sarkozy on 22 June 2009 at: http://www.youtube.com/watch?v=hbzdpKi_TSY (last accessed 10 January 2013). Certainly, what happened on 22 June 2009 is similar to the State of the Union address in the USA. However, one may want to consider that in Britain too the head of state speaks in Parliament. On the day of its annual opening, the Monarch gives the representatives a list of issues that her government will deal with rather than 'informing' Parliament of what is happening. Therefore, the French model of a semi-presidential system of government should remain ambivalent and 'in between presidential and parliamentary'. That said, it highlights the possibility I explore here and after that the Fifth Republic, instead of becoming more 'presidential', is reinforcing its monarchical elements. See also D. Marrani, 'The importance of the symbolic role of the head of state', *European Journal of Law Reform*, 13 (1), 2011, pp. 40–58.

20. Instead of using article 89 which concerns constitutional revision, De Gaulle used article 11 in dealing with constitutional matters in 1962 and 1969. This practice was widely criticised, notably by Mitterrand, in Mitterrand, *Le Coup d'État Permanent*, Paris: Plon, 1964.

21. G. Agamben, *State of Exception*, Chicago: University of Chicago Press, 2005, p. 14.

22. Ibid.

23. Article 54 allows the President to refer an international agreement to the *Conseil constitutionnel* if it contains a clause that might be contrary to the Constitution, while under article 61 he may also refer a bill to the *Conseil constitutionnel*.

24. Since the 2008 constitutional reform, the President needs the advice of a parliamentary commission, in accordance to the new paragraph 4 of article 13 of the Constitution.

25. Presidential regulation (*non délibéré en Conseil des Ministres*) 64-46, 14 January 1964 *relatif aux forces aeriennes stratégiques*, JORF, 19 January 1964, 722, last modified by regulation (*en Conseil des Ministres*) 96-520, 12 June 1996 *portant détermination des responsabilités concernant les forces nucléaires*, JORF, 15 June 1996, 8921.

26. For a romanticised account of the event, see the famous novel by F. Forsyth, *The Day of the Jackal*, 40th anniversary edition, London: Arrow, 2011.

27. In fact, he was re-elected as he had been President since 1958. To be precise, we should note that this was not the first election of a President of a French Republic by universal suffrage. The President of the Second Republic (1848–52), Louis Napoleon Bonaparte, the future Napoleon III, became President in 1848 elected directly. His term of office was four years.

28. A representative is supposed to be involved in the law-making process and as such the President formally passes the law, changing it from a bill to an act, but is not, strictly speaking, part of the process. *Faire la loi* is, according to Brunet, a *prerogative essentielle*. P. Brunet, 'La représentation', in M. Troper and D. Chagnollaud (eds.), *Traité International de Droit Constitutionnel*, Paris: Dalloz, 2012, pp. 608–41.

29. In a way, the thesis of Habermas concerning public opinion and the mediation of civil society and the state may find a strong illustration here. Even if the President is not legally a representative, because of his or her direct election by the people, the President is considered by public opinion to be a strong institution, to be a representative, to incarnate the state.

30. He declared in his speech of 25 April 1969: 'Your answer will engage the fate of France, because if I am disowned by a majority of you solemnly on this capital matter and whatever may be the number, hard work, dedication of the army of those who support me and anyway, hold the future of the country, my current task of head of state will obviously become impossible and I will cease immediately to perform my duties.' Online at: http://www.ina.fr/media/petites-phrases/video/CAF87002504/allocution-du-general-de-gaulle-President-de-la-republique.fr.html (last accessed 10 January 2013).

31. The people's support for the project was weak. Article 89 of the Constitution was used. The *Assemblée nationale* adopted the proposals by 466 votes to 28 (with 9 abstentions) and the *Sénat* by 228 to 34 (with 8 abstentions). On 24 September 2000, a referendum was held with a result of 73.21 per cent for, 26.79 per cent against (and 16.09 per cent void), but with a large number of abstentions (69.81 per cent).

32. It was also, as mentioned above, the foundation of the seven-year mandate that created the Republican head of state while waiting for the death of one of the royal pretenders.

33. G. Gouzes, *Rapport 2463 fait au nom de la Commission des Lois Constitutionnelles, de la Legislation et de l'Administration Générale de la République sur le Projet de Loi Constitutionnelle (N° 2462), relatif à la durée du mandat du Président de la République.* One may want to consider the contrast between those times and recent elections (2012) and the suggested difference between telepresident (Sarkozy) and normal president (Hollande).

34. It was said at the time that there should be a five-year mandate but that everything should be done to avoid synchronisation occurring: a 'quinquennat avec délai suffisant entre l'élection et celle des députés de l'Assemblée nationale, évitant toute simultanéité'.

35. 'Le mandat présidentiel sera ramené à cinq ans renouvelable une fois, ou limité à 7 ans sans possibilité d'être renouvelé.'

36. '7 ans, je suis en train de m'en apercevoir, c'est court'.

37. Reported by Professor Duhamel in: http://www.brookings.edu/articles/2001/03 france_duhamel.aspx (last accessed 10 January 2013).

38. See *Rapport* 2463: 'l'instauration du quinquennat permettrait de revenir à la conception initiale de la Ve République telle qu'elle a fonctionné de 1962 à 1986'.

39. *Projet de loi constitutionnelle relatif à la durée du mandat du Président de la République J Larché, Rapport 426 (1999–2000), Commission des lois.* 'En dehors de l'élection, le Président n'est donc soumis à un contrôle que de sa propre initiative. Telle sera la pratique répétée du Général De Gaulle au travers de dissolutions et de référendums, parfois contestés, dont la conséquence ultime sera son départ en 1969.'

40. 'Le peuple anglais pense être libre. Il se trompe fort: il ne l'est que durant l'élection des membres du parlement.' J. J. Rousseau, *Du Contrat Social*, Livre 3, Ch XV. In fact for Rousseau the English people are free only one day every seven years.

41. It seems that the situation may be more complex and confusing from time to time. For instance, during President Chirac's last term of office (2002–5), Sarkozy was the leader of the party supporting Chirac and was the equivalent of Home Secretary. He was therefore not the head of government.

42. Indeed, when one is not well, one has to force oneself to take tablets!

43. The moderate right-wing political parties at that time were the Rassemblement Pour La République (RPR) and the centre-right Union pour la Démocracie Française (UDF).

44. 'Raymond Barre est mort', *Libération* (Paris, 25 August 2007). Online at: http://www.liberation.fr/politiques/010119118-raymond-barre-est-mort (last accessed 10 January 2013). Accord to d'Estaing, he was 'le meilleur économiste français, en tout cas un des tout premiers'.

45. D. Wilsford, *Political Leaders of Contemporary Western Europe: A Biographical Dictionary*, Wesport, CT: Greenwood Press, 1995, pp. 103–4.

46. Mitterrand, *Le Coup d'Etat Permanent*.

47. Wilsford, *Political Leaders*, p. 104.

48. When De Gaulle was President, Debré in April 1962 and Pompidou in July 1968 were certainly asked to do so; likewise Chaban Delmas in July 1972 during the Pompidou presidency, and Rocard in 1991 and Cresson in 1992 with Mitterrand as President. More recently we had the example of Chirac for Raffarin in 2005.

49. Wislford, *Political Leaders*, pp. 103–4.

50. J. Chapsal, *La vie politique sous la Ve République 2 1974–1987*, 3rd edn, Paris: PUF Thémis, 1987, p. 534.

51. One may want to consider an analogy between the period 1967–8 and the situation in 2002 and 2005. In 2002 Chirac won dramatically the election against J. M. Le Pen. In the end all institutions were in the hands of the right. In 2005 a series of riots were seen all across France.

52. The traditional electoral system for deputies since 1958 has been the majoritarian system over two rounds. In 1986, proportional representation was used and elections organised on a single day.

53. Jospin was so damaged by the non-synchronisation that, as the PS candidate to the presidential election in 2002, he did not even reach the second round. As previously mentioned, in a classical parliamentary system of government, the Prime Minister is supposed to be the one in the political game, working and fighting, the President hiding behind the Prime Minister. Mitterrand in 1988 and Chirac in 2002 were re-elected after a period of non-synchronisation, a period of classical parliamentary operation of the Constitution, which seemed to help them be re-elected as President.

54. These concerned the privatisation of public enterprises on 13 July 1986, the remodelling of constituencies on 2 October 1986 and the management of working time on 17 December 1986.

55. See R. F. Howell, 'The philosopher Alain and French classical radicalism', *Western Political Quarterly*, 18 (3), 1965, pp. 594–614.

56. President Chirac, during an interview given on 14 July 1999, called his experience of 1974–6 (and that of Rocard, 1988–91) a 'cohabitation voilée', a masked non-synchronisation. He also confessed that he rather liked working as the Prime Minister of President Mitterrand. Online at: http://www.ladocumentationfrancaise. fr/dossiers/d000132-la-cohabitation-dans-la-vie-politique-francaise (last accessed 10 January 2013); http://www.ladocumentationfrancaise.fr/dossiers/cohabitation/ chirac.shtml (last accessed 5 November 2011).

57. *Loi organique* 2001-419, 15 May 2001 *modifiant la date d'expiration des pouvoirs de l'Assemblée nationale*, JORF 113, 16 May 2001, p. 7776.

58. *Rapport de M. Christian Bonnet au nom de la commission des lois*, 186 (2000–2001).

59. *Lois organiques* are acts of the French parliament that complete the Constitution without the need to amend it via the procedure of article 89. Although they are similar to normal legislative statutes, they also differ from them: conformity to the Constitution of such organic statutes is automatically controlled by the *Conseil constitutionnel*.

60. *Cons. const.*, *Décision* 2001-444 DC, 9 May 2001, *Loi organique modifiant la date d'expiration des pouvoirs de l'Assemblée nationale*, JORF 113, 16 May 2001, p. 7806: 'en raison de la place de l'élection du Président de la République au suffrage universel direct dans le fonctionnement des institutions de la cinquième République'

61. Ibid.: 'qu'il était souhaitable que l'élection présidentielle précède, en règle générale, les élections législatives et que cette règle devait s'appliquer dès l'élection présidentielle prévue en 2002'. Online at: http://www.conseil-constitutionnel.fr/conseil-constitutionnel/francais/les-decisions/acces-par-date/ decisions-depuis-1959/2001/2001-444-dc/decision-n-2001-444-dc-du-09-mai-2001.501.html (last accessed 10 January 2013).

62. This is why the *Conseil constitutionnel* mentioned in its decision the notion of 'general rule' because it is still theoretically possible to end up with a non-synchronisation although the probability of such an occurrence has dramatically diminished.

63. F. Jost and D. Muzet, *Le Téléprésident: Essai sur un pouvoir médiatique*, Paris: L'Aude, 2008.

64. A. Badiou, *Le Monde*, 'L'intellectuel de gauche va disparaître, tant mieux', 14 July 2007. Online at: http://www.lemonde.fr/web/imprimer_element/ 0,40-0,50-935544,0.html (last accessed 10 January 2013).

65. V. Le Guay and J. Esperandieu, *Le Journal du Dimanche*, 8 July 2007, Paris.
66. *Ministre d'État, ministre de l'Environnement, du Développement durable, de l'Énergie et des Transports*
67. Juppé: 'Si je pouvais crever, vous seriez contents.' Online at: http://www.liberation.fr/actualite/politiques/legislative/261896.FR.php (last accessed 10 January 2013). 'Je présenterai dès demain matin au président de la République et au premier ministre ma démission.' Since then, Alain Juppé has been appointed Minister of State, Minister of Defence and Veterans Affairs (2010–11) and Minister of State, Minister of Foreign and European Affairs (since February 2011).
68. http://www.leparisien.fr/politique/en-direct-pour-cope-hollande-est-l-homme-d-un-clan-16-05-2012-2002887.php (last accessed 10 January 2013).
69. http://lesrapports.ladocumentationfrancaise.fr/BRP/074000697/0000.pdf (last accessed 10 January 2013).

2 The greening of the French Republic

1. This is a revised, amended and updated version of a paper delivered to the environmental law subject section meeting at the 2006 Keele Annual conference of the Society of Legal Scholars (UK) which was published as 'The Second Anniversary of the Constitutionalisation of the French Charter for the Environment: Constitutional and Environmental Implications', *ENV L REV*, 10 (1), 2008, pp. 9–27.
2. As provided by article 89 of the 1958 Constitution. Online at: http://www.legifrance.gouv.fr (last accessed 10 January 2013).
3. The 4th article of the constitutional bill was supposed to create an exception to the application of the new article 88-5. This article was meant to make compulsory a referendum regarding future inclusion of member states to the EU. The exception meant that this would not apply to Bulgaria, Romania and Croatia.
4. Hereafter referred to as the Charter.
5. The first paragraph of the Preamble was completed by 'ainsi que les droits et devoirs définis dans la Charte de l'environnement de 2004' (and to the rights and duties as defined in the Charter for the Environment of 2004) and is now as follows: 'The French people solemnly proclaim their attachment to the Rights of Man and the principles of national sovereignty as defined by the Declaration of 1789, confirmed and complemented by the 1946 Constitution Preamble, and to the rights and duties as defined in the Charter for the Environment of 2004.' The Charter has been adopted as statute law in 2004 and became part of the constitutional norm in 2005.
6. The result of the *Congrés*'s vote was 730 for and 66 against.
7. 'La France devient le premier pays européen à rejeter la Constitution', *Le Monde* (Paris), 30 May 2005. The *Ministère de l'intérieur*, or French home office, gave an official result of 54.87 per cent no and 45.13 per cent yes.
8. The result of the *Congrés*'s vote was 531 for and 23 against.
9. See the answer of the *Ministre de l'écologie et du développement durable, Réponse à la question écrite n° 05714 of 13 February 2003, posée par M. Oudin (Jacques) from the groupe UMP, JO Sénat 31 July 2003, p. 2468.*
10. http://www.congreso.es/constitucion/ficheros/c78/cons_ingl.pdf (last accessed 10 January 2013).

11. http://www.quirinale.it/qrnw/statico/costituzione/costituzione.htm and http://www.parlamento.pt/Legislacao/Documents/Constitution7thRev2010EN.pdf (last accessed 10 January 2013).

12. https://www.btg-bestellservice.de/pdf/80201000.pdf (last accessed 10 January 2013).

13. http://www.hellenicparliament.gr/UserFiles/f3c70a23-7696-49db-9148-f24dce6a27c8/001-156%20aggliko.pdf (last accessed 10 January 2013).

14. Since 1958, a bill may be referred to the *Conseil constitutionnel* by the head of state, the Prime Minister, the president of both chambers of parliament or, since the constitutional amendment of 1974, by 60 members of either parliament chamber for an 'ante' control of conformity to the Constitution. Since the 2008 revision, it is possible for the *Conseil* to control 'ex post' conformity of a statute that has been promulgated. Indeed the *question prioritaire de constitutionnalité* (QPC) has been introduced under article 61-1 as a procedure allowing for a control of the conformity of promulgated acts to the rights and freedoms protected by the Constitution.

15. *Cons. const.*, *Décision* 71-44 DC 16 July 1971, *Loi complétant les dispositions des articles 5 et 7 de la loi du 1er juillet 1901 relative au contrat d'association*, JORF 18, July 1971, p. 7114. Online at: http://www.conseil-constitutionnel.fr/conseil-constitutionnel/francais/les-decisions/depuis-1958/decisions-par-date/1971/71-44-dc/decision-n-71-44-dc-du-16-juillet-1971.7217.html (last accessed 10 January 2013).

16. L. Favoreu and L. Philip, *Index thématique des Grandes décisions du Conseil constitutionnel*, Paris: Dalloz, 1999. L. Favoreu, 'Bloc de constitutionnalité', in O. Duhamel and Y. Meny (eds), *Dictionnaire constitutionnel*, Paris: PUF, 1992, pp. 87–9.

17. Ibid.

18. M. Verpeaux, 'L'enfer constitutionnel est pavé de bonnes intentions', *AJDA* Chroniques, 2004, p. 1209. Since 2008 the control may applied to promulgated laws although before it was only possible to control non-promulgated ones.

19. As mentioned in Chapter 1, Jacques Chirac served a first term of seven years from 1995 to 2002 and a second term of five years from 2002 to 2007 (the duration of the presidential term was amended in 2000).

20. Speech by J. Chirac, Orléans, 3 May 2001. Online at: http://www.jacqueschirac-asso.fr/fr/wp-content/uploads/2010/04/Quest-ce-que-l%C3%A9cologie-humaniste.pdf (last accessed 10 January 2013).

21. Speech by J. Chirac, Avranches, 18 March 2002 (*Campagne électorale pour l'élection présidentielle*). Online at: http://www.jacqueschirac-asso.fr/fr/wp-content/uploads/2011/04/Discours-18-mars-2002.pdf (last accessed 10 January 2013).

22. The 'Commission Coppens' was named after Professor Coppens who chaired it.

23. In accordance with article 89 of the 1958 Constitution, the procedure was initiated by the President of the Republic on the proposal of the Prime Minister, then the bill was passed by the two Assemblies in identical terms. The project of the bill (*projet de loi constitutionnelle relatif à la Charte de l'environnement*) n. 992 was presented before the *Assemblée nationale* on 27 June 2003. Online at: http://www.assemblee-nationale.fr/12/projets/pl0992.asp (last accessed 10 January 2013).

24. The result was 328 votes for and 10 against (194 abstentions).

25. The result was 172 votes for and 92 against (47 abstentions).

26. As provided by article 89 of the 1958 Constitution, an amendment shall become definitive after approval by referendum although the proposed amendment shall not be submitted to a referendum when the President of the Republic decides to submit it to Parliament convened in Congress; in this case, the proposed amendment shall be approved only if it is accepted by a three-fifths majority of the votes cast. Online at: http://www.legifrance.gouv.fr. The President then promulgated the Act on 1 March 2005. *Loi constitutionnelle* 2005-205 of 1 March 2005 (*Loi constitutionnelle relative à la Charte de l'environnement (1)*), JORF, 2 March 2005, p. 3697.

27. As mentioned previously, the constitutional council since 1971 considers the Preamble of the Constitution as part of the Constitution.

28. G. Deleuze, 'Le Devenir révolutionnaire et les créations politiques', *Futur Anterieur*, May 1990, p. 1.

29. D. Bourg, *Les Scénarios de l'Ecologie*, Paris: Hachette, 1996, and H. Jonas, *Le Principe Responsabilité. Une éthique pour la civilisation technologique*, Paris: Cerf, 1990.

30. A. Dowson and P. Lucardie, *The Politics of Nature*, London: Routledge, 1993.

31. See Chirac, speech at Orléans (see note 19).

32. Article 17: 'Each people has the right to use the common patrimony of humanity such as the high seas, the sea floor and celestial space'. Universal Declaration of Human Rights (United Nations, 1948).

33. See Dowson and Lucardie, *The Politics of Nature*.

34. Even after the new decentralisation laws of 1982–3 devolving partially the competence of education to a sub-national level of administration, the State remained responsible for the curriculum. J. Zajda, *Decentralisation and Privatisation in Education*, Dordrecht: Springer, 2006, p. 83. See also: http://www.education.gouv.fr/pid289/le-ministere-de-l-education-nationale-de-1789-a-nos-jours.html (last accessed 10 January 2013).

35. Durkheim, who first considered studying education with his sociology of education in the nineteenth century, was convinced that the *instituteurs* were the recipients of a part of 'holiness' leftover from the priest, thus positioning education at the same level as religion. F. Dubet, 'La laïcité dans les mutations de l'école', in M. Wieviorka (ed.), *Une société fragmentée? Le multiculturalisme en débat*, Paris: La Découverte, 1996. Also, M. de Saint Martin, 'Les principales tendances de la sociologie de l'éducation en France', *Revue Internationale de l'Education*, 18 (1), 1972, pp. 100–7.

36. Péguy, C ., De Jean Coste, Arles: Actes Sud, 1993, p. 95. See also the comments made by the philosopher Alain Finkielkraut during the 2003 debates on wearing religious symbols at school. 'Je vais essayer de réfléchir avec vous à la question de la laïcité, et je commencerai par une définition que j'irai chercher chez un auteur auquel on ne pense pas toujours quand on réfléchit à ces problèmes. C'est pourtant l'auteur d'une formule laïque par excellence. Il s'agit de Péguy parlant des hussards noirs de la République. A la fin de l'un de ses textes intitulé « De Jean Coste » qui, dans les Cahiers de la Quinzaine, servait d'introduction à l'autobiographie romancée d'un instituteur – Jean Coste –, Péguy écrit ceci: "Il ne faut pas que l'instituteur soit dans la commune le représentant du gouvernement. Il convient qu'il y soit le représentant du l'humanité. Ce n'est pas un président du Conseil, si considérable que soit un président du Conseil, ce n'est pas une majorité qu'il faut que l'instituteur dans la commune représente, il est le représentant né de personnes moins transitoires, il est le seul et l'inestimable représentant des poètes et des artistes, des philosophes

et des savants, des hommes qui ont fait et qui maintiennent l'humanité. Il doit assurer la représentation de la culture, c'est pour cela qu'il ne peut pas assurer la représentation de la politique, parce qu'il ne peut cumuler les deux représentations" http://www.assemblee-nationale.fr/12/dossiers/laicite_CR.asp. (last accessed 25 May 2013).

37. Article 6: 'Public policies must promote a sustainable development. To this purpose, they conciliate protection and valorisation of the environment, economic development and social progress.' Article 8: 'Education and training on the environment have to contribute to the exercise of rights and duties listed in the present charter.'

38. There is here a parallel with the 1789 Declaration, which was also a philosophical reference until 1971.

39. *Circulaire* 2004-110 of 8 July 2004, BOEN 28, 15 July 2004, p. 1473 (*Généralisation d'une éducation à l'environnement pour un développement durable (EEDD) – rentrée 2004*). It has to be noted that this document replaces a previous one, *Circulaire* 77-300 of 29 August 1977, BOEN 31, 9 September 1977, p. 2507 (*Instruction générale sur l'éducation des élèves en matière d'environnement*). The requirement to develop teaching on environmental protection was always present in the curriculum through specific educational programmes (on forests and animals for example) but never on a general basis. This generalisation of environmental education follows the first law adopted in 1976 on environmental protection (*Loi n° 76-629 du 10 juillet 1976 relative à la protection de la nature*, JORF, 13 July 1976, p. 4203).

40. The Brundtland Report – also known as *Our Common Future* – was a work carried out by the UN World Commission on Environment and Development in 1987. It introduced the idea of sustainable development, linking environment and development. Report of the World Commission on Environment and Development: Our Common Future, Annex to Document A/42/427 – Development and International Co-operation: Environment. Online at: http://www.un-documents.net/wced-ocf.htm (last accessed 10 January 2013).

41. See F. Luchaire, 'Brèves remarques sur une création du Conseil constitutionnel: l'objectif de valeur constitutionnelle', *Revue Française de Droit Constitutionnel*, n° 64, October 2005, pp. 675–84, and the *Rapport fait au nom de la Commission des lois constitutionnelles, de la législation et de l'administration générale de la République sur le projet de loi constitutionnelle (N° 992) relatif à la Charte de l'environnement.* Online at: http://www.assemblee-nationale.fr/12/rapports/r1595.asp (last accessed 10 January 2013).

42. The Rio Declaration is often considered the path towards sustainable development also thought of as the start of the third generation of human rights. Online at: http://www.unep.org/Documents.Multilingual/Default.asp?documentid=78&articleid=1163 (last accessed 10 January 2013).

43. Introduced under the *Loi 92-654 du 13 juillet 1992 relative au contrôle de l'utilisation et de la dissémination des organismes génétiquement modifiés et modifiant la loi 76-663 du 19 juillet 1976 relative aux installations classées pour la protection de l'environnement*, JORF, 16 July 1992, p. 9461. Then again the most important step was the codification operated under the *Loi 95-101 du 2 février 1995 Loi relative au renforcement de la protection de l'environnement*, JORF, 3 February 1995. Since *Loi 2002-276 du 27 février 2002 art. 132*, JORF, 28 February 2002, it appears in the first article (Article L.110-1) of the environment code, *Code de l'environnement*, enshrining the general principles of environmental law

(precautionary, prevention, participation). Accessible in English at: http://www. legifrance.gouv.fr/Traductions/en-English/Legifrance-translations (last accessed 10 January 2013).

44. Luchaire, 'objectif de valeur constitutionnelle'.
45. However, if a private company is allowed to experiment it may face responsibility under article 4 of the Charter.
46. Y. Jegouzo, 'La Charte de l'environnement', *AJDA* Chroniques, 2005, p. 1156.
47. Speech by J. Chirac, Palais de l'Élysée, 1 March 2006 (*premier anniversaire de la promulgation de la charte de l'environnement*), See: http://discours.vie-publique.fr/ notices/067000825.html (last accessed 10 January 2013).
48. Perhaps it worth comparing this to some extent with the Human Rights Act 1998 (HRA) in the UK and its guiding purpose for public authorities. The main difference would probably be that the comparison might well differentiate the notion's political effect and unclear legal effect. Section 19 of the Human Rights Act 1998 requires that for every government bill the minister in charge in each House make a statement that in his or her view the bill's provisions are compatible with the Convention rights. In addition, it is stated that an ECHR Memorandum setting out the bill's compatibility with the Convention rights must be produced for the Legislation Committee before it will approve a bill for introduction or publication in draft. In fact, this is the sort of quality control ex ante that the Charter obliges the public authorities to provide.
49. Chirac, Élysée speech.
50. Ibid.
51. Verpeaux, 'L'enfer constitutionnel', p. 1209.
52. H. Groud and S. Pugeault, 'Le droit à l'environnement, nouvelle liberté fondamentale', *AJDA* Jurisprudence, 2005, p. 1357. This was already stated by article L.521-1 of the *Code de justice administrative*.
53. *Cons. const.*, Décision 2000-441 DC, 28 December 2000, *Loi de finances rectificative pour 2000*, JORF, 31 December 2000, p. 21204. Online at: http://www.conseil-constitutionnel.fr/conseil-constitutionnel/francais/les-decisions/2000/2000-441-dc/decision-n-2000-441-dc-du-28-decembre-2000.460.html (last accessed 10 January 2013).
54. D. Marrani, 'How to end an attempt to institute a carbon tax: the Conseil constitutionnel declares that article 7 of the 2010 Budget instituting a carbon tax does not conform to the Constitution of the French Republic', *Env. Law Rev.*, 13, 2011, pp. 50–5.
55. *Cons. const.*, *Décision* 71-44 DC, 16 July 1971, *Loi complétant les dispositions des articles 5 et 7 de la loi du 1er juillet 1901 relative au contrat d'association*, JORF, 18 July 1971, p. 7114. Online at: http://www.conseil-constitutionnel.fr/conseil-constitutionnel/francais/les-decisions/depuis-1958/decisions-par-date/1971/71-44-dc/decision-n-71-44-dc-du-16-juillet-1971.7217.html (last accessed 10 January 2013). See notes 14 to 16 above.
56. *Cons. const.*, *Décision* 24 March 2005 REF, *Decision sur des requêtes présentées par Monsieur Stéphane Hauchemaille et par Monsieur Alain Meyet*, JORF, 31 March 2005, p. 5834. Online at: http://www.conseil-constitutionnel.fr/conseil-constitution-nel/francais/les-decisions/acces-par-date/decisions-depuis-1959/2005/2005-31-ref/decision-n-2005-31-ref-du-24-mars-2005.107222.html (last accessed 10 January 2013).
57. Ibid., para. 4.
58. Ibid., para. 7.

59. *Cons. const.*, *Décision* 2005-514 DC, 28 April 2005, *Loi relative à la création du registre international français*, JORF, 4 May 2005, p. 7702. This bill was declared in conformity with the Constitution. Online at: http://www.conseil-constitutionnel.fr/conseil-constitutionnel/francais/les-decisions/acces-par-date/decisions-depuis-1959/2005/2005-514-dc/decision-n-2005-514-dc-du-28-avril-2005.967.html (last accessed 10 January 2013).

60. *Cons. const.*, *Décision* 2005-516 DC, 7 July 2005, *Loi de programme fixant les orientations de la politique énergétique*, JORF, 14 July 2005, p. 11589. This bill was declared in conformity with the Constitution. Online at: http://www.conseil-constitutionnel.fr/conseil-constitutionnel/francais/les-decisions/acces-par-date/decisions-depuis-1959/2005/2005-516-dc/decision-n-2005-516-dc-du-07-juillet-2005.968.html (last accessed 10 January 2013).

61. Ibid., para. 23.

62. Ibid., para. 25.

63. *Cons. const.*, *Décision* 2005-513 DC, 14 April 2005, *Loi relative aux aéroports*, JORF, 21 April 2005, p. 6974. Online at: http://www.conseil-constitution-nel.fr/conseil-constitutionnel/francais/les-decisions/depuis-1958/decisions-par-date/2005/2005-513-dc/decision-n-2005-513-dc-du-14-avril-2005.966.html (last accessed 10 January 2013). This bill was declared in conformity with the Constitution (paragraph 12 of the decision concerned the modulations of a tax based on reducing or compensating for impacts on the environment).

64. *Cons. const.*, *Décision* 2005-530 DC, 29 December 2005, *Loi de finances pour 2006*, JORF, 31 December 2005, p. 20705. Online at: http://www.conseil-constitutionnel.fr/conseil-constitutionnel/francais/les-decisions/depuis-1958/decisions-par-date/2005/2005-530-dc/decision-n-2005-530-dc-du-29-decem-bre-2005.975.html (last accessed 10 January 2013). This bill was declared partially not to be in conformity with the Constitution.

65. Ibid., paras 11–14.

66. *Cons. const.*, *Décision* 2006-543 DC, 30 November 2006, *Loi relative au secteur de l'énergie*, JORF, 8 December 2006, p. 18544. Online at: http://www.conseil-constitutionnel.fr/conseil-constitutionnel/francais/les-decisions/acces-par-date/decisions-depuis-1959/2006/2006-543-dc/decision-n-2006-543-dc-du-30-no-vembre-2006.1014.html (last accessed 10 January 2013). This bill was declared partially not to be in conformity with the Constitution.

67. *Cons. const.*, *Décision* DC 2007-548, *Loi relative aux règles d'urbanisme applicables dans le périmètre de l'opération d'intérêt national de La Défense et portant création d'un établissement public de gestion du quartier d'affaires de La Défense*, JORF, 28 February 2007, p. 3683. This bill was declared to be in conformity with the Constitution. Online at: http://www.conseil-constitutionnel.fr/conseil-constitutionnel/francais/les-decisions/acces-par-date/decisions-depuis-1959/2007/2007-548-dc/decision-n-2007-548-dc-du-22-fevrier-2007.1174.html (last accessed 10 January 2013).

68. Remarkably, the *Conseil d'État* was using a similar method to protect the environment even before the transposition of the precautionary principle in French law. See CE, 4 January 1995, *Ministère de l'Interieur c/Rossi*, n. 94967.

69. CE, 25 September 1998, *Association Green Peace France*, n. 194348.

70. CE, 29 October 1999, *Société Rustica Programme Génétique SA et autres*, n. 206687 and 206373.

71. CAA Marseilles, 13 June 2002, *Association AIPE c/Commune de Cagnes sur Mer*, n. 97MA05052.

72. CE, 22 August 2002, *SFR c/ Commune de Valauris*, n. 245624.

73. TA Châlons-sur-Marne 29 April 2005, *AJDA*, 2005, p. 978.
74. The airport of Marigny witnesses the presence of many species of communitarian interest and is designated as an important area of bird conservation by the directive 79-409 79/409/CEE, 2 April 1979, modified. The site is now integrated into the Natura 2000 network (*Arrêté du 10 mars 2006 portant désignation du site Natura 2000 Marigny, Superbe, vallée de l'Aube (zone de protection spéciale), JO n° 60 du 11 mars 2006 page 3726, texte n° 48*).
75. Three major associations were involved: *Conservatoire du Patrimoine Naturel de Champagne-Ardenne, la Ligue de Protection des Oiseaux* and *la Fédération des Conservatoires d'Espaces Naturels*.
76. Article L.521-2 of the *Code de justice administrative*.
77. Two conditions are set up by article L.521-2 of the *Code de justice administrative* to initiate the emergency summary procedure: the seriousness of the 'attack' on the fundamental freedom and the obvious illegality of the decision.
78. It was commented by the judge that the Charter contains the right to live in a balanced environment respectful of health (*le droit de chacun de vivre dans un environnement équilibré et respectueux de la santé*), and that the right to environment (*le droit á l'environnement*) is a fundamental freedom according to the meaning of article L.521-2 du *Code de justice administrative*.
79. The *Conseil d'État* has, since the innovation of the *référé liberté* in 2000, considered as fundamental freedoms the freedom of reunion, the right of asylum and the right to own a property. It seems that the *Conseil d'État* is once again the protector of civil and political rights. It is the role of creator, discoverer and protector of freedoms it had before the creation of the *Conseil constitutionnel*. (Indeed the *Conseil d'État* was the main source of protection of civil and political rights and freedoms during the French third and fourth Republics.)
80. *Ordonnance du juge des référés du 9 mai* 2006, *Fédération Transpyrénéenne des Éleveurs de Montagne et autres*, n. 292398. Online at: http://www.conseil-etat.fr/fr/ communiques-de-presse/-rejet-demande-suspension-decision-d-introduire-cinq-ours.html (last accessed 10 January 2013).
81. CE, 28 April 2006, *Fédération des Syndicats Agricoles MODEF*, n. 274458 and 274459. Online at: http://www.legifrance.gouv.fr/affichJuriAdmin.do?oldActi on=rechJuriAdmin&idTexte=CETATEXT000008258937&fastReqId=496061 826&fastPos=11 (last accessed 10 January 2013). CE, 28 April 2006, *Association Générale des Producteurs de Mais et autres*, n. 269103, 269109, 269686, 269722, 269959 and 270004. Online at: http://www.legifrance.gouv.fr/affichJuriAdmin. do?oldAction=rechJuriAdmin&idTexte=CETATEXT000008223967&fastReqI d=342302874&fastPos=1 (last accessed 10 January 2013).
82. CE, 6 April 2006, *Ligue pour la protection des oiseaux (LPO)*, n. 283103 and CE, 19 June 2006, *Association Eau et Rivières de Bretagne*, n. 282456. Online at: http://www.legifrance.gouv.fr/affichJuriAdmin.do?oldAction=rechJuriAdmin& idTexte=CETATEXT000008255798&fastReqId=1946444090&fastPos=1 (last accessed 10 January 2013).
83. The first 'operation' of field cutting of GMO crops was held in France on 7 June 1997 in Saint-Georges d'Esperanche. Three activists were sentenced in Vienne on 23 April 2003. The *Cour d'Appel de Grenoble* invoked the presidential amnesty of 2002 to annul the judgement of the first court (26 October 2005).
84. *Cour d'appel de Toulouse*, 15 November 2005, n. 004/01065. Online at: http:// legimobile.fr/fr/jp/j/ca/31555/2005/11/15/6947321/ (last accessed 10 January 2013).

85. H. Kempf, 'La Cour de cassation statuera le 7 février sur le sort judiciaire de José Bové ' *Le Monde* (Paris), 12 January 2007.
86. C.Cass. (crim.), *7 February 2007,* Actes dits de 'fauchage volontaire', n. 06-80.108. Arrêt n° 220 du 7 février 2007. *Online at: http://www.courdecassation.fr/jurisprudence_2/chambre_criminelle_578/fauchage_volontaire_9879.html (last accessed 10 January 2013).*
87. *Dégradation grave de bien d'autrui commise en réunion.*
88. However, they were held to be civilly responsible and required to pay compensation to Monsanto for the civil offence caused.
89. CE, 28 April 2006, *Fédération des Syndicats Agricoles MODEF*, n. 274458 and 274459. Online at: http://www.legifrance.gouv.fr/affichJuriAdmin.do?oldActio n=rechJuriAdmin&idTexte=CETATEXT000008258937&fastReqId=4960618 26&fastPos=11 (last accessed 10 January 2013).
90. *Destruction de bien d'un charge de mission de service public.*
91. http://www.international.inra.fr/the_institute/organisation/management (last accessed 10 January 2013).
92. Although Monsanto appeared to be still present 'behind' INRA.
93. They were held to be civilly responsible and had to pay no compensation.
94. *Cons. const.*, *Décision* 2009-599 DC, 29 December 2009, *Loi de finances pour 2010*, JORF, 31 December 2009, p. 22995. Online at: http://www.conseil-constitutionnel.fr/conseil-constitutionnel/francais/les-decisions/acces-par-date/decisions-depuis-1959/2009/2009-599-dc/decision-n-2009-599-dc-du-29-decembre-2009.46804.html (last accessed 10 January 2013). See also Marrani, 'Carbon tax'.
95. *Cons. const.*, *Décision* 2008-564 DC, 19 June 2008, *OGM*, JORF, 26 June 2008, p. 10228. Online at: http://www.conseil-constitutionnel.fr/conseil-constitutionnel/francais/les-decisions/acces-par-date/decisions-depuis-1959/2008/2008-564-dc/decision-n-2008-564-dc-du-19-juin-2008.12335.html (last accessed 10 January 2013).
96. *Cons. const.*, *Décision* 2011-116 QPC, 8 April 2011, *M. Michel Z. et autre {Troubles du voisinage et environnement}*, JORF, 9 April 2011, p. 6361. Online at: http://www.conseil-constitutionnel.fr/conseil-constitutionnel/francais/les-decisions/acces-par-date/decisions-depuis-1959/2011/2011-116-qpc/decision-n-2011-116-qpc-du-08-avril-2011.95732.html (last accessed 10 January 2013), and 2011-183/184 QPC, 14 October 2011, *Association France Nature Environnement {Projets de nomenclature et de prescriptions générales relatives aux installations classées pour la protection de l'environnement}*, JORF, 15 October 2011, p. 17466. Online at: http://www.conseil-constitutionnel.fr/conseil-constitutionnel/francais/les-decisions/acces-par-date/decisions-depuis-1959/2011/2011-183/184-qpc/decision-n-2011-183-184-qpc-du-14-octobre-2011.100273.html (last accessed 10 January 2013).
97. *Loi constitutionnelle n° 2005-205 du 1er mars 2005 relative à la Charte de l'environnement (1), JO n° 51 du 2 mars 2005 page 3697.* Unofficial translation by the author.

3 Human rights (in practice) and the French Republic

1. This chapter is a version of the article published as 'Exclusion and Human Rights: The French Case', *University of San Francisco Journal of Law and Social Challenges (JLSC)*, 12, pp. 69–94.

2. Institut National d'Etudes Démographiques, *Statistiques des flux d'immigration en France – Année 2005*, Paris: INED, 2005, p. 2.

3. Ibid.

4. C. Borrel, 'Enquêtes annuelles de recensement 2004 et 2005, Près de 5 millions d'immigrés à la mi-2004', Insee Première n°1098 – août 2006, Cellule Statistiques et études sur l'immigration, Paris: Insee, 2006. Online at: http://www.insee.fr/fr/ffc/ipweb/ip1098/ip1098.pdf (last accessed 10 January 2013).

5. *Ordonnance n° 45-2658 du 2 novembre 1945 relative aux conditions d'entrée et de séjour des étrangers en France*. Online at: http://www.legifrance.gouv.fr/affichTexte.do?c idTexte=LEGITEXT000006069184&dateTexte=20080130 (last accessed 10 January 2013).

6. Hereinafter referred to as CESEDA. Online at: http://www.legifrance.gouv. fr/affichCode.do?cidTexte=LEGITEXT000006070158&dateTexte=20130115 (last accessed 10 January 2013).

7. See U. Beck, *Risk Society: Towards a New Modernity*, London: Sage, 1992; U. Beck, *Democracy Without Enemy*, Cambridge: Polity Press, 1998.

8. The Schengen area represents a territory where the free movement of persons is guaranteed. See the Schengen Area and Cooperation, online at: http://europa.eu/legislation_summaries/justice_ freedom_security/free_movement_of_persons_asylum_immigration/l33020_en.htm (last accessed 10 January 2013). The Treaty of Amsterdam modified the Treaty creating the European Union. See Treaty of Amsterdam Amending the Treaty on European Union, the Treaties Establishing the European Communities and Related Acts, November 10, 1997. Online at: http://eur-lex.europa.eu/en/treaties/dat/11997D/htm/11997D.html (last accessed 10 January 2013).

9. *Cons. const.*, *Décision* 93–325 DC, 13 August 1993, *Loi relative à la maîtrise de l'immigration et aux conditions d'entrée, d'accueil et de séjour des étrangers en France*, JORF, 18 August 1993, p.11722. Online at: http://www.conseil-constitu-tionnel.fr/conseil-constitutionnel/francais/les-decisions/acces-par-date/decisions-depuis-1959/1993/93-325-dc/decision-n-93-325-dc-du-13-aout-1993.10495. html (last accessed 10 January 2013).

10. http://www.gisti.org/IMG/pdf/norintk0600058c-2.pdf (last accessed 10 January 2013).

11. *Cons. const.*, *Décision* 79-109 DC, 9 January 1980, *Loi relative à la prévention de l'immigration clandestine et portant modification de l'ordonnance n° 45-2658 du 2 novembre 1945 relative aux conditions d'entrée et de séjour en France des étrangers et portant création de l'office national d'immigration*, JORF, 11 January 1980, p. 84. Online at: http://www.conseil-constitutionnel.fr/conseil-constitutionnel/francais/les-decisions/acces-par-date/decisions-depuis-1959/1980/79-109-dc/decision-n-79-109-dc-du-09-janvier-1980.7765.html (last accessed 10 January 2013).

12. The constitutional council can operate both an ex ante (since 1958) and an ex post constitutional control (since the 2008 constitutional amendment).

13. *Cons. const.*, *Décision* 71-44 DC, 16 July 1971, *Loi complétant les dispositions des articles 5 et 7 de la loi du 1er juillet 1901 relative au contrat d'association*, JORF, 18 July 1971, p. 7114. Online at: http://www.conseil-constitutionnel.fr/conseil-constitutionnel/francais/les-decisions/depuis-1958/decisions-par-date/1971/71-44-dc/decision-n-71-44-dc-du-16-juillet-1971.7217.html (last accessed 10 January 2013).

14. L. Favoreu and L. Philip, *Index thématique des grandes décisions du Conseil cons-titutionnel*, Paris: Dalloz, 1999. L. Favoreu, 'Bloc de constitutionnalité', in

O. Duhamel and Y. Meny, *Dictionnaire constitutionnel*, Paris: PUF, 1992, pp. 87–9. See note 1 above.

15. J.-F. Renucci, *Droit Européens des Droits de l'Homme*, 3rd edn, Paris: LGDJ, 2002, p. 59.

16. Ibid., p. 61.

17. CE, 26 January 2007, *Société Arcelor Atlantique et Lorraine et autres*, N° 287110.

18. CE, 26 January 2007, *M.X.*, N° 279522.

19. *Cons. const.*, *Décision* 93–325 DC, 13 August 1993, *Loi relative à la maîtrise de l'immigration et aux conditions d'entrée, d'accueil et de séjour des étrangers en France*, JORF, 18 August 1993, p.11722. Online at: http://www.conseil-constitutionnel.fr/conseil-constitutionnel/francais/les-decisions/acces-par-date/decisions-depuis-1959/1993/93-325-dc/decision-n-93-325-dc-du-13-aout-1993.10495.html (last accessed 10 January 2013).

20. 'Le Conseil constitutionnel, Vu la Déclaration des droits de l'homme et du citoyen du 26 août 1789; Vu le Préambule de la Constitution du 27 octobre 1946; Vu la Constitution du 4 octobre 1958; Vu la Convention de Genève du 28 juillet 1951 sur le statut des réfugiés, ensemble la loi n° 54-290 du 17 mars 1954 autorisant sa ratification; Vu le protocole relatif au statut des réfugiés, signé à New York le 31 janvier 1967, ensemble la loi n° 70-1076 du 25 novembre 1970 autorisant l'adhésion de la France à ce protocole; Vu la Convention signée à Dublin le 15 juin 1990 relative à la détermination de l'Etat responsable de l'examen d'une demande d'asile présentée auprès d'un Etat membre des Communautés européennes; Vu la Convention d'application de l'accord de Schengen signée le 19 juin 1990; Vu l'ordonnance n° 45-2658 du 2 novembre 1945 modifiée relative aux conditions d'entrée et de séjour des étrangers en France; Vu le code civil, ensemble la loi n° 93-333 du 22 juillet 1993 réformant le droit de la nationalité; Vu le code pénal; Vu le code de la construction et de l'habitation; Vu le code de la famille et de l'aide sociale; Vu le code de procédure pénale, et notamment son article 78-2; Vu le code de la sécurité sociale; Vu le code du travail; Vu le code de la santé publique; Vu la loi n° 52-893 du 25 juillet 1952 modifiée portant création d'un office français de protection des réfugiés et apatrides; Vu la loi n° 73-548 du 27 juin 1973 modifiée relative à l'hébergement collectif; Vu la loi n° 78-17 du 6 janvier 1978 modifiée relative à l'informatique, aux fichiers et aux libertés; Vu les décisions n° 91-294 DC du 25 juillet 1991 et n° 92-307 DC du 25 février 1992.'

21. The Charter for the Environment cannot really be considered in the context of this chapter.

22. *Cons. const.*, *Décision* 89-269 DC, 22 January 1990, *Loi portant diverses dispositions relatives à la sécurité sociale et à la santé*, JORF, 24 January 1990, p. 972. Online at: http://www.conseil-constitutionnel.fr/conseil-constitutionnel/francais/les-decisions/acces-par-date/decisions-depuis-1959/1990/89-269-dc/decision-n-89-269-dc-du-22-janvier-1990.8711.html (last accessed 10 January 2013). 'Considérant que l'exclusion des étrangers résidant régulièrement en France du bénéfice de l'allocation supplémentaire [...], méconnaît le principe constitutionnel d'égalité.'

23. Ibid.

24. C. Borrel, '5 millions d'immigrés'. Of the residence permits delivered in 2005 94,500 were on the basis of the right to family reunification. Family migration is the largest immigration sector in France above students (48,900) and workers (13,650). It worth noting that the masculine gender became the minority gender in 2004.

25. Case C-127/08 *Metock and Others* v. *Minister for Justice, Equality and Law Reform* [2008] ECR I-6241.

26. INED (2005), p. 23.

27. Renucci, *Droits de l'Homme*, pp. 319; see also pp. 407–10.

28. CE, 8 December 1978, *Groupe d'Intervention et de Soutien des Travailleurs Immigrés et a.* Rec., p. 493.

29. *Cons. const.*, *Décision* 93-325 DC, 13 August 1993, *Loi relative à la maîtrise de l'immigration et aux conditions d'entrée, d'accueil et de séjour des étrangers en France*, JORF, 18 August 1993, p.11722. Online at: http://www.conseil-constitutionnel.fr/conseil-constitutionnel/francais/les-decisions/acces-par-date/decisions-depuis-1959/1993/93-325-dc/decision-n-93-325-dc-du-13-aout-1993.10495.html (last accessed 10 January 2013), and *Cons. const.*, *Décision* 2005-528 DC, 15 December 2005, *Loi de financement de la sécurité sociale pour 2006*, JORF, 20 December 2005, JORF, 20 December 2005, p. 19561. Online at: http://www.conseil-constitutionnel.fr/conseil-constitutionnel/francais/les-decisions/acces-par-date/decisions-depuis-1959/2005/2005-528-dc/decision-n-2005-528-dc-du-15-decembre-2005.974.html (last accessed 10 January 2013).

30. 'Le ressortissant étranger qui séjourne régulièrement en France depuis au moins dix-huit mois, sous couvert d'un des titres d'une durée de validité d'au moins un an prévus par le présent code ou par des conventions internationales, peut demander à bénéficier de son droit à être rejoint, au titre du regroupement familial, par son conjoint si ce dernier est âgé d'au moins dix-huit ans et les enfants du couple mineurs de dix-huit ans.'

31. CE, 29 juin 1990 *GISTI* JCP 1991 II 61.

32. *Loi n° 2007-1631 du 20 novembre 2007 relative à la maîtrise de l'immigration, à l'intégration et à l'asile*, JORF, n° 270, 21 November 2007, p.18993.

33. *Loi n° 2003-1119 du 26 novembre 2003 relative à la maîtrise de l'immigration, au séjour des étrangers en France et à la nationalité*, JORF, n° 274, 27 November 2003, p. 20136 and *Loi n° 2006-911 du 24 juillet 2006 relative à l'immigration et à l'intégration*, JORF, n° 170, 25 July 2006, p. 11047.

34. Council Directive (EC) 2003/86 on the right to family reunification [2003] OJ L 251/12).

35. *Décret n° 2008-1115 du 30 octobre 2008 relatif à la préparation de l'intégration en France des étrangers souhaitant s'y installer durablement*, JORF 0256, 1 November 2008, p. 16689.

36. The values listed in the regulation are: gender equality, secularisation (*laïcité*), respect for individuals and collective rights and duties, public/civil liberties, security and safety of persons and goods, rules relating to education (for parents).

37. *Décret n° 2009-331 du 25 mars 2009 substituant la dénomination « Office français de l'immigration et de l'intégration » à la dénomination « Agence nationale de l'accueil des étrangers et des migrations »*, JORF 0073, 27 March 2009, p. 5480.

38. V. Tchen, *Droit des Etrangers*, Paris: Ellipses, 2006, pp. 74–6.

39. *Cons. const.*, *Décision* 99-423 DC, 13 January 2000, *Loi relative à la réduction négociée du temps de travail*, JORF, 20 January 2000, p. 992. Online at: http://www.conseil-constitutionnel.fr/conseil-constitutionnel/francais/les-decisions/depuis-1958/decisions-par-date/2000/99-423-dc/decision-n-99-423-dc-du-13-janvier-2000.11855.html (last accessed 10 January 2013).

40. *Loi n° 2008-496 du 27 mai 2008 portant diverses dispositions d'adaptation au droit communautaire dans le domaine de la lutte contre les discriminations*, JORF, n° 0123,

28 May 2008, p. 8801. This statute transposed the 'Directive 2000/43/CE du Conseil du 29 juin 2000 relative à la mise en œuvre du principe de l'égalité de traitement entre les personnes sans distinction de race ou d'origine ethnique; Directive 2000/78/CE du Conseil du 27 novembre 2000 portant création d'un cadre général en faveur de l'égalité de traitement en matière d'emploi et de travail; Directive 2002/73/CE du Parlement européen et du Conseil du 23 septembre 2002 modifiant la directive 76/207/CEE du Conseil relative à la mise en œuvre du principe de l'égalité de traitement entre hommes et femmes en ce qui concerne l'accès à l'emploi, à la formation et à la promotion professionnelles, et les conditions de travail; Directive 2004/113/CE du Conseil du 13 décembre 2004 mettant en œuvre le principe de l'égalité de traitement entre les femmes et les hommes dans l'accès à des biens et services et la fourniture de biens et services; Directive 2006/54/CE du Parlement européen et du Conseil du 5 juillet 2006 relative à la mise en œuvre du principe de l'égalité des chances et de l'égalité de traitement entre hommes et femmes en matière d'emploi et de travail.'

41. *Circulaire n° NOR: IMI/N/07/00011/C relative aux autorisations de travail délivrées au ressortissants des nouveaux États membres de l'Union européenne pendant la période transitoire et des États tiers, sur la base de listes de métiers connaissant des difficultés de recrutement.* Online at: http://www.gisti.org/IMG/pdf/norimin0700011c.pdf (last accessed 10 January 2013).

42. The administrative agency HALDE examined all matters brought to its attention in the area of discrimination (broadly speaking). The HALDE examined and investigated the case and informed the applicant of its rights and may act, after determining it was within its jurisdiction. Furthermore, article 15 of the 30 December 2004 law that created HALDE stated that the agency may recommend all modifications (legislatives or regulations). The HALDE ceased to exist in 2011 and was replaced by the *défenseur des droits*, a new institution set up by the 2008 constitutional amendment (new article 71.1 of the 1958 constitution).

43. HALDE *Déliberation* 2008-149, 15 septembre 2008.

44. See my comments on education in Chapter 2.

45. CE, 23 October 1987, *Consort Metrat*, AJDA, 1987, p. 758.

46. *Loi n° 2006-911 du 24 juillet 2006 relative à l'immigration et à l'intégration*, JORF, no° 170, 25 July 2006, p. 11047.

47. INED (2005), p. 11.

48. http://www.gisti.org/IMG/pdf/norintk0600058c-2.pdf (last accessed 10 January 2013). They must also fulfil the following conditions: have at least one school-age child; have a child born in France or currently resident in France since the child was 13; at least one parent effectively contributes to the maintenance and education of the child; the family shows a real will to integrate into French society, particularly by showing their willingness to master the French language; absence of any links with the country where he or she is a national.

49. http://www.ldh-toulon.net/spip.php?article1404 (last accessed 10 January 2013).

50. http://www.gisti.org/doc/textes/2005/INTD0500097C.pdf (last accessed 10 January 2013).

51. This was only an option offered to applicants: they had to decide whether to go back or not. If they agreed, financial support was also offered in 2005 and was raised by the new *circulaire* from €150 to €2,000 for an adult, €3,000 for a couple, €1,000 per minor child (up to three children), then €500 per child.

It was indicated that all amounts would change if the families were to decide to return before 13 August 2006. Indeed, the *circulaire* of 13 June 2006 indicated more attractive figures: €4,000 for adults, €7,000 for a couple, €2,000 per child (up to three children), then €1,000 per child.

52. Six (objective and subjective) criteria were laid down to assess their situation: the family had been in France for at least two years; a child had been in school at least since September 2005; the child had been born in France or arrived in France when a toddler or when he or she was a maximum of 13 years of age; family life was essentially in France and not in the country of origin; the parents contributed effectively to the maintenance and education of the child; the family showed a real wish to integrate.

53. http://www.ldh-toulon.net/spip.php?article1528 (last accessed 10 January 2013).

54. http://www.ilo.org/ilolex/english/reportforms/pdf/22e118.pdf (last accessed 10 January 2013).

55. *Cons. const.*, *Décision* 89-269 DC, 22 January 1990, *Loi portant diverses dispositions relatives à la sécurité sociale et à la santé*, JORF, 24 January 1990, p. 972. Online at: http://www.conseil-constitutionnel.fr/conseil-constitutionnel/francais/les-decisions/acces-par-date/decisions-depuis-1959/1990/89-269-dc/decision-n-89-269-dc-du-22-janvier-1990.8711.html (last 10 January 2013).

56. Available at: http://www.legifrance.gouv.fr/affichCode.do?cidTexte=LEGIT EXT000006073189 (last accessed 10 January 2013).

57. Article L.161-25-1, *Code de la Sécurité Sociale*.

58. Article L.115-6, *Code de la Sécurité Sociale*.

59. Article D.115-6, *Code de la Sécurité Sociale*, lists the documents necessary to certify the condition of residency: permanent resident permit; temporary resident permit; Algerian resident permit; document acknowledging the demand for renewal of one of the documents above; document acknowledging the demand for a temporary resident permit granted to refugees (*reconnu réfugié*), to be used as authorisation to remain, renewable every three months; document acknowledging the demand for a temporary resident permit granted to asylum-seekers (*étranger admis au titre de l'asile*), valid for six months, renewable; document acknowledging the demand for refugee status (*demandé le statut de réfugié*), valid for three months, renewable; temporary work permit for persons resident in France under a visa of three months or less, or if not covered by a visa, of less than three months; temporary resident authorisation together with a temporary work permit.

60. Article L.161-25-2, *Code de la Sécurité Sociale*. Article D.161-25-2 lists the documents that may be used to certify the residency in that case: permanent resident permit; temporary resident permit; Algerian resident permit; document acknowledging the demand for renewal of one of the documents above; document acknowledging the first demand of a resident permit, together with either the certificate of medical control delivered by the *Office des migrations internationales* for family reunification (*regroupement familial*), or a state document certifying that the person is a member of a French national's family; document acknowledging the demand for a temporary resident permit used as authorisation to remain, renewable every three months (*reconnu réfugié*); document acknowledging the demand for a temporary resident permit (*étranger admis au titre de l'asile*), valid for six months, renewable; temporary resident permit.

61. Article L.311-2, *Code de la Sécurité Sociale*.

62. *Loi n° 98-349 du 11 mai 1998 relative à l'entrée et au séjour des étrangers en France et au droit d'asile*, JORF, 12 May 1998, p. 7087, especially article 41 I. Article L.311-7, *Code de la Sécurité Sociale.*

63. Article L.308-1, *Code de la Sécurité Sociale.*

64. Article R 380-1, *Code de la Sécurité Sociale.*

65. Article D.374-6, *Code de la Sécurité Sociale.*

66. As modified by *Loi* 86-1307, 29 December 1986, art. 7 I, JORF, 30 December 1986, *Loi* 2005-1579, 19 December 2005, art. 89, JORF, 20 December 2005. Article L512-2, *Code de la Sécurité Sociale.* Their children either have to be born in France, or have entered the French territory legally via the family reunification procedure (*Livre* IV CESEDA); or they must be children of refugees; or have, as non-national children, a resident permit of paragraph 10° article L.313-11 CESEDA; or they must have a resident permit under CESEDA, article L.313-13; or a resident permit under article L.313-8 or 5° article L.313-11 CESEDA; or a resident permit of 7° article L.313-11 CESEDA if children have entered France with their parents and their parents held a resident permit.

67. Article D.512-1, *Code de la Sécurité Sociale* as inserted by *Décret* 2006-234, 27 February 2006, art. 1, JORF, 28 February 2006.

68. Ibid. Article D.512-2, *Code de la sécurité sociale.* The list of documents required is slightly different: birth certificate attesting to birth in France; certificate of medical control from the *Agence nationale de l'accueil des étrangers et des migrations*, after the beginning of the family reunification procedure; family booklet delivered by OFPRA, or birth certificate prepared by OFPRA when the child is a refugee or stateless family member. When the child is a refugee or stateless family member, the birth certificate is given with the ruling of a court giving care of the child to the non-national seeking social benefits; a visa given by the consulate naming the child of a non-national with a resident permit of article L.313-8 or 5° article L.313-11 CESEDA; a certificate delivered by the *Préfet* that the child has entered French territory with parents who are documented under 7° of article L.313-11 of CESEDA, or 5° article 6 of the Franco-Algerian modified agreement of 27 December 1968; a resident permit delivered to 16–18 year-old non-nationals under CESEDA, article L.311-3. The *Office français des réfugiés et apatrides* (OFPRA) is now an agency attached to the new *Ministre de l'immigration, de l'intégration, de l'identité nationale et du codéveloppement*, and considers that the presidential decree (see note 1 above) gives power to the minister over asylum matters. This includes the files of decisions to definitely reject asylum applications (Article 9 3° modifying article L.722-4 CESEDA). The French foreign affairs minister will share with the new minister the power of nomination of OFPRA's director (Article 9 2° modifying article L.722-2 CESEDA).

69. For basic cover see article L.380-1 and s. *Code de la Sécurité Sociale* and for complementary cover Article L.861-1 and s. *Code de la Sécurité Sociale.*

70. *Loi n° 2002-1576 du 30 décembre 2002 art. 57 III finances rectificative pour 2002*, JORF, 31 December 2002 ; *Loi n° 2003-1312 du 30 décembre 2003 art. 97 1° finances rectificative pour 2003*, JORF, 31 December 2003.

71. CE, 7 June 2006, *Association Aides et autres*, com. Aubert, AJDA, 22/2006, 1189.

72. *International Federation of Human Rights Leagues (FIDH)* v. *France* (14/2003), (2005) 40 EHRR SE25. The Committee of Ministers adopted Resolution ResChS(2005)6 on 4 May 2005 and thus acknowledged the move.

73. S. Boyron, *The Constitution of France: A Contextual Analysis*, Oxford: Hart, 2012, especially pp. 204–5.

74. http://www.immigration-professionnelle.gouv.fr/sites/default/files/fckupload/ Circulaire_Prefets_du_31-05-2011.pdf (last accessed 10 January 2013.

4 The French Republic and its supranational offspring

1. This is a revised version of an article published as 'A love–hate relationship: France and European law', *Columbia Journal of European Law*, 16 (2), 2010, pp. 1–19.
2. S. Freud, 'Analysis of a phobia in a five-year-old boy', in *Case Histories 1: Dora and Little Hans*, vol. 8, Pelican Freud Library, Harmondsworth: Penguin, 1977, pp. 165–303, especially p. 207.
3. Ibid., note under p. 204.
4. As mentioned previously, according to the final results published by the Ministry of the Interior, 54.68 per cent of the French voted 'no' while 45.32 per cent voted in favour.
5. See the rejection of the Nice Treaty in 2001 (online at: http://news.bbc.co.uk/1/ hi/world/europe/1376379.stm) and the rejection of the Lisbon Treaty (online at: http://news.bbc.co.uk/1/hi/world/europe/7453560.stm (last accessed 10 January 2013)).
6. Many commentators have noted that domestic problems have contributed to this rejection. There is an obvious correlation between the 'no' vote and the unemployment rate for instance. See *Le Monde* (Paris), 1 June 2005, p. 7.
7. N. Bobbio, *Liberalism and Democracy*, London: Verso Radical Thinkers, 2005, pp. 25–30.
8. I am here referring both to communitarian law and to conventional law.
9. This was born under the Fourth French Republic, which was in place from 1946 to 1958.
10. P. Craig and G. de Burca, *EU Law, Text, Cases and Materials*, Oxford: Oxford University Press, 2003, p. 7.
11. This chapter is only considering the relevant Constitutions of the Fourth and Fifth Republics.
12. 1946 Constitution, Preamble, para. 14: 'La République française, fidèle à ses traditions, se conforme aux règles du droit public international. Elle n'entreprendra aucune guerre dans des vues de conquête et n'emploiera jamais ses forces contre la liberté d'aucun people'; para. 15: 'Sous réserve de réciprocité, la France consent aux limitations de souveraineté nécessaires à l'organisation et à la défense de la paix'.
13. The hierarchy established by the Constitution is explained in article 55: 'Les traités ou accords régulièrement ratifiés ou approuvés ont dés leur publication, une autorité supérieure à celle des lois, sous réserve, pour chaque accord ou traité, de son application par l'autre partie.'
14. There were some forms of political control in past systems and particularly in previous Republics, with the particularity of quasi-judiciary control by the *Comité constitutionnel* under the Fourth Republic (articles 91–3, 1946 Constitution).
15. 'A regulation shall have general application. It shall be binding in its entirety and directly applicable in all Member States. A directive shall be binding, as to the result to be achieved, upon each Member State to which it is addressed, but shall leave to the national authorities the choice of form and methods.' Consolidated version of the Treaty on the Functioning of the European Union

(TFEU), Article 288 (ex Article 249 TEC). Official Journal 115, 09/05/2008, p. 0171–0172. Online at: http://eur-lex.europa.eu/LexUriServ/LexUriServ. do?uri=CELEX:12008e288:en:HTML (last accessed 10 January 2013).

16. As the *Francovich* case highlighted. Joined Cases C-6/90 & 9/90, *Andrea Francovich and Danila Bonifaci and others* v. *Italian Republic* [1991] ECR I 5357.

17. U. Beck, 'The silence of words and political dynamics in the world risk society', *Logos*, 1 (4), 2002. Online at: http://logosonline.home.igc.org/beck.htm (last accessed 10 January 2013). U. Beck, 'The cosmopolitan perspective: sociology of the second age of modernity', *British Journal of Sociology*, 51 (1), 2000, pp. 79–105.

18. *Cons. const., Décision* 92-308 DC, 9 April 1992 (I), *Traité sur l'Union européenne (I)*, JORF, 11 April 1992, p. 5354. Online at: http://www.conseil-constitution-nel.fr/conseil-constitutionnel/francais/les-decisions/depuis-1958/decisions-par-date/1992/92-308-dc/decision-n-92-308-dc-du-09-avril-1992.8798.html (last accessed 10 January 2013). *Cons. const., Decision* 92-312 DC, 2 September 1992, *Traité sur l'Union européenne (II)*, JORF, 3 September 1992, p. 12095. Online at: http://www.conseil-constitutionnel.fr/conseil-constitutionnel/francais/les-decisions/acces-par-date/decisions-depuis-1959/1992/92-312-dc/decision-n-92-312-dc-du-02-septembre-1992.8800.html (last accessed 10 January 2013). *Cons. const., Décision* 92-313 DC, 23 September 1992, *Loi autorisant la ratification du traité sur l'Union européenne (III)*, JORF, 25 September 1992, p. 13337. Online at: http://www.conseil-constitutionnel.fr/conseil-constitutionnel/francais/les-decisions/acces-par-date/decisions-depuis-1959/1992/92-313-dc/decision-n-92-313-dc-du-23-septembre-1992.8822.html (last accessed 10 January 2013).

19. As mentioned previously, it seems that since 1982 the *Conseil constitutionnel* has referred to the so called *principes à valeur constitutionnel* and *objectifs à valeur constitutionnel*. For Professor F. Luchaire, the principles of constitutional value are directly applicable and can be invoked by an individual before a court, while objectives of constitutional value are imposed on the legislative power but are never directly invoked before a court. See *Revue Française de Droit Constitutionnel*, n° 64, October 2005, pp. 675–84 and the *Rapport fait au nom de la Commission des lois constitutionnelles, de la législation et de l'administration générale de la République sur le projet de loi constitutionnelle (N° 992) relatif à la Charte de l'environnement*. Online at: http://www.assemblee-nationale.fr/12/rapports/r1595.asp (last accessed 10 January 2013).

20. During the period 1958–68, the French legal order operated more or less in the same way as the political leadership: a national awakening provoked by a strong leader.

21. The term 'court' may not quite explain the real nature of the *Conseil constitutionnel*, but in the context of this article and since the adoption of an ex post constitutional control type procedure in 2008, this approximation will suffice.

22. *Cons. const., Décision* 74-54 DC, 15 January 1975, *Loi relative à l'interruption volontaire de la grossesse*, JORF, 16 January 1975, p. 671. Online at: http://www.conseil-constitutionnel.fr/conseil-constitutionnel/francais/les-decisions/1975/74-54-dc/decision-n-74-54-dc-du-15-janvier-1975.7423.html (last accessed 10 January 2013).

23. Ibid. In fact, 'decisions [taken] in application of article 61 of the Constitution have absolute and definite characteristics, as a result of article 62, which impeaches promulgation and enforcement of every disposition declared

unconstitutional. On the contrary, the superiority of treaties on statute laws, a principle found at article 55 [...], presents a relative and contingent characteristic, as, on the one hand, it is limited to the scope of the treaty, and on the other hand, it is subordinated to the condition of reciprocity which depends on its variable realisation based on the behaviour of one or more states' signatories and the moment when the respect of this condition has to be appreciated.' In this case, the *Conseil constitutionnel* considered that 'a law contradicting a treaty [did] not automatically contradict the Constitution' and in consequence the control could not be activated.

24. *Cons. const.*, *Décision* 2004-496 DC, 10 June 2004, *Loi pour la confiance dans l'économie numérique*, JORF, 22 June 2004, p. 11182. Online at: http://www. conseil-constitutionnel.fr/conseil-constitutionnel/francais/les-decisions/acces-par-date/decisions-depuis-1959/2004/2004-496-dc/decision-n-2004-496-dc-du-10-juin-2004.901.html (last accessed 10 January 2013).

25. Directive 2000/31/CE [2000] OJ L178, pp. 1–16.

26. Case 100/77, *Commission* v. *Italy* [1978] EUECJ C-100/77; Rec. 879 and Case 102/79 *Commission of the European Communities* v. *Kingdom of Belgium* [1981] 1 CMLR 282; [1980] EUECJ C-102/79.

27. The text of this article has been modified.

28. 'la transposition en droit interne d'une directive communautaire résulte d'une exigence constitutionnelle à laquelle il ne pourrait être fait obstacle qu'en raison d'une disposition expresse contraire de la Constitution'.

29. 'qu'en l'absence d'une telle disposition, il n'appartient qu'au juge communautaire, [...], de contrôler le respect par une directive communautaire [...]'.

30. See *Cons. const.*, *Décision* 92-308 DC, 9 April 1992 (I), *Traité sur l'Union européenne (I)*, JORF, 11 April 1992, p. 5354. Online at: http://www.conseil-constitution-nel.fr/conseil-constitutionnel/francais/les-decisions/depuis-1958/decisions-par-date/1992/92-308-dc/decision-n-92-308-dc-du-09-avril-1992.8798.html (last accessed 10 January 2013). *Cons. const.*, *Décision* 92-312 DC, 2 September 1992, *Traité sur l'Union européenne (II)*, JORF, 3 September 1992, p. 12095. Online at: http://www.conseil-constitutionnel.fr/conseil-constitutionnel/francais/les-decisions/acces-par-date/decisions-depuis-1959/1992/92-312-dc/decision-n-92-312-dc-du-02-septembre-1992.8800.html (last accessed 10 January 2012). *Cons. const.*, *Décision* 92-313 DC, 23 September 1992, *Loi autorisant la ratification du traité sur l'Union européenne (III)*, JORF, 25 September 1992, p. 13337. Online at: http://www.conseil-constitutionnel.fr/conseil-constitutionnel/francais/les-decisions/acces-par-date/decisions-depuis-1959/1992/92-313-dc/decision-n-92-313-dc-du-23-septembre-1992.8822.html (last accessed 10 January 2013).

31. *Loi constitutionnelle* 92-554, 25 June 1992, *ajoutant à la Constitution un titre: 'Des communautés européennes et de l'Union européenne'*, JORF, 26 June 1992, p. 147.

32. See *Cons. const.*, *Décision* 92-308 DC, 9 April 1992 (I), *Traité sur l'Union européenne (I)*, JORF, 11 April 1992, p. 5354. Online at: http://www.conseil-constitution-nel.fr/conseil-constitutionnel/francais/les-decisions/depuis-1958/decisions-par-date/1992/92-308-dc/decision-n-92-308-dc-du-09-avril-1992.8798.html (last accessed 10 January 2013). *Cons. const.*, *Décision* 92-312 DC, 2 September 1992, *Traité sur l'Union européenne (II)*, JORF, 3 September 1992, p. 12095. Online at: http://www.conseil-constitutionnel.fr/conseil-constitutionnel/francais/les-decisions/acces-par-date/decisions-depuis-1959/1992/92-312-dc/decision-n-92-312-dc-du-02-septembre-1992.8800.html (last accessed 10 January 2013).

Cons. const., *Décision* 92-313 DC, 23 September 1992, *Loi autorisant la ratification du traité sur l'Union européenne (III)*, JORF, 25 September 1992, p. 13337. Online at: http://www.conseil-constitutionnel.fr/conseil-constitutionnel/francais/les-decisions/acces-par-date/decisions-depuis-1959/1992/92-313-dc/decision-n-92-313-dc-du-23-septembre-1992.8822.html (last accessed 10 January 2013).

33. In reality, EU law is 'somewhere else' than the domestic hierarchy. It seems that in fact this hierarchy does not mean anything anymore. On paper, EU law will be considered as supra legislative and infra constitutional, pleasing everyone when the Constitution is amended. This seems to have added a new pressure on the French legal order and the Constitution has to be amended each time it clashes with EU law, to allow the move towards a more supra-national integration. But this is not a 'new' mechanism. Indeed, a similar one was used under the Fourth French Republic as a means of control of constitutionality. In that case a statute contrary to the Constitution always obliged the Constitution to be amended. This aimed to reinforce the precedence of (substantial) norms voted on by the French parliament over the Constitution, while keeping the hypocrisy of the hierarchy of norms alive (in form). If we use similar reasoning, there is no doubt that there exists a precedence of EC/EU law over the Constitution.

34. Joined Cases C-6/90 and 9/90, *Andrea Francovich and Danila Bonifaci and others* v. *Italian Republic* [1991] ECR I 5357.

35. CE, Ass. 30 October 1998, *M. Sarran, Levacher et autres*, Rec. p. 369; *RFDA* (1998), p. 1091.

36. See also the development of Kelsen's argument in H. Kelsen, *Theorie Général des Normes*, Paris: PUF, 1996, pp. 161–6.

37. CE, 15 March 1972, *Dame veuve Sadok Ali* Rec. p. 213.

38. See *Cons. const.*, *Décision* 74-54 DC, 15 January 1975, *Loi relative à l'interruption volontaire de la grossesse*, JORF, 16 January 1975, p. 671. Online at: http://www.conseil-constitutionnel.fr/conseil-constitutionnel/francais/les-decisions/1975/74-54-dc/decision-n-74-54-dc-du-15-janvier-1975.7423.html (last accessed 10 January 2013).

39. Cass., Ch. Mixte, 24 May 1975, *Société des Cafés Jacques Vabre*, *Dalloz* 1975 conc. Touffait.

40. 'au motif que celui-ci, en vertu de l'article 55 de la Constitution, a une autorité supérieure à celle de la loi interne, même postérieure'.

41. 'Mais attendu que le traité du 25 mars 1957, qui, en vertu de l'article susvisé de la Constitution, a une autorité supérieure à celle des lois, institue un ordre juridique propre intègre à celui des Etats membres; qu'en raison de cette spécificité, l'ordre juridique qu'il a créé est directement applicable aux ressortissants de ces États et s'impose à leurs jurisdictions.'

42. See also Michael Gueldry, *France and European Integration: Towards a Transnational Polity?*, New York: Greenwood Press, 2001, pp. 51–3.

43. CE, Ass., 30 May 1952, *Dame Kirkwood* Rec. p. 291.

44. It is even more complicated in the case of the administrative supreme court, as it could be considered a branch of the executive interfering with the work of the legislature.

45. CE, Ass., 20 October 1989, *Nicolo* Rec. p. 190, conc. Frydman.

46. CE, 24 September 1990, *M. Boisdet* Rec. p. 251.

47. This requires some further comment. Regulations, contrary to statute law, are more or less not adopted by the elected parliamentary body but by appointed civil servants. In the system thereby in effect, they have precedence over domestic

pieces of legislation that are the creation of democratically elected institutions. The logic of secondary European norms has to be seen through the delegation process to supra-national entities, and has to confront the idea of accountability, with the chain of accountability mirroring the chain of delegation. Citizens elect parliament, which delegates to supra-national agents the power to enact law. In this logic, regulations and directives are pure products of transnational institutions, themselves the creation of cosmopolitan western societies. If this chain is not present in the mind of the people and/or the elite, the system may not receive the required legitimacy.

48. CE, Ass., 3 February 1989, *Compagnie Alitalia* Rec. p. 44.
49. CE, Ass., 28 February 1992, *S.A. Rothmans International France et S.A. Philip Morris France* Rec. p. 81.
50. These seem to bring a major change in the relationship.
51. *Cons. const.*, *Décision* 2006-540 DC, 27 July 2006, *Loi relative au droit d'auteur et aux droits voisins dans la société de l'information*, JORF, 3 August 2006, p. 11541. Online at: http://www.conseil-constitutionnel.fr/conseil-constitutionnel/francais/les-decisions/acces-par-date/decisions-depuis-1959/2006/2006-540-dc/decision-n-2006-540-dc-du-27-juillet-2006.1011.html (last accessed 10 January 2013). *Cons. const.*, *Décision* 2006-543 DC, 30 November 2006, *Loi relative au secteur de l'énergie*, Rec. p. 120, JORF, 8 December 2006, p. 18544.Online at: http://www.conseil-constitutionnel.fr/conseil-constitutionnel/francais/les-decisions/acces-par-date/decisions-depuis-1959/2006/2006-543-dc/decision-n-2006-543-dc-du-30-novembre-2006.1014.html (last accessed 10 January 2013).
52. 'la transposition en droit interne d'une directive communautaire résulte d'une exigence constitutionnelle'.
53. 'Considérant [...] que la transposition d'une directive ne saurait aller à l'encontre d'une règle ou d'un principe inhérent à l'identité constitutionnelle de la France, sauf à ce que le constituant y ait consenti.'
54. CE, 8 February 2007, *Arcelor*, N° 287110.
55. 'Considérant que si, aux termes de l'article 55 de la Constitution, "les traités ou accords régulièrement ratifiés ou approuvés ont, dès leur publication, une autorité supérieure à celle des lois, sous réserve, pour chaque accord ou traité, de son application par l'autre partie", la suprématie ainsi conférée aux engagements internationaux ne saurait s'imposer, dans l'ordre interne, aux principes et dispositions à valeur constitutionnelle.'
56. Now article 267 TFEU. Online at: http://eur-lex.europa.eu/LexUriServ/LexUriServ.do?uri=CELEX:12008E267:fr:HTML (last accessed 10 January 2013).
57. *Allocution de M. le président de la République, Après le vote de la Loi autorisant la ratification du Traité de Lisbonne, Palais de l'Élysée*, 10 February 2008. 'Pendant la campagne présidentielle, je m'étais engagé à tout faire pour convaincre nos partenaires de tourner la page de la Constitution européenne qui ne pouvait plus entrer en vigueur alors que deux pays, la France et les Pays-Bas, l'avaient rejetée par référendum et qu'il n'était pas question de demander au peuple français et au peuple néerlandais de se déjuger.'
58. 'J'ai dit pendant la campagne présidentielle que c'est ce que je ferais si j'étais élu. Cela faisait partie, mes chers concitoyens, du mandat que vous m'avez confié en m'élisant Président de la République. Cet engagement que j'avais pris solennellement devant vous, je l'ai tenu.'

59. *Loi* 2008-125, 13 February 2008, *autorisant la ratification du traité de Lisbonne modifiant le traité sur l'Union européenne, le traité instituant la Communauté européenne et certains actes connexes*, JORF 0038, 14 February 2008, p. 2712, text n° 1.

60. http://european-council.europa.eu/media/639235/st00tscg26_en12.pdf (last accessed 10 January 2013).

61. *Loi constitutionnelle* 2008-103, 4 February 2008, *modifiant le titre XV de la Constitution*, JORF 0030, 5 February 2008, p. 2202, text n° 1.

62. *Cons. const.*, *Décision* 2012-653 DC, 9 August 2012, JORF, 11 August 2012, p. 13283, *Traité sur la stabilité, la coordination et la gouvernance au sein de l'Union économique et monétaire*. Online at: http://www.conseil-constitutionnel. fr/conseil-constitutionnel/francais/les-decisions/acces-par-date/decisions-depuis-1959/2012/2012-653-dc/decision-n-2012-653-dc-du-09-aout-2012.115444. html (last accessed 10 January 2013).

63. *Conférence de Presse de M. Nicolas Sarkozy Président de la République, Sommet Informel des Chefs d'Etat et de Gouvernement de l'Union Europeénne, Session de la Conférence Intergouvernementale, Centre International de Lisbonne*, 19 October 2007. 'Sur le référendum, j'ai dit pendant la campagne que je me battrai pour l'adoption du Traité simplifié et que si j'arrivais à convaincre nos 26 partenaires que le Traité simplifié était la solution, je le soumettrai à la voie parlementaire. [...] Donc non, c'est parlementaire, et par ailleurs ce n'est pas une Constitution, ce n'est pas le Traité issu de la Convention.'

64. J. Monnet, *Mémoires*, Paris: Fayard, 1976, p. 360: 'Rien n'est possible sans les hommes, rien n'est durable sans les institutions.'

65. U. Beck and A. Giddens, 'Nationalism has now become the enemy of Europe's nations', *The Guardian* (London), 4 October 2005.

5 Principle of indivisibility of the French Republic and the people's right to self-determination

1. The present chapter is a revised, amended and updated version of an article published as 'Principle of indivisibility of the French Republic and the people's right to self-determination: the "New Caledonia test"', *Journal of Academic Legal Studies*, 2, 2006, pp. 16–29.

2. The unity of the people and indivisibility of the Republic were first enshrined in article 1 of the 1793 Constitution (known as the Constitution of the First Republic). This confirms that the problem remained unsolved for approximately four years (1789–93). J.-J. Chevallier, *Histoire des Institutions et des Régimes Politiques de la France de 1789 à Nos Jours*, 7th edn, Paris: Dalloz, 1985, especially p. 69.

3. J. Bell and S. Boyron, *Principles of French Law*, Oxford: Oxford University Press, 1998, especially p. 162.

4. The freedom of administration of local authorities is a principle recognised by article 72 of the 1958 Constitution. This was commented on and interpreted by the *Conseil constitutionnel* in *Cons. const.*, *Décision* 79-104 DC, 23 May 1979, *Loi modifiant les modes d'élection de l'Assemblée territoriale et du Conseil de gouvernement du territoire de la Nouvelle-Calédonie et dépendances et définissant les règles générales de l'aide technique et financière contractuelle de l'État*, JORF, 25 May 1979, online at: http://www.conseil-constitutionnel.fr/conseil-constitutionnel/ francais/les-decisions/acces-par-date/decisions-depuis-1959/1979/79-104-dc/

decision-n-79-104-dc-du-23-mai-1979.7722.html (last accessed 10 January 2013); and *Cons. const.*, *Décision* 82-137 DC, 25 February 1982, *Loi relative aux droits et libertés des communes, des départements et des régions*, JORF, 3 March 1982, p. 759, online at: http://www.conseil-constitutionnel.fr/conseil-constitutionnel/francais/les-decisions/acces-par-date/decisions-depuis-1959/1982/82-137-dc/decision-n-82-137-dc-du-25-fevrier-1982.7990.html (last accessed 10 January 2013).

5. W. Safran, 'The context of French politics', in M. Donald Hancock, Raphael Zariski and David P. Conradt (eds), *Politics in Western Europe*, Washington, DC: CQ Press, 1993, pp. 93–5.

6. J. L. Sibert, *Le Plus Petit Atlas du Monde*, Paris: Lac, 1940, pp. 47–8.

7. New Caledonia is translated as *Nouvelle-Calédonie* in French. Geographically, the Atlas of 1940 estimates the size of the territory to be 20,000 km². Located in the Pacific Ocean, New Caledonia has an accurate area of 18,575 km² and belongs to Melanesia. It consists of a large island, *Grande-Terre* (400 km by 50 km), the *île des Pins*, the archipels of *Belep*, *Huon* and *Surprise*, the *îles de Chesterfield* and *recif* of *Bellone*, the four *îles Loyauté* (Ouvéa, Lifou, Tiga et Maré), the *îles Warpole, de l'Astrolabe, Matthew* et *Fearn, Hunter* and some remote little islands. The Economic Exclusive Zone covers 1.4 million km². Demographically, this colony comprised 60,000 inhabitants in 1940 but after the census of 1996 the population reached 196,836 inhabitants, with an estimated 216,132 in 2001. The population of the territory is currently as follows: (a) *Province Sud*: 134,546 inhabitants; (b) *Province Nord*: 41,413 inhabitants; and (c) *Province des îles Loyauté*: 20,877 inhabitants (source: *Institut Territorial de la Statistique et des Etudes Economiques*).

8. Preamble, Nouméa Agreement of 5 May 1998, JORF, 27 May 1998, pp. 8039–44 (*Accord sur la Nouvelle-Calédonie signé a Nouméa le 5 mai 1998*).

9. R. Elgie, *Political Institutions in Contemporary France*, Oxford: Oxford University Press, 2003, p. 211.

10. *Loi constitutionnelle* 2003-276, *relative à l'organisation décentralisée de la République*, 28 March 2003, JORF 75, 29 March 2003, p. 5568.

11. Article 1 of the Fifth French Republic Constitution [1958 Const.] states: 'La France est une République indivisible, laïque, démocratique et sociale. Elle assure l'égalité devant la loi de tous les citoyens sans distinction d'origine, de race ou de religion. Elle respecte toutes les croyances. Son organisation est décentralisée.'

12. Hereinafter referred to as R/D/C.

13. *Cons. const.*, *Décision* 82-138 DC, 25 February 1982, *Loi portant statut particulier de la région Corse*, JORF, 27 February 1982, p. 697. Online at: http://www.conseil-constitutionnel.fr/conseil-constitutionnel/francais/les-decisions/depuis-1958/decisions-par-date/1982/82-138-dc/decision-n-82-138-dc-du-25-fevrier-1982.7992.html (last accessed 10 January 2013).

14. C. Debbasch, *Constitution Ve République*, Paris: Dalloz, 2005, p. 391.

15. Article 34 limits the legislative attribution of the French parliament to a list of specific competences.

16. *Loi organique* 2004-192 *portant statut d'autonomie de la Polynésie française*, 27 February 2004, JORF, 2 March 2004, p. 4183 and *Loi* 2004-193 *complétant le statut d'autonomie de la Polynésie française*, 27 February 2004, JORF, 2 March 2004, p. 4213.

17. I. Brownlie, *Principles of Public International Law*, 6th edn, Oxford: Oxford University Press, 2003, p. 553.

18. 'En vertu de ces principes et de celui de la libre détermination des peuples, la République offre aux territories d'Outre-mer qui manifestent la volonté d'y adhérer des institutions nouvelles fondées sur l'idéal commun de liberté, d'égalité et de fraternité et concues en vue de leur évolution démocratique.'

19. 'Nulle cession, nul échange, nulle adjonction de territoire n'est valable sans le consentement des populations interessées.'

20. *Cons. const.*, *Décision* 2000-428 DC, 4 May 2000, *loi organisant une consultation de la population de Mayotte* JORF, 10 May 2000, p. 6976. Online at: http://www.conseil-constitutionnel.fr/conseil-constitutionnel/francais/les-decisions/acces-par-date/decisions-depuis-1959/2000/2000-428-dc/decision-n-2000-428-dc-du-04-mai-2000.448.html (last accessed 10 January 2013).

21. Article. 17, 1946 Const.: 'L'Union française est composée de nations et de peuples qui mettent en commun ou coordonnent leurs ressources et leurs efforts pour développer leurs civilisations respectives, accroître leur bien-être et assurer leur sécurité'.

22. TOM disappeared with the 2003 amendment of the 1958 Constitution. COM is now the updated version of TOM.

23. *Loi 56-619 autorisant le gouvernement à mettre en œuvre les réformes et à prendre les mesures propres à assurer l'évolution des territoires relevant du ministère de la France d'Outre-Mer*, 23 June 1956, JORF, 23 June 1956, p. 5782.

24. *Décret 57-811 organisation des pouvoirs publics en Nouvelle-Calédonie*, 22 July 1957, JORF 23 July 1957, p. 7252.

25. See generally G.A. Res. 1514, U.N. GAOR, 15th Sess., Supp. No. 16, U.N. Doc. A/4684 (1960). (In that respect, the Declaration on the Granting of Independence to Colonial Countries and People adopted by the UN General Assembly in 1960 remains one of the most significant.)

26. *Loi 63-1246 organisation des pouvoirs publics en Nouvelle-Calédonie*, 21 December 1963, JORF, 22 December 1963, p. 11451.

27. *Loi 69-4 modifiant la règlementation minière en Nouvelle-Calédonie*, 3 January 1969, JORF, 5 January 1969, p. 196; *Loi 69-5 relative à la création et à l'organisation des communes dans le territoire de la Nouvelle-Calédonie et dépendances*, 3 January 1969, JORF, 5 January 1969, p. 197; *Loi 69-6 portant régime fiscal de certains investissements dans le territoire de la Nouvelle-Calédonie*, 3 January 1969, JORF, 5 January 1969, p. 199.

28. *Loi 76-1222 relative à l'organisation de la Nouvelle-Calédonie et dépendances*, 28 December 1976, JORF, 22 December 1976, p. 7530.

29. Norm-making but not precisely law-making in that case as France remains a unitary state.

30. *Loi 84-821 portant statut du territoire de Nouvelle-Calédonie et dépendances*, 6 September 1984, JORF, 7 September 1984, p. 2840.

31. *Loi 85-892 sur l'évolution de la Nouvelle-Calédonie*, 23 August 1985, JORF, 24 August 1985, p. 9775.

32. *Loi 86-844 relative à la Nouvelle-Calédonie*, 17 July 1986, JORF, 19 July 1986, p. 8930.

33. *Loi 88-82 portant statut du territoire de la Nouvelle-Calédonie*, 22 January 1988, JORF, 26 January 1988, p. 1243.

34. *Loi* 88-808 *relative à l'administration de la Nouvelle-Calédonie*, 12 July 1988, JORF, 14 July 1998, p. 9142.

35. *Loi* 88-1028 *portant dispositions statutaires et préparatoires à l'autodétermination de la Nouvelle-Calédonie en 1998*, 9 November 1988, JORF, 10 November 1988, pp. 14096–9.

36. Ibid., article 2 'Entre le 1er mars et le 31 décembre 1998, les populations intéressées de la Nouvelle-Calédonie seront appelées à se prononcer par un scrutin d'autodétermination, conformément aux dispositions de l'article 53 de la Constitution, sur le maintien du territoire dans la République ou sur son accession à l'indépendance.'

37. Part 1 *Rapport d'information du sénat* 216 of 16 February 2004. Online at: http://www.senat.fr/rap/r03-216/r03-216_mono.html (last accessed 10 January 2013).

38. Nouméa Agreement, 5 May 1998, JORF, 27 May 1998, pp. 8039–44 (*Accord sur la Nouvelle-Calédonie signé à Nouméa le 5 mai 1998*).

39. *Décret* 98-733 *portant organisation de la consultation des populations de Nouvelle-Calédonie prévue par l'article 76 de la Constitution*, 20 August 1998, JORF, 22 August 1998, pp. 12844–7 and *Décision proclamant les résultats de la consultation des populations de Nouvelle-Calédonie du dimanche 8 novembre 1998*, 9 November 1998, JORF, 10 November 1998, p. 16956.

40. Commentators have considered that *Cons. const.*, *Décision* 99-410 DC, *Loi organique relative à la Nouvelle-Calédonie*,15 March 1999, interpreted the Nouméa Agreement as incorporated into the French constitutional norms (see O. Gohin, 'L'apport de l'évolution institutionnelle de l'outre-mer non départementalisé au droit constitutionnel depuis 1998', *Cahiers du Conseil constitutionnel 12, Dossier: Le droit constitutionnel des collectivités territoriales, Mai 2002*. Online at: http://www.conseil-constitutionnel.fr/conseil-constitutionnel/francais/nouveaux-cahiers-du-conseil/cahier-n-12/l-apport-de-l-evolution-institutionnelle-de-l-outre-mer-non-departementalise-au-droit-constitutionnel-depuis-1998.52103.html (last accessed 10 January 2013).

41. *Loi* 99-209 *organique relative à la Nouvelle-Calédonie*, 19 March 1999, JORF, 21 March 1999, pp. 4197–226 rect. 16 April 1999, p. 5610, hereinafter referred to as L.99-209, and *Loi* 99-210 *relative à la Nouvelle-Calédonie*, 19 March 1999, JORF, 21 March 1999, pp. 4226–33, hereinafter referred to as L.99-210.

42. The National Assembly comprises *députés* (elected members of the constituency) who are normally never referred to as *députés* of any constituency but as representatives of the French nation as a whole. To represent the local authorities, the Senate has members from each constituency. New Caledonia is divided into two constituencies which return one *député* each and one *sénateur* for the whole territory.

43. Article 7 of the *Loi organique* 2010-704 *relative au Conseil économique, social et environnemental*, 28 June 2010, JORF 0148, 29 June 2010, p. 11633 creates 11 councillors for the socio-economic activities of DOM, ROM, COM and New Caledonia. Online at: http://www.legifrance.gouv.fr/affichTexte.do?cidTexte=JORFTEXT000022402454&dateTexte=&categorieLien=id (last accessed 10 January 2013).

44. Article 21 L.99-209.

45. Article 26 L.99-209.

46. *Titre* III L.99-209.

47. Article 62 L.99-209.

48. Article 186 L.99-209; article 14 L.99-210.
49. In the design R/D/C, the elected members of the different councils are all *conseiller*.
50. Article 65 L.99-209.
51. Article 66 L.99-209.
52. Article 63.
53. It could be assumed that *Loi du pays* will become a generic terminology for norms created by overseas authorities COM. Specifically for New Caledonia, these are *Loi du pays de Nouvelle-Calédonie*. Here again the words used are extremely important as they relate to vocabulary used to describe an act of a state parliament or perhaps regional parliaments in some countries with high levels of devolution. The expression could be translated as 'law of the country of New Caledonia'. If *loi* (statute) may indicate a legislative act, adopted by a national or a regional parliament (for example in the case of regional states like Spain or Italy), *pays* (country) is used in French either for a local area like a village or a region, or as a synonym of the state.
54. Article 73 L.99-209.
55. As defined in articles 99 to 107 L.99-209.
56. Article 99 L.99-209.
57. *Décret* 99-842 *relatif à la promulgation des lois du pays en Nouvelle-Calédonie*, 27 September 1999, JORF, 30 September 1999, p. 14492.
58. The first constitutional control of these *loi de pays* took place in 2000 on a matter of taxation, *Cons. const.*, *Décision* 2000-1 LP, *Loi du pays relative à l'institution d'une taxe générale sur les services*, 27 January 2000, JORF, 29 January 2000, p. 1536. Online at: http://www.conseil-constitutionnel.fr/conseil-constitutionnel/francais/les-decisions/2000/2000-1-lp/decision-n-2000-1-lp-du-27-janvier-2000.463.html (last accessed 10 January 2013). The second and last one at the date of the publication of this work, April 2006, *Cons. const.*, *Décision* 2006-2 LP *Loi du pays relative à la représentativité des organisations syndicales de salariés*, 5 April 2006, JORF, 11 April 2006, p. 5439. Online at: http://www.conseil-constitutionnel.fr/conseil-constitutionnel/francais/les-decisions/acces-par-date/decisions-depuis-1959/2006/2006-2-lp/decision-n-2006-2-lp-du-05-avril-2006.1018.html (last accessed 10 January 2013).
59. R. Cornes, 'Devolution and England: what is on offer?', in N. Bamforth and P. Leyland (eds), *Public Law in a Multi-layered Constitution*, Oxford: Hart, 2003, pp. 109–10.
60. Article 109 L.99-209.
61. Article 110 L.99-209.
62. Article 126 L.99-209.
63. Article 115 L.99-209.
64. Article 122 L.99-209.
65. Article 123 L.99-209.
66. Article 137 L.99-209.
67. There are eight councils for the eight areas: Hoot Ma Whaap, Paici Camuki, Ajie Aro, Xaracuu, Djubea-Kapone, Iaai, Drehu, Nengone. Article 149 L.99-209.
68. Article 138 L.99-209.
69. Article 139 L.99-209.
70. Article 143 L.99-209.

71. Article 142 L.99-209.
72. Article 144 L.99-209.
73. Article 145 L.99-209.
74. Article 154 L.99-209.
75. Article 153 L.99-209.
76. Article 155 L.99-209.
77. The provinces are defined under *Titre* IV L.99-209.
78. Article 186 L.99-209; article 14 L.99-210.
79. Article 173 L.99-209.
80. Article 20 L.99-209.
81. *Loi* 90-1247 *portant suppression de la tutelle administrative et financière sur les communes de Nouvelle-Calédonie et dispositions diverses relatives à ce territoire*, 29 December 1990, JORF, 3 January 1991, p. 98.
82. Vœu 1, 13 July 2010, *Journal Officiel de la Nouvelle-Calédonie*, 22 July 2010, p. 6341. Online at: http://emblemes.free.fr/site/index.php?option=com_content &task=view&id=2817&Itemid=258. Last accessed 10 January 2013.
83. Article 219 IV L.99-209 details that three hours are allocated in both radio and television broadcasts of the French public services.
84. Article 219 II L.99-209.
85. R. Lafargue, 'La coutume judiciaire en Nouvelle-Calédonie. Aux sources d'un droit commun coutumier', ɪ, 2002. Also online at: http://www.gip-recherche-justice.fr/catalogue/PDF/rapports/78-RF_Lafargue_Nlle_Caledonie.pdf (last accessed 10 January 2013).
86. Article 18 L.99-209.
87. Article 1.2.4, Nouméa Agreement.
88. *Ordonnance* 82-877 *instituant des assesseurs coutumiers dans le territoire de la Nouvelle-Calédonie et Dépendances au tribunal civil de première instance et à la cour d'appel*, 15 October 1982, JORF, 17 October 1982, p. 3106.
89. Article 4 L.99-209.
90. *Cons. const.*, 91-290 DC, *Loi portant statut de la collectivité territoriale de Corse*, 9 May 1991, para. 37, JORF, 14 May 1991, p. 6350. Online at: http://www.conseil-constitutionnel.fr/conseil-constitutionnel/francais/les-decisions/acces-par-date/decisions-depuis-1959/1991/91-290-dc/decision-n-91-290-dc-du-09-mai-1991.8758.html (last accessed 10 January 2013).
91. Ibid., para. 13.
92. Ibid. See also *Cons. const.*, 87-226 DC, *Loi organisant la consultation des populations intéressées de la Nouvelle-Calédonie et dépendances prévue par l'alinéa premier de l'article 1er de la loi n° 86-844 du 17 juillet 1986 relative à la Nouvelle-Calédonie*, 2 June 1987, JORF, 4 June 1987, p. 6058. Online at: http://www.conseil-constitutionnel.fr/conseil-constitutionnel/francais/les-decisions/acces-par-date/decisions-depuis-1959/1987/87-226-dc/decision-n-87-226-dc-du-02-juin-1987.8337.html (last accessed 10 January 2013).
93. In the Nouméa Agreement (article 1) the Kanak identity seems to have been a priority for the negotiators.
94. Article 28 L.99-209.
95. Article 29 L.99-209.
96. Article 33 L.99-209.
97. U. Beck and J. Willms, *Conversation with Ulrich Beck*, Oxford: Polity, 2004, p. 16.

6 The French Republic, its language and the paradigm of unity

1. This is a revised version of a paper 'Language and Republic: The Paradigm of Unity' presented at the conference on French Republicanism Today: 1958–2008 Fifty Years of the Fifth French Republic Constitution, held at the University of Essex in December 2008. I wish to thank Professor John Packer for his help.
2. http://www.dglf.culture.gouv.fr/publications/francais-monde.pdf (last accessed 10 January 2013).
3. For an overview of the organisation of central government in France, see R. Elgie, *Political Institutions in Contemporary France*, Oxford: Oxford University Press, 2003, pp. 129–51.
4. *Décret* 89-403 2 June 1989 *instituant un Conseil supérieur de la langue française et une délégation générale à la langue française*, JORF, 22 June 1989, p. 7729.
5. *Décret* 2001-950 16 October 2001 *modifiant le décret n°89-403 du 2 juin 1989 instituant un Conseil supérieur de la langue française et une délégation générale à la langue française*, JORF, 19 October 2001, p. 16497, particularly article 1: 'la délégation générale à la langue française devient la délégation générale à la langue française et aux langues de France'. The DGLFLF is now under the direct authority of the *Conseil supérieur de la langue française*, according to article 8 of the *Décret* 2004-822 18 August 2004 *modifié relatif à l'organisation et aux missions de l'administration centrale du ministère de la culture et de la communication*, JORF 193, 20 August 2004, p. 14902.
6. P. Brunet, 'Humpty Dumpty à Babel? Les juges et le vocabulaire juridique européen', *Chronique De Droit Européen & Comparé*, 17, 2008, Centre d'études juridiques européennes et comparées (CEJEC – Université Paris Ouest – Nanterre La Défense), 'Approche Critique du Vocabulaire Juridique Européen: Le Pouvoir des Juges', 2. 'On mesure ainsi combien appliquer le droit c'est exercer un pouvoir le pouvoir de décider du sens des mots.'
7. See article 1 of the *Loi constitutionnelle* 92-554 25 June 1992 *ajoutant à la Constitution un titre: 'Des Communautés européennes et de l'Union européenne'*, JORF 147, 26 June 1992, p. 8406, which adds a paragraph to article 2 of the 1958 Constitution. According to Roland Debbasch, the initial formulation was that French is the official language of the Republic, 'La Reconnaissance constitutionnelle de la langue francaise ', *RFDC*, 11, 1992, p. 457.
8. *La langue de la République est le français.*
9. *Loi* 94-665 4 August 1994 *relative à l'emploi de la langue française*, JORF, 5 August 1994, p. 11392.
10. *Cons. Const.* 94-345 DC, *Loi relative à l'emploi de la langue française*, JORF, 2 August 1994, p. 11240. Online at: http://www.conseil-constitutionnel.fr/conseil-constitutionnel/francais/les-decisions/acces-par-date/decisions-depuis-1959/1994/94-345-dc/decision-n-94-345-dc-du-29-juillet-1994.10568.html (last accessed 10 January 2013).
11. See article 2 *Décret* 2001-950 concerning the DGLFLF which states the requirement to 'préserver et valoriser les langues de France, à savoir les langues autres que le français qui sont parlées sur le territoire national et font partie du patrimoine culturel national'.
12. J. Lacan, *Le Séminaire Livre II: Le Moi dans le Théorie de Freud et dans la Technique de la Psychanalyse*, Paris: Seuil, 1978), p. 202: 'La nomination constitue un pacte, par lequel deux sujets en même temps s'accordent à reconnaître le même objet.'

13. M. Heidegger, *The Basic Problems of Phenomenology*, Bloomington, IN: Indiana University Press, 1982, p. 208.
14. Ferdinand de Saussure, *Cours de Linguistique Générale*, Paris: Payot, 1972, p. 21: 'le language est un fait social'.
15. Ibid., p. 30: 'ce qui est social de ce qui est individual'.
16. Ibid., p. 31.
17. Ibid., pp. 112–13.
18. Ibid.
19. E. Balibar, *We, The People of Europe: Reflections on Transnational Citizenship*, Princeton, NJ: Princeton University Press, 2004, pp. 19–20.
20. C. Levi-Strauss, *Totemism*, London: Merlin, 1964, pp. 85–91.
21. Unity (*unité*) and unicity (*unicité*) will be considered as being similar in this chapter. See, for example, the *Déclaration sur l'unicité et l'universalité salvifique de Jésus-Christ et de l'Église – Dominus Iesus* (*Declaratio de Iesu Christi atque Ecclesiae unicitate et universalitate salvifica*), 6 August 2000. See especially Chapter IV, Unicité et Unité de l'Église. It is, of course, not a simple coincidence to find similarities between the Catholic Church and the Republic. Many actors in the Revolution were priests, and the model of Port Royal is often cited as the one for the parliamentary system of representation: http://www.vatican.va/roman_curia/congregations/cfaith/documents/rc_con_cfaith_doc_20000806_dominus-iesus_fr.html (last accessed 10 January 2013).
22. P. Ives, *Language and Hegemony in Gramsci*, London: Pluto Press, 2004.
23. Ibid., p. 46.
24. A. Gramsci, *Selections from Cultural Writings*, Cambridge, MA: Harvard University Press, 1985, p. 187.
25. Saussure, *Cours*, pp. 40–1: 'la langue fait la nation'.
26. Ibid.: 'Des grands faits historiques comme la conquête romaine, ont eu une portée incalculable pour une foule de faits linguistiques. La colonisation, qui n'est qu'une forme de la conquête, transporte un idiome dans des milieux différents, ce qui entraîne des changements dans cet idiome. On pourrait citer à l'appui toute espèce de faits: ainsi la Norvège a adopté le Danois en s'unissant politiquement au Danemark; il est vrai qu'aujourd'hui les Norvégiens essaient de s'affranchir de cette influence linguistique. La politique intérieure des Etats n'est pas moins importante pour la vie des langues: certains gouvernements, comme la Suisse, admettent la coexistence de plusieurs idiomes; d'autres, comme la France, aspirent à l'unité linguistique.'
27. L. Oakes, 'Multilingualism in Europe: an effective French identity strategy?', *Journal of Multilingual and Multicultural Development*, 23 (5), 2002, pp. 371–87, especially p. 371. He adds '[t]he extent to which any overt action on the part of the French authorities can influence the linguistic environment of the European arena is highly debatable, especially considering the economic dominance of (American) English even in the European context.'
28. Ibid.
29. As commented earlier in Chapter 2. Education contributed to the violence of the imposition of French as a unique language.
30. S. Žižek, *Violence*, London: Profile Books, 2008, pp. 52–3.
31. Therefore, the work of the translator is of importance. It implies an immersion in the other, in his world, while remaining in one's own world. The work of the translator is open to the other without letting his or her 'mind go'. The translator operates a projector into another world. Umberto Eco suggests that 'translating

signifies understanding the internal system of a language and the structure of a text in this language and constructing a double of a textual system that under a certain description may produce similar effects in the reader, in a semantic way, syntaxic way, stylistic way, metric and phono symbolic to passionate effects towards which the text source was supposed to aim.' U. Eco, *Quase a Mesma Coisa*, Rio de Janeiro: Record, 2007, p. 17. The semiotic approach of Lamizet considers that the objective of fidelity in the translation goes through a process of teleological interpretation, allowing the reader imaginary representation to get closer to the underlying initial signifying chain (B. Lamizet, *Sémiotique de l'évènement*, Paris: Lavoisier, 2006). Imposing a language on a group of individuals as their medium of communication when this group has developed and communicated through another medium of communication (their original language) is far from being a pleasant experience of translation. It certainly does not regard the other kindly.

32. J. Derrida, *Le Monolinguism de l'Autre, ou la Prothése d'Origine*, Paris: Gallilée, 1996, p. 53.
33. http://www.opsi.gov.uk/acts/acts1993/Ukpga_19930038_en_1 (last accessed 10 January 2013).
34. http://www.opsi.gov.uk/legislation/scotland/acts2005/asp_20050007_en_1 (last accessed 10 January 2013).
35. See, for example, the comments on Spain and the UK in R. Cornes, 'Devolution and England: what is on offer?', in N. Bamforth and P. Leyland (eds), *Public Law in a Multi-layered Constitution*, Oxford: Hart, 2003, pp. 107–21.
36. M. Nic Craith, 'Politicised linguistic consciousness: the case of Ulster-Scots', *Nations and Nationalism*, 7 (1), 2001, pp. 21–37, especially p. 23.
37. Article 8 of the 1937 Constitution of Ireland specifically refers to the two languages. However, the Constitution confers a certain value to the languages. Article 8.1 classifies Irish as the first official language and 8.2 classifies English as the second. As highlighted by Casey, '[t]he "national" status of Irish is further emphasised by article 25.5.4 which provides that should a conflict arise between the two texts of the Constitution the one in Irish prevails' J. Casey, *Constitutional Law in Ireland*, 3rd edn, Dublin: Round Hall Sweet & Maxwell, 2000, p. 74.
38. Saussure, *Cours*, p. 266: 'En Irlande on parle le celtique et l'anglais.'
39. As Casey mentioned, the Constitution Review Group criticised 'Art. 8 as unrealistic, "given that English is the language currently spoken as their vernacular by 98% of the population of the state".' See Casey, *Constitutional Law in Ireland*, p. 74.
40. Article 111 of the *ordonnance* specifically refers to language in the first part of the article: 'Et pour ce que telles choses sont souvent advenues sur l'intelligence des mots latins contenus dans les dits arrêts.' This sentence has to be viewed in conjunction with what is said in article 110 about interpretation: 'Afin qu'il n'y ait cause de douter sur l'intelligence des arrêts de justice, nous voulons et ordonnons qu'ils soient faits et écrits si clairement, qu'il n'y ait, ni puisse avoir, aucune ambiguïté ou incertitude, ni lieu à demander interprétation.' Online at: http://www.assemblee-nationale.fr/histoire/villers-cotterets.asp (last accessed 10 January 2013).
41. As translated from old to modern French by the *Académie Française*: 'nous voulons dorénavant que tous arrêts, ensemble toutes autres procédures, soit de nos cours souveraines et autres subalternes et inférieures, soit de registres, enquêtes, contrats, commissions, sentences, testaments, et autres quelconques

actes et exploits de justice, soient prononcés, enregistrés et délivrés aux parties, en langage maternel français et non autrement.'

42. Gramsci, *Cultural Writings*, p. 188.
43. See Chapter 5. The *Girondins* were in favour of a federal state. The physical elimination of the *Girondins* in June 1793 marked the end of the possibility of a Republic organised as a federal state. The state became unitary; the French Republic became one and indivisible. The people's sovereign legitimated the idea of a unitary state: one people, one nation, one Republic. Article 1 of the Fifth French Republic Constitution proclaimed the indivisibility of the Republic as stated in 1793.
44. See F. Ost, 'Les Détours de Babel', paper presented at the Colloque International 'interpréter et traduire', 25–26 November 2005, USTV Toulon, France.
45. Ibid.: 'A la base du "sens commun linguistique", l'idée de langage se ramène, pour l'essentiel, et au moins dans l'idéal, a un immense lexique [qui] ne serait autre que l'héritage de celui qui prévalait au Jardin d'Eden ou Dieu avait nommé toutes les chose selon leur nature, sans ambiguïté, lacune, ni redondance.'
46. *Décret 2 thermidor An II 20 juillet 1794 sur la langue française*.
47. Article 1 1794 Décret.
48. Article 2 1794 Décret.
49. Articles 3 and 4 1794 Décret.
50. *Rapport et projet de décret sur l'organisation des écoles primaires présentés à la Convention nationale, au nom de son Comité d'instruction publique* (1792). 'L'enseignement public sera partout dirigé de manière qu'un de ses premiers bienfaits soit que la langue française devienne en peu de temps la langue familière de toutes les parties de la République.'
51. Gramsci, *Cultural Writings*, p. 248.
52. Ibid., p. 256.
53. In 1860, the county of Nice was attached to France at the same time as Savoy; the result was the decreasing use of Nissart and Italian to the advantage of French; the name Nizza (Italianisation of the name Nissa or Niça) was changed to Nice.
54. S. Jones, *The French State in Question, Public Law and Political Argument in the Third Republic*, Cambridge: Cambridge University Press, 1993, p. 9.
55. J. Derrida, *Force de Loi, Le 'Fondement mystique de l'autorité'*, Paris: Galilée, 1994, p. 47: 'une des violences fondatrices de la loi ou de l'imposition du droit étatique consiste à imposer une langue à des minorités nationales ou ethniques regroupées par l'Etat'.
56. Ibid.
57. http://news.bbc.co.uk/2/hi/europe/6738037.stm (last accessed 10 January 2013).
58. F. Wilmer, 'Minority rights and Charles Tilly's "statelessness"', *ConWEB*, 3, 2006, pp. 1–30, especially p. 11. Online at: http://www.qub.ac.uk/schools/SchoolofPoliticsInternationalStudiesandPhilosophy/FileStore/ConWEBFiles/Filetoupload,38374,en.pdf (last accessed 10 January 2013).
59. Ibid., p. 12.
60. See Chapter 5.
61. *Loi* 2000-1207 13 December 2000 *d'orientation pour l'outre-mer*, JORF, 14 December 2000, p. 19760.
62. Marrani, *Indivisibility*.

63. *Loi organique* 96-312, 12 April 1996 *portant statut d'autonomie de la Polynésie française*, JORF, 13 April 1996, p. 5705.

64. *Cons. Const.*, *Décision* 96-373DC, 9 April 1996, *Loi organique portant statut d'autonomie de la Polynésie française*, JORF, 13April 1996, p. 5724. Online at: http://www.conseil-constitutionnel.fr/conseil-constitutionnel/francais/ les-decisions/acces-par-date/decisions-depuis-1959/1996/96-373-dc/decision-n-96-373-dc-du-09-avril-1996.10806.html (last accessed 10 January 2013).

65. *Loi organique* 2004-192, 27 February 2004 *portant statut d'autonomie de la Polynésie française*, JORF, 2 March 2004, p. 4183.

66. 'Le français, le tahitien, le marquisien, le paumotu et le mangarevien sont les langues de la Polynésie française.'

67. 'Son usage s'impose aux personnes morales de droit public et aux personnes de droit privé dans l'exercice d'une mission de service public ainsi qu'aux usagers dans leurs relations avec les administrations et services publics.'

68. 'Les personnes physiques et morales de droit privé en usent librement dans leurs actes et conventions; ceux-ci n'encourent aucune nullité au motif qu'ils ne sont pas rédigés dans la langue officielle.'

69. 'Le français s'impose donc toujours dans la sphère publique.' *Cons. const.*, *Décision* 2004-490 DC, 12 February 2004, *Loi organique portant statut d'autonomie de la Polynésie française*, *Rec.* 41, JORF, 2 March 2004, p. 4220. See particularly paragraph 68. Online at: http://www.conseil-constitutionnel.fr/conseil-constitutionnel/francais/les-decisions/2004/2004-490-dc/decision-n-2004-490-dc-du-12-fevrier-2004.892.html (last accessed 10 January 2013).

70. CE 29 March 2006, Haut-commissaire de la République en Polynésie française, M. Fritch, n° 282335.

71. *Loi organique* 2004-192.

72. 'Le français est la langue officielle de la Polynésie française. Son usage s'impose aux personnes morales de droit public et aux personnes de droit privé dans l'exercice d'une mission de service public ainsi qu'aux usagers dans leurs relations avec les administrations et services publics.'

73. 'La langue tahitienne est un élément fondamental de l'identité culturelle: ciment de cohésion sociale, moyen de communication quotidien, elle est reconnue et doit être préservée, de même que les autres langues polynésiennes, aux côtés de la langue de la République, afin de garantir la diversité culturelle qui fait la richesse de la Polynésie française.'

74. 'La langue de la République est le français.'

75. On the ideas of nation and people, Gramsci considered that 'in France the meaning of "national" already includes a more politically elaborated notion of "popular" because it is related to the concept of "sovereignty"' (Gramsci, *Cultural Writings*, p. 208); see also Troper, commenting on article 3 of the 1958 Constitution, 'la souveraineté national appartient au people' (M. Troper, *La Théorie du Droit, le Droit, l'État*, Paris: PUF Leviathan, 2001, pp. 299–313).

76. *Cons. const.*, *Décision* 91-290 DC, 9 May 1991, *Loi portant statut de la collectivité territoriale de Corse*, JORF, 14 May 1991, p. 6350. Online at: http:// www.conseil-constitutionnel.fr/conseil-constitutionnel/francais/les-decisions/ acces-par-date/decisions-depuis-1959/1991/91-290-dc/decision-n-91-290-dc-du-09-mai-1991.8758.html (last accessed 10 January 2013).

77. *Cons. const.*, *Décision* 2000-428 DC, 4 May 2000, *Loi organisant une consultation de la population de Mayotte*, JORF, 10 May 2000, p. 6976, in particular

this paragraph: 'Considérant que la Constitution de 1958 a distingué le peuple français des peuples des territoires d'outre-mer, auxquels est reconnu le droit à la libre détermination et à la libre expression de leur volonté.' Online at: http://www.conseil-constitutionnel.fr/conseil-constitutionnel/francais/ les-decisions/acces-par-date/decisions-depuis-1959/2000/2000-428-dc/ decision-n-2000-428-dc-du-04-mai-2000.448.html (last accessed 10 January 2013).

78. *Cons. const.*, *Décision* 99-412 DC, 15 June 1999, *Charte européenne des langues régionales ou minoritaires*, JORF, 18 June 1999, p. 8964. Online at: http:// www.conseil-constitutionnel.fr/conseil-constitutionnel/francais/les-decisions/ 1999/99-412-dc/decision-n-99-412-dc-du-15-juin-1999.11825.html (last accessed 10 January 2013). See also K. Oellers-Frahm, 'Charte européenne des langues régionales ou minoritaires, Decision 99- 412 DC', *American Journal of International Law*, 93 (4), 1999, pp. 938–42, and S. K. Määttä, 'The European Charter for Regional or Minority Languages, French language laws, and national identity', *Language Policy*, 4 (2), 2005, pp. 167–86.

79. 'La France est une République indivisible, laïque, démocratique et sociale. Elle assure l'égalité devant la loi de tous les citoyens sans distinction d'origine, de race ou de religion. Elle respecte toutes les croyances.'

80. 'Le principe d'unicité du peuple français, dont aucune section ne peut s'attribuer l'exercice de la souveraineté nationale, a également valeur constitutionnelle.'

81. 'Considérant que ces principes fondamentaux s'opposent à ce que soient reconnus des droits collectifs à quelque groupe que ce soit, défini par une communauté d'origine, de culture, de langue ou de croyance.'

82. 'La libre communication des pensées et des opinions est un des droits les plus précieux de l'homme: tout citoyen peut donc parler, écrire, imprimer librement, sauf à répondre de l'abus de cette liberté dans les cas déterminés par la loi, doit être conciliée avec le premier alinéa de l'article 2 de la Constitution selon lequel "La langue de la République est le français".'

83. 'Aux principes constitutionnels d'indivisibilité de la République, d'égalité devant la loi et d'unicité du peuple français.'

84. 'Au premier alinéa de l'article 2 de la Constitution en ce qu'elle tend à reconnaître un droit à pratiquer une langue autre que le français non seulement dans la "vie privée" mais également dans la "vie publique".'

85. See R. J. Blackwood, 'Compulsory Corsican language classes in school as a method for reversing the language shift to French?', *Transactions of the Philological Society*, 102 (3), 2004, pp. 307–33.

86. CE 22 February 2007 M. F. et autres Requête n° 299649.

87. 'Aux principes constitutionnels d'indivisibilité de la République, d'égalité devant la loi et d'unicité du peuple français.'

88. *Loi constitutionnelle* 2008-724 23 July 2008 *de modernisation des institutions de la Ve République*, JORF 0171, 24 July 2008, p. 11890.

89. Après l'article 75 de la Constitution, il est inséré un article 75-1 ainsi rédigé: 'Art. 75-1. – Les langues régionales appartiennent au patrimoine de la France.'

90. *Projet de Loi Constitutionnelle de modernisation des institutions de la Ve République*. Online at: http://www.assemblee-nationale.fr/13/projets/pl0820.asp (last accessed 10 January 2013).

91. http://www.assemblee-nationale.fr/13/amendements/0820/082000605.asp (last accessed 10 January 2013).

92. 'Les langues régionales appartiennent à son patrimoine.'

93. Some MPs wanted to amend article 2, which specifically refers to the language of the Republic (French). That reasoning was clearly an attempt to break its foundation, discussed throughout this chapter (of unity/indivisibility). The government did not allow anything but the addition of a sentence in article 1, later moved to the section on local authorities.

94. http://www.assemblee-nationale.fr/13/ta/ta0150.asp (last accessed 10 January 2013).

95. http://www.senat.fr/leg/pjl07-365.html (last accessed 10 January 2013).

96. http://www.senat.fr/leg/tas07-116.html (last accessed 10 January 2013).

97. http://www.assemblee-nationale.fr/13/projets/pl0993.asp (last accessed 10 January 2013).

98. 'Son organisation [the Republican one] est décentralisée. Les langues régionales appartiennent à son patrimoine.'

99. http://www.assemblee-nationale.fr/13/ta/ta0172.asp (last accessed 10 January 2013).

100. http://www.senat.fr/leg/pjl07-459.html (last accessed 10 January 2013).

101. http://www.senat.fr/leg/tas07-137.html (last accessed 10 January 2013).

102. http://www.assemblee-nationale.fr/13/amendements/0993/099300038.asp (last accessed 10 January 2013).

103. The transcript of the debate between MP Myard and the minister of justice is clear on this point:
    M. *Jacques Myard* – 'Vous me permettrez de m'interroger, même si cela doit rompre ce beau consensus… Nul ne peut contester que les langues régionales appartiennent à notre patrimoine national. Ces langues sont là, elles sont parlées par certains de nos concitoyens, et elles nous apportent une richesse linguistique supplémentaire, sans que cela fragilise pour autant la primauté de la langue française, qui est reconnue par l'article 2 de la Constitution.
    'Toutefois, il ne faudrait oublier que ce texte n'est pas le seul en jeu: il y a aussi la charte des langues dites minoritaires, issue des travaux menés dans l'entre-deux-guerres par la SDN en faveur des nations enclavées dans d'autres pays. À l'origine, il n'était pas du tout question d'une protection des langues régionales…
    'Je ne voterai pas cette disposition, car on ne mesure pas bien les dangers de l'utilisation politique des langues. La Charte nous y expose, sans que nous mesurions la dynamique qui nous attend. Le Gouvernement peut-il d'ailleurs nous indiquer s'il envisage de ratifier ce texte? Ce serait mettre la main dans un engrenage que nous ne maîtrisons pas.'
    Mme *Rachida Dati, garde des sceaux* – 'Il n'en est pas question.'

104. 'I. – Dans le titre XIV de la Constitution, il est rétabli un article 87 ainsi rédigé: Art. 87. – "La République participe au développement de la solidarité et de la coopération entre les États et les peuples ayant le français en partage"; II. – L'intitulé du titre XIV de la Constitution est ainsi rédigé: "De la francophonie et des accords d'association"'.

105. *Rapport d'information de la Commission des Lois Constitutionnelles, de la Législation et de l'administration générale de la République sur les implications constitutionnelles d'une ratification par la France de la Charte européenne des langues régionales ou*

minoritaires, M. Jean-Jacques Urvoas, 12 December 2012. Online at: http://www.assemblee-nationale.fr/14/rap-info/i0489.asp (last accessed 10 January 2013).

106. R. Sacco, *Anthropologie Juridique, Apport à une Macro-Histoire du Droit*, Paris: Dalloz, L'esprit du Droit, 2008), pp. 41–53.

Conclusion

1. 'Nos jeunes maîtres étaient beaux comme des hussards noirs. Sveltes; sévères; sanglés. Sérieux, et un peu tremblants de leur précoce, de leur soudaine omnipotence' (C. Péguy, in 'L'Argent' in *Œuvres Complètes de Charles Péguy*, Vol. III, Paris: NRF, 1913, p. 403).

2. This idea of a block was introduced in a commentary written by two scholars about the decision of 20 November 1969 concerning the internal regulation of the National Assembly, and later developed by Professor Favoreu. See C. Emeri and J. L. Sevrin, *Revue du droit public*, 1971, Jur., p. 172.

3. *Loi constitutionnelle de modernisation des institutions de la Ve République, n° 2008-724*, 23 July 2008, JORF 171, 24 July 2008.

4. M. Kelly, *A Short History of Western Legal Theory*, 1st edn, Oxford: Oxford University Press, 1992, p. 123.

5. U. Beck, 'The silence of words and political dynamics in the world risk society', *Logos*, Fall 2002. Online at: http://logosonline.home.igc.org/beck.htm (last accessed 10 January 2013).

6. U. Beck, 'The cosmopolitan perspective: sociology of the second age of modernity', *British Journal of Sociology*, 5 (1), 2000, pp. 79–105, especially p. 90.

7. U. Beck, 'The terrorist threat', *Theory, Culture and Society*, 19 (4), 2002, pp. 39–55, at p. 53.

8. Beck, 'Cosmopolitan perspective', p. 84. 'Let us not forget that law is subject to a possible deconstruction while justice is un-deconstructed and un-deconstructible. The change in Modernity may modify "the law"; it will not modify justice. Justice cannot be deconstructed, because justice is the deconstruction, the impossible' (J. Derrida, *Force de Loi*, Paris: Galilée, 1994, p. 35). In the same way, 'Un catholique vraiment formé dans le catholicisme est inanalysable' (J. Aubert, 'Sur James Joyce', *Mélanges, Analytica*, 4, 1992, pp. 3–18.

9. This is signalled by the new relationship between the individual and society, where the idea of belonging to a community is part of a bottom-up process, not the other way around (U. Beck, *Democracy Without Enemy*, Cambridge: Polity Press, 1998, p. 35).

10. Beck, *World Risk Society*, p. 10.

11. http://www.gouvernement.fr/gouvernement/comite-de-reflexion-et-de-proposition-sur-la-modernisation-et-reequilibrage-des-institu (last accessed 15 December 2011).

12. http://www.commission-rdvp.gouv.fr/Rapport_Commission_RDVP.pdf.

13. http://www.senat.fr/rap/l07-387/l07-3871.html (last accessed 15 December 2011): 'le meilleur gage de la pérennité du lien qui unit les Français à la Ve République.'

References

Books

Constitutional law

Ardant, P. and Mathieu, B., *Institutions politiques et droit constitutionnel*, 21st edn, Paris: LGDJ, 2009.

Chantebout, B., *Droit constitutionnel*, 26th edn, Paris: LGDJ, 2009.

Duverger, M., *Institutions politiques et droit constitutionnel*, Paris: PUF Thémis, 1990.

Duverger, M., *Le système politique français*, Paris: PUF Thémis, 1996.

Favoreu, L., Ghevontian, R., Scoffoni, G. and Pfersmann, O., (ed.), *Droit constitutionnel*, 12th edn, Paris: Dalloz Précis Droit Public, 2009.

Gicquel, J. E. and Gicquel J., *Droit constitutionnel et institutions politiques*, 23rd edn, Paris: Montchretien Domat Droit Public, 2009.

Hamon, F. and Troper, M., *Droit constitutionnel*, 31st edn, Paris: LGDJ, 2009.

Pactet, P. and Mélin-Soucramanien, F., *Droit constitutionnel*, 28th edn, Paris: Dalloz Sirey Université, 2009.

Rousseau, D. and Viala, A., *Droit constitutionnel*, Paris: Montchretien, 2004.

Vlad Constantinesco, V. and Pierré-Caps, S., *Droit constitutionnel*, 4th edn, Paris: PUF Thémis, 2009.

Administrative law

Braibant, G. and Stirn, B., *Le droit administratif français*, 7th edn, Paris: Presses de Sciences-Po et Dalloz Amphi, 2005.

Morand-Deviller, J., *Cours de Droit administratif*, 9th edn, Paris: Montchrestien, 2005.

Seiller, B., *Droit administratif*, Vol. 1 (*Les sources et le juge*) and Vol. 2 (*L'Action administrative*), Paris: Flammarion, 2005.

Miscellaneous

Agamben, G., *State of Exception*, Chicago: University of Chicago Press, 2005.

Aristotle, *The Politics*, Harmondsworth: Penguin Classics, 1981.

Balibar, E., *We, The People of Europe: Reflections on Transnational Citizenship*, Princeton, NJ: Princeton University Press, 2004.

Beck, U., *Risk Society: Towards a New Modernity*, London: Sage, 1992.

Beck, U., *Democracy Without Enemy*, Cambridge: Polity Press, 1998.

Beck, U. and Willms, J., *Conversation with Ulrich Beck*, Oxford: Polity, 2004.

Bell, J. and Boyron, S., *Principles of French Law*, Oxford: Oxford University Press, 1998.

Bobbio, N., *Liberalism and Democracy*, London: Verso Radical Thinkers, 2005.

Bourg, D., *Les Scénarios de l'Ecologie*, Paris: Hachette, 1996.

Boyron, S., *The Constitution of France: A Contextual Analysis*, Oxford: Hart, 2012.

Brownlie, I., *Principles of Public International Law*, 6th edn, Oxford: Oxford University Press, 2003.

Brunet, P., 'La représentation', in M. Troper and D. Chagnollaud (eds), *Traité International de Droit Constitutionnel*, Paris: Dalloz, 2012, pp. 608–41.

Carre de Malberg, R., *Contribution à la théorie générale de l'Etat*, 1st edn, 1920, Paris: Dalloz, 2003.

Casey, J., *Constitutional Law in Ireland*, 3rd edn, Dublin: Round Hall Sweet & Maxwell, 2000.

Cassese, A., *I Diritti Umani Oggi*, Rom: Laterza, 2007.

Chapsal, J., *La vie politique sous la Ve République: 2 1974–1987*, 3rd edn, Paris: PUF Thémis, 1987.

Chevallier, J.-J., *Histoire des Institutions et des Regimes Politiques de la France de 1789 à Nos Jours*, 7th edn, Paris: Dalloz, 1985.

Cicero, *The Republic, and The Laws*, Oxford: Oxford University Press, 1998.

Cornes, R., 'Devolution and England: what is on offer?', in N. Bamforth and P. Leyland (eds), *Public Law in a Multi-layered Constitution*, Oxford: Hart, 2003, pp. 107–21.

Craig, P. and de Burca, G., *EU Law, Text, Cases and Materials*, Oxford: Oxford University Press, 2003.

de Saussure, F., *Cours de Linguistique Générale*, Paris: Payot, 1972.

Debbasch, C., *Constitution Ve Republique*, Paris: Dalloz, 2005.

Debord, G., *La Société du Spectacle*, Paris: Folio Gallimard, 1992.

Derrida, J., *Force de Loi*, Paris: Galilée, 1994.

Derrida, J., *Le Monolinguism de l'Autre, ou la Prothése d'Origine*, Paris: Gallilée, 1996.

Dowson, A. and Lucardie, P., *The Politics of Nature*, London: Routledge, 1993.

Dubet, F., 'La laïcité dans les mutations de l'école', in M. Wieviorka (ed.), *Une société fragmentée? Le multiculturalisme en débat*, Paris: La Découverte, 1996.

Duhamel, O. and Meny, Y., *Dictionnaire constitutionnel*, Paris: PUF, 1992.

Duverger, M., *Échec au Roi*, Paris: Albin Michel, 1978.

Eco, U., *Quase a Mesma Coisa*, Rio de Janeiro: Record, 2007.

Elgie, R., *Political Institutions in Contemporary France*, Oxford: Oxford University Press, 2003.

Elgie, R., *Semi-presidentialism in Europe*, New York: Oxford University Press, 1999.

Favoreu, L. and Philip, L., *Index thématique des Grandes décisions du Conseil constitutionnel*, Paris: Dalloz, 1999.

Feldstein, R., Fink, B. and Jaanus, M., *Reading Seminars I and II: Lacan's Return to Freud*, New York: SUNY Press, 1996.

Foucault, M., *Surveiller et Punir*, Paris: Tel Gallimard, 1975.

Freud, S., *Case Histories: 1 Dora and Little Hans*, Vol. 8, Harmondsworth: Pelican Freud Library, 1977.

Freud, S., 'Moses and monotheism: three essays', *SE*, Vol. 23, London: Hogarth, 1939.

Freud, S., *Totem and Taboo*, London: Ark, 1983.

Gramsci, A., *Selections from Cultural Writings*, Cambridge, MA: Harvard University Press, 1985.

Gueldry, M., *France and European Integration: Towards a Transnational Polity?* New York: Greenwood Press, 2001.

Hans, J., *European Environmental Law*, 1st edn, Amsterdam: Europa Law, 2000.

Heidegger, M., *The Basic Problems of Phenomenology*, Bloomington, IN: Indiana University Press, 1982.

Ives, P., *Language and Hegemony in Gramsci*, London: Pluto Press, 2004.

Jonas, H., *Le Principe Responsabilité. Une éthique pour la civilisation technologique*, Paris: Cerf, 1990.

Jones, H. S., *The French State in Question: Public Law and Political Argument in the Third Republic*, Cambridge: Cambridge University Press, 1993.

Joset, F. and Muzet, D., *Le Téléprésident: Essai sur un pouvoir médiatique*, Paris: L'Aude, 2008.

Kelly, M., *A Short History of Western Legal Theory*, 1st edn, Oxford: Oxford University Press, 1992.

Kelsen, H., *Theorie Général des Normes*, Paris: PUF, 1996.

Lacan, J., *Ecrit 1*, Paris: Seuil, 1999.

Lacan, J., *Le Seminaire Livre II: Le Moi dans le Theorie de Freud et dans la Technique de la Psychanalyse*, Paris: Seuil, 1978.

Laclau, E., *Emancipation(s)*, London, Verso, 2007.

Levi-Strauss, C., *Totemism*, London Merlin 1964.

Leyland, P., *The Constitution of the United Kingdom: A Contextual Analysis*, Oxford: Hart, 2007.

Mitterand, F., *Le Coup d'État Permanent*, Paris: Plon, 1964.

Monnet, J., *Mémoires*, Paris: Fayard, 1976.

Montesquieu, Baron de, *The Spirit of the Laws*, Cambridge: Cambridge University Press, 1989.

Péguy, C., 'L'Argent', in *Œuvres Complètes de Charles Péguy*, Vol. III, Paris: NRF, 1913.

Péguy, C., *De Jean Coste*, Arles: Actes Sud, 1993.

Plato, *The Republic*, New York: Plain Label Books, 1946.

Renucci, J. F., *Droit Européens des Droits de l'Homme*, 3rd edn, Paris: LGDJ, 2002.

Rousseau, J.-J., *Du Contrat Social*, Paris: Larousse, 1973.

Sacco, R., *Anthropologie Juridique, Apport à une Macro-Histoire du Droit*, Paris: Dalloz, L'esprit du Droit, 2008.

Safran, W., 'The context of French politics', in M. D. Hancock, R. Zariski, D. P. Conradt (eds), *Politics in Western Europe*, Chatham, NJ: Chatham House, 1993, pp. 93–5.

Sartori, G., *Comparative Constitutional Engineering: An Inquiry into Structures, Incentives and Outcomes*, 2nd edn, New York: New York University Press, 1997.

Sellers, M. N. S., *Republican Legal Theory: The History, Constitution and Purposes of Law in a Free State*, London: Palgrave, 2003.

Sibert, J. L., *Le Plus Petit Atlas du Monde*, Lyon: IAC, 1940.

Sueur, J.-J., *Histoire du Droit Public Francais, Xve–XVIIIe siecle, Tome 1 La Constitution Monarchique*, 4th edn, Paris: PUF Thémis, 1989.

Tchen, V., *Droit des Etrangers*, Paris: Ellipses, 2006.

Troper, M., *La Théorie du Droit, le Droit, l'État*, Paris: PUF Leviathan, 2001.

Weyembergh, M., *Charles Maurras et la Révolution française*, Paris: VRIN, 1992.

Wieviorka, M., (ed), *Une société fragmentée? Le multiculturalisme en débat*, Paris: La Découverte, 1996.

Wilsford, D., *Political Leaders of Contemporary Western Europe: A Biographical Dictionary*, Westport, CT: Greenwood Press, 1995.

Wittgenstein, L., *Tractatus Logico Philosophicus*, London: Routledge, 2001.

Žižek, S., *Violence*, London: Profile Books, 2008.

Articles

Academic journals

See generally: *Actualité Juridique du Droit Administrative, Revue Française de Droit Public, Revue du Droit Public, Revue Française d'Administration Publique*.

Barbé, V., 'Le droit de l'environnement en droit constitutionnel comparé: contribution à l'étude des effets de la constitutionnalisation', http://www.droitconstitutionnel. org/congresParis/comC8/BarbeTXT.pdf, Association française de droit constitutionnel VIIe Congrès français de droit constitutionnel, 50e anniversaire de la Constitution de 1958, 25, 26 and 27 September 2008, p. 1.

Beck, U., 'The cosmopolitan perspective: sociology of the second age of modernity', *British Journal of Sociology*, 51 (1), 2000, pp. 79–105.

Beck, U., 'The silence of words and political dynamics in the world risk society', *Logos*, 1 (4), 2002, http://logosonline.home.igc.org/beck.htm (last accessed 10 February 2009).

Beck, U., 'The terrorist threat', *Theory, Culture and Society*, 19 (4), 2002, pp. 39–55.

Blackwood, R. J., 'Compulsory Corsican language classes in school as a method for reversing the language shift to French?', *Transactions of the Philological Society*, 102 (3), 2004, pp. 307–33.

Borrel, C., 'Enquêtes annuelles de recensement 2004 et 2005. Près de 5 millions d'immigrés à la mi-2004', Insee Première n° 1098. Paris: INSEE, Cellule Statistiques et études sur l'immigration, 2006. Online at: http://www.insee.fr/fr/ffc/ipweb/ip1098/ip1098.pdf (last accessed 10 January 2013).

Brunet, P., 'Humpty Dumpty à Babel? Les juges et le vocabulaire juridique Européen', 17 *Chronique de Droit Européen & Comparé* (2008) Centre d'études juridiques européennes et comparées (CEJEC – Université Paris Ouest – Nanterre La Défense) 'Approche Critique Du Vocabulaire Juridique Européen: Le Pouvoir Des Juges', 2.

de Saint Martin, M., 'Les principales tendances de la sociologie de l'éducation en France', *Revue Internationale de l'Education*, 18 (1), 1972, pp. 100–7.

Debbasch, R., 'La Reconnaissance constitutionnelle de la langue francaise', *RFDC*, 11, 1992, p. 457.

Déclaration sur l'unicité et l'universalité salvifique de Jésus-Christ et de l'Église – *Dominus Iesus* (*Declaratio de Iesu Christi atque Ecclesiae unicitate et universalitate salvifica*), 6 August 2000. Online at: http://www.vatican.va/roman_curia/congregations/cfaith/documents/rc_con_cfaith_doc_20000806_dominus-iesus_fr.html (last accessed 10 January 2013).

Deleuze, G., 'Le Devenir révolutionnaire et les créations politiques', *Futur Anterieur*, May, 1990, p. 1.

Emeri, C. and Sevrin, J. L., *Revue du droit public*, Jur., 1971, p. 172.

Freud, S., 'Moses and monotheism: three essays', *SE*, 23, 1939, pp. 1–138.

Groud, H. and Pugeault, S., 'Le droit à l'environnement, nouvelle liberté fondamentale', *AJDA* Jurisprudence, 2005, p. 1357.

Howell, R. F., 'The philosopher Alain and French classical radicalism', *Western Political Quarterly*, 18 (3), 1965, pp. 594–614.

Jegouzo, Y., 'La Charte de l'environnement', *AJDA* Chroniques, 2005.

Lafargue, R., 'La coutume judiciaire en Nouvelle-Calédonie. Aux sources d'un droit commun coutumier', 2002, p. 1. Online at: http://www.gip-recherche-justice.fr/recherches/syntheses/78-lafargue.pdf.

Määttä, S., 'The European Charter for Regional or Minority Languages, French language laws, and national identity', *Language Policy*, 4 (2), 2005, pp. 167–86.

Marrani, D., 'How to end an attempt to institute a carbon tax: the Conseil constitutionnel declares that article 7 of the 2010 Budget instituting a carbon tax does not conform to the Constitution of the French Republic', *Env. Law Rev.*, 13, 2011, pp. 50–5.

Marrani, D., 'Principle of indivisibility of the French Republic and the People's Right to Self-determination: The "New Caledonia Test"', *JOALS*, 2, 2006, pp. 16–29.

Marrani, D., 'The importance of the symbolic role of the head of state', *European Journal of Law Reform*, 13 (1), 2011, pp. 40–58.

Nic Craith, M., 'Politicised linguistic consciousness: the case of Ulster-Scots', *Nations and Nationalism*, 7 (1), 2001, pp. 21–37.

Oakes, L., 'Multilingualism in Europe: an effective French identity strategy?', *Journal of Multilingual and Multicultural Development*, 23 (5), 2002, pp. 371–87.

Oellers-Frahm, K., 'Charte européenne des langues regionales ou minoritaires, Decision No 99- 412 DC', *American Journal of International Law*, 93 (4), 1999, pp. 938–42.

Olin, Mme N., Conseil des ministres, communication 1 March 2006. Online at: http://www.ecologie.gouv.fr/article.php3?id_article=5253 (last accessed 20 October 2006).

Rapport 2463 fait au nom de la Commission des Lois Constitutionnelles, de la Legislation et de l'Adminsitration Générale de la République sur le Projet de Loi Constitutionnelle (N° 2462), relatif à la durée du mandat du Président de la République.

Rapport 426, Projet de loi constitutionnelle relatif à la durée du mandat du Président de la République J. Larché, (1999–2000), Commission des lois.

Rapport de M. Christian Bonnet au nom de la commission des lois, 186 (2000–2001).

Rapport fait au nom de la Commission des lois constitutionnelles, de la législation et de l'administration générale de la République sur le projet de loi constitutionnelle (N° 992) relatif à la Charte de l'environnement. Online at: http://www.assemblee-nationale.fr/12/rapports/r1595.asp (last accessed 10 January 2013).

'Statistiques des flux d'immigration en France – Année 2005', Paris: INED, 2005, p. 2. Online at: http://www.ined.fr/fichier/t_telechargement/34419/telechargement_fichier_fr_immigration05.pdf (last accessed 10 January 2013).

Verpeaux, M., 'L'enfer constitutionnel est pavé de bonnes intentions', *AJDA* Chroniques, 2004, p. 1209.

Wilmer, F., 'Minority rights and Charles Tilly's "statelessness"', *ConWEB*, 3, 2006, pp. 1–30, at p. 11. Online at: http://www.qub.ac.uk/schools/SchoolofPolitics

InternationalStudiesandPhilosophy/FileStore/ConWEBFiles/Filetoupload, 38374,en.pdf (last accessed 10 January 2013).

Newspapers

Le Journal du Dimanche (Paris):
—— 8 July 2007, V. Le Guay and J. Esperandieu, http://www.lejdd.fr/cmc/politique/200727/sarkozy-je-l-avais-reve-je-le-mets-en-oeuvre_36389.html (last accessed 10 January 2013).

Libération (Paris):
—— 12 May 2007, C. Coroller, 'Paris: expulsions quotidiennes dans le Xxe, Série de reconduites à la frontière de sans-papiers aux enfants scolarisés', http://www.liberation.fr/actualite/societe/253342.FR.php (last accessed 28 October 2008).
—— 25 May 2007, C. Coroller, 'Paris: sans-papiers arrêtés, enfants caches'.
—— 'Juppé: "Si je pouvais crever, vous seriez contents"', http://www.liberation.fr/actualite/politiques/legislative/261896.FR.php (last accessed 10 January 2013).
—— http://www.liberation.fr/actualite/societe/256008.FR.php (last accessed 28 October 2008).

Le Monde (Paris):
—— 26 September 1981, 'Première conférence de presse a l'Elysée'.
—— 30 May 2005, 'La France devient le premier pays européen à rejeter la Constitution'.
—— 12 January 2007, H. Kempf, 'La Cour de cassation statuera le 7 février sur le sort judiciaire de José Bové'.
—— 25 August 2007, 'L'ancien premier ministre français Raymond Barre est mort', http://www.lemonde.fr/web/article/0,1-0@2-3224,36-947468,0.html (last accessed 26 August 2007).
—— 13 September 2007, 'Des maires refusent d'obéir aux préfets sur les sans-papiers'.http://www.lemonde.fr/societe/article/2007/07/12/m-sarkozy-inscrit-ses-projets-dans-la-tradition-gaulliste_934993_3224.html (last accessed 10 January 2013).

BBC (London):
—— http://news.bbc.co.uk/2/hi/europe/6738037.stm (last accessed 10 January 2013).
—— http://news.bbc.co.uk/1/hi/world/europe/1376379.stm, and recently the rejection of the Lisbon treaty, http://news.bbc.co.uk/1/hi/world/europe/7453560.stm (last accessed 15 June 2009).

Daily Telegraph (London):
—— 31 January 2009, T. Finan and J. Copping, 'Asbestos-laden warship to set sail for Britain: a French warship deemed too toxic to be broken up in India is to set sail for Britain to be dismantled', http://www.telegraph.co.uk/news/worldnews/europe/france/4409964/Asbestos-laden-warship-to-set-sail-for-Britain.html (last accessed 10 January 2013).

The Guardian (London):
—— 4 October 2005, U. Beck and A. Giddens, 'Nationalism has now become the enemy of Europe's nations'.

Legislation

Statutes

Loi 56-619, 23 June 1956, *autorisant le gouvernement a mettre en œuvre les reformes et a prendre les mesures propres a assurer l'évolution des territoires relevant du ministère de la France d'Outre Mer*, JORF, 23 June 1956, p. 5782.

Loi 58-520, 3 June 1958, *relative aux pleins pouvoirs accordés au gouvernement du Général de Gaulle (durée six mois)*, JORF, 4 June 1958, p. 5327.

Loi constitutionnelle 3 June 1958, *portant derogation transitoire aux dispositions de l'art. 90 de la Constitution et prévoyant un referendum*, JORF, 4 June 1958, p. 5326.

Loi 62-1292, 6 November 1962, *relative à l'élection du Président de la République au suffrage universel*, JORF, 7 November 1962.

Loi 63-1246, 21 December 1963, *organisation des pouvoirs publics en Nouvelle-Calédonie*, JORF, 22 December 1963, p.11451.

Loi 69-4, 3 January 3 1969, *modifiant la reglementation minière en nouvelle-Calédonie*, JORF, 5 January 1969, p. 196.

Loi 69-5, 3 January 1969, *relative à la creation et à l'organisation des communes dans le territoire de la Nouvelle-Calédonie et dependances*, JORF, 5 January 1969, p. 197.

Loi 69-6, 3 January 1969, *portant régime fiscal de certains investissements dans le territoire de la Nouvelle-Calédonie*, JORF, 5 January 1969, p. 199.

Loi 76-629, 10 July 1976, *relative à la protection de la nature*, JORF, 13 July 1976, p. 4203.

Loi 76-1222, 28 December 1976, *relative à l'organisation de la Nouvelle-Calédonie et dépendances*, JORF, 22 December 1976, p. 7530.

Loi 84-821, 6 September 1984, *portant statut du territoire de Nouvelle-Calédonie et dépendances*, JORF, 7 September 1984, p. 2840.

Loi 85-30, 9 January 1985, *relative au développement et à la Protection de la Montagne*, JORF, 10 January 1985, p. 320.

Loi 85-892, 23 August 1985, *sur l'évolution de la Nouvelle-Calédonie*, JORF, 24 August 1985, p. 9775.

Loi 86-2, 3 January 1986, *relative à l'aménagement, la protection et la mise en valeur du littoral*, JORF, 4 January 1986, p. 200.

Loi 86-844, 17 July 1986, *relative à la Nouvelle-Calédonie*, JORF, 19 July 1986, p. 8930.

Loi 86-1307, 29 December 1986, art. 7 I, JORF, 30 December 1986.

Loi 88-82, 22 January 1988, *portant statut du territoire de la Nouvelle-Calédonie*, JORF, 26 January 1988, p. 1243.

Loi 88-808, 12 July 1988, *relative à l'administration de la Nouvelle-Calédonie*, JORF, 14 July 1998, p. 9142.

Loi 88-1028, 9 November 1988, *portant dispositions statutaires et préparatoires à l'autodétermination de la Nouvelle-Calédonie en 1998*, JORF, 10 November 1988, pp. 14096–9.

Loi 90-1247, 29 December 1990, *portant suppression de la tutelle administrative et financière sur les communes de Nouvelle-Calédonie et dispositions diverses relatives à ce territoire*, JORF, 3 January 1991, p. 98.

Loi constitutionnelle 92-554, 25 June 1992, *ajoutant à la Constitution un titre: 'Des Communautés européennes et de l'Union européenne'*, JORF, 147, 26 June 1992, p. 8406.

Loi 92-654, 13 July 1992, *relative au contrôle de l'utilisation et de la dissémination des organismes génétiquement modifiés et modifiant la loi 76-663 du 19 juillet 1976 relative aux installations classées pour la protection de l'environnement*, JORF, 16 July 1992, p. 9461.

Loi 94-665, 4 August 1994, *relative à l'emploi de la langue française*, JORF, 5 August 1994, p. 11392.

Loi 95-101, 2 February 1995, *relative au renforcement de la protection de l'environnement*, JORF, 3 February 1995.

Loi organique 96-312, 12 April 1996, *portant statut d'autonomie de la Polynésie française*, JORF, 13 April 1996, p. 5705.

Nouméa Agreement, 5 May 1998, JORF, 27 May 1998, pp. 8039–44.

Loi 98-349, 11 May 1998, *relative à l'entrée et au séjour des étrangers en France et au droit d'asile*, JORF, 12 May 1998, p. 7087.

Loi 99-209, 19 March 1999, *organique relative à la Nouvelle-Calédonie*, JORF, 21 March 1999, pp. 4197–226 rect. 16 April 1999, p. 5610.

Loi 99-210, 19 March 1999, *relative à la Nouvelle-Calédonie*, JORF, 21 March 1999, pp. 4226–3.

Loi 2000-1207, 13 December 2000, *d'orientation pour l'outre-mer*, JORF, 14 December 2000, p. 19760.

Loi constitutionnelle 2000-964, 2 October 2000, *relative à la durée du mandat du Président de la République*, JORF, 229, 3 October 2000, p. 15582.

Loi organique 2001-419, 15 May 2001, *modifiant la date d'expiration des pouvoirs de l'Assemblée nationale*, JORF, 113, 16 May 2001, p. 7776.

Loi constitutionnelle 2003-276, 28 March 2003, *relative à l'organisation décentralisée de la République*, JORF, 75, 29 March 2003, p. 5568.

Loi 2003-1119, 26 November 2003, *relative à la maîtrise de l'immigration, au séjour des étrangers en France et à la nationalité*, JORF, 274, 27 November 2003, p. 20136.

Loi 2002-1576, 30 December 2002, art. 57 III *finances rectificative pour 2002*, JORF, 31 December 2002.

Loi 2003-1312, 30 December 2003, art. 97 1° *finances rectificative pour 2003*, JORF, 31 December 2003.

Loi organique 2004-192, 27 February 2004, *portant statut d'autonomie de la Polynésie française*, JORF, 2 March 2004, p. 4183.

Loi 2004-193, 27 February 2004, *complétant le statut d'autonomie de la Polynésie française*, JORF, 2 March 2004, p. 4213.

Loi 2005-157, 23 February 2005, *relative au développement des territoires ruraux*, JORF, 46 24 February 2005, p. 3073, texte n° 1.

Loi constitutionnelle 2005-205, 1 March 2005, *relative à la Charte de l'environnement (1)*, JORF, 2 March 2005, p. 3697.

Loi 2005-1579, 19 December 2005, art. 89, JORF, 20 December 2005.

Loi 2006-911, 24 July 2006, *relative à l'immigration et à l'intégration*, JORF, 170, 25 July 2006, p. 11047.

Loi 2007-1631, 20 November 2007, *relative à la maîtrise de l'immigration, à l'intégration et à l'asile*, JORF, 270, 21 November 2007, p. 18993.

Loi constitutionnelle 2008-103, 4 February 2008, modifiant le titre XV de la Constitution, JORF, 0030, 5 February 2008, p. 2202, text. n° 1.

Loi 2008-125, 13 February 2008, *autorisant la ratification du traité de Lisbonne modifiant le traité sur l'Union européenne, le traité instituant la Communauté européenne et certains actes connexes*, JORF, 0038, 14 February 2008, p. 2712, text. n° 1.

Loi 2008-496, 27 May 2008, *portant diverses dispositions d'adaptation au droit commu-nautaire dans le domaine de la lutte contre les discriminations*, JORF, 0123, 28 May 2008, p. 8801.

Loi constitutionnelle 2008-724, 23 July 2008, *de modernisation des institutions de la Ve République*, JORF, 24 July 2008, p. 11890.

Regulations

Décret qui abolit la royauté en France, 21–22 septembre 1792, Journal officiel de la Convention Nationale – La Convention Nationale (1792–1793), Procès-verbaux officiels des séances depuis le 21 septembre 1792, Constitution de la grande assemblée révolution-naire, jusqu'au 21 janvier 1793, exécution du roi Louis XVI, seule édition authentique et inaltérée contenant les portraits des principaux conventionnels et des autres personnages connus de cette sublime époque, auteur non mentionné, Librairie B. Simon & Cie, Paris, sans date, pp. 10–11. http://www.fordham.edu/halsall/french/royaute.htm (last accessed 10 January 2013).

Décret 2 *thermidor An II* 20 July 1794 *sur la langue française.*

Décret 57-811, 22 July 1957, *organisation des pouvoirs publics en Nouvelle-Calédonie*, JORF, 23 July 1957, p.7252.

Décret (non délibéré en Conseil des Ministres) 64-46, 14 January 1964, *relatif aux forces aeriennes stratégiques*, JORF, 19 January 1964, p. 722, last modified by regulation (en Conseil des Ministres) 96-520, 12 June 1996, *portant détermination des responsa-bilités concernant les forces nucléaires*, JORF, 15 June 1996, p. 8921

Ordonnance 82-877, 15 October 1982, *instituant des assesseurs coutumiers dans le territoire de la Nouvelle-Calédonie et Dépendances au tribunal civil de première instance et à la cour d'appel*, JORF, 17 October 1982, p. 3106.

Décret 89-403, 2 June 1989, *instituant un Conseil supérieur de la langue française et une délégation générale à la langue française*, JORF, 22 June 1989, p. 7729.

Décret 98-733, 20 August 1998, *portant organisation de la consultation des populations de Nouvelle-Calédonie prévue par l'article 76 de la Constitution*, JORF, 22 August 1998, pp. 12844–7.

Décret 99-842, 27 September 1999, *relatif à la promulgation des lois du pays en Nouvelle-Calédonie*, JORF, 30 September 1999, p. 14492

Décret 2001-950, 16 October 2001, *modifiant le Décret n° 89-403 du 2 juin 1989 instituant un Conseil supérieur de la langue française et une délégation générale à la langue française*, JORF, 19 October 2001, p. 16497.

Décret 2004-822, 18 August 2004, *modifié relatif à l'organisation et aux missions de l'administration centrale du ministère de la culture et de la communication*, JORF, 193, 20 August 2004, p. 14902.

Décret 2006-234, 27 February 2006, JORF, 28 February 2006.

Décret 2006-993, 1 August 2006, *relatif aux lacs de montagne pris pour l'application de l'article L. 145-1 du code de l'urbanisme*, JORF, 180, 5 August 2006, p. 11719, text. n° 4.

Arrêté, 10 March 2006, *portant désignation du site Natura 2000 Marigny, Superbe, vallée de l'Aube (zone de protection spéciale)*, JORF, 60, 11 March 2006, p. 3726, text. 48.

Décret 2008-328, 9 April 2008, *portant création d'un comité de réflexion sur le Préambule de la Constitution.*

Décret 2008-1115, 30 October 2008, *relatif à la préparation de l'intégration en France des étrangers souhaitant s'y installer durablement*, JORF, n° 0256, 1 November 2008, p. 16689.

Circulaire 2004-110 of 8 July 2004, BOEN 28, 15 July 2004, p. 1473 (*Généralisation d'une éducation à l'environnement pour un développement durable (EEDD) – rentrée 2004*). It has to be noted that this document replaces a previous one, *Circulaire* 77-300 of 29 August 1977, BOEN 31, 9 September 1977, p. 2507 (*Instruction générale sur l'éducation des élèves en matière d'environnement*).

Cases

Conseil constitutionnel

Décision 71-44 DC, 16 July 1971, *Loi complétant les dispositions des articles 5 et 7 de la loi du er juillet 1901 relative au contrat d'association*, JORF, 18 July 1971, p. 7114.

Décision 74-54 DC, 15 January 1975, *Loi relative à l'interruption volontaire de la grossesse*, Recueil, 19; RJC, I-30, JORF, 16 January 1975, p. 671.

Décision 79-104 DC, 23 May 1979, RJC, I-69, Loi modifiant les modes d'élection de l'Assemblée territoriale et du Conseil de gouvernement du territoire de la Nouvelle-Calédonie et dépendances et définissant les règles générales de l'aide technique et financière contractuelle de l'État.

Décision 79-109 DC, 9 January 1980, JORF, 11 January 1980, p. 84.

Décision 82-138 DC, 25 February 1982, *Loi portant statut particulier de la région Corse*, JORF, 27 February 1982, p. 697.

Décision 82-137 DC, 25 February 1982, *Loi relative aux droits et libertés des communes, des départements et des régions*, JORF, 3 March 1982, 759, RJC, I-177.

Décision 87-226 DC, 2 June 1987, *Loi organisant la consultation des populations intéressées de la Nouvelle-Calédonie et dépendances prévue par l'alinéa premier de l'article 1er de la loi n° 86-844 du 17 juillet 1986 relative à la Nouvelle-Calédonie*, JORF, 4 June 1987, p. 6058.

Décision 89-269 DC, 22 January 1990, JORF, 24 January 1990, p. 972.

Décision 91-290 DC, 9 May 1991, *Loi portant statut de la collectivité territoriale de Corse*, JORF, 14 May 1991, p. 6350.

Décision 92-308 DC, 9 April 1992 (I), *Traité sur l'Union européenne (I)*, Recueil, p. 55; RJC, I-496, JORF, 11 April 1992, p. 5354.

Décision 92-312 DC, 2 September 1992, *Traité sur l'Union européenne (II)*, Recueil, 76; RJC, I-505, JORF, 3 September 1992, p. 12095.

Décision 92-313 DC, 23 September 1992, *Loi autorisant la ratification du traité sur l'Union européenne (III)*, Recueil, p. 94; RJC, I-510, JORF, 25 September 1992, p. 13337.

Décision 93–325 DC, 13 August 1993, JORF, 18 August 1993, 11722.

Décision 94-345 DC, *Loi relative à l'emploi de la langue française*, Rec. 106; RJC, I-595, JORF, 2 August 1994, p. 11240.

Décision 96-373 DC, 9 April 1996, *Loi organique portant statut d'autonomie de la Polynésie française*, Rec. 43; RJC, I-660, JORF, 13April 1996, p. 5724.

Décision 99-412 DC, 15 June 1999, *Charte européenne des langues régionales ou minoritaires*, Rec. 71.

Décision 99-423 DC, 13 January 2000, JORF, 20 January 2000, p. 1992.

Décision 2000-1 LP, 27 January 2000, *Loi du pays relative à l'institution d'une taxe générale sur les services*, JORF, 29 January 2000, p. 1536.

Décision 2000-428 DC, 4 May 2000, *Loi organisant une consultation de la population de Mayotte*, Rec. 70, JORF, 10 May 2000, p. 6976.

Décision 2000-441 DC, 28 December 2000, *Loi de finances rectificative pour 2000*, JORF, 31 December 2000, p. 21204.

Décision 2001-444 DC, 9 May 2001, *Loi organique modifiant la date d'expiration des pouvoirs de l'Assemblée nationale*, JORF, 113, 16 May 2001, p. 7806.

Décision 2004-490 DC, 12 February 2004, *Loi organique portant statut d'autonomie de la Polynésie française*, Rec. 41, JORF, 2 March 2004, p. 4220.

Décision 2004-496 DC, 10 June 2004, *Loi pour la confiance dans l'économie numérique*, JORF, 22 June 2004, p. 11182.

Décision 24 March 2005, *sur des requêtes présentées par Monsieur Stéphane Hauchemaille et par Monsieur Alain Meyet*, JORF, 31 March 2005, p. 5834.

Décision 2005-514 DC, 28 April 2005, *Loi relative à la création du registre international français*, JORF, 4 May 2005, p. 7702.

Décision 2005-516 DC, 7 July 2005, *Loi de programme fixant les orientations de la politique énergétique*, JORF, 14 July 2005, p. 11589.

Décision 2005-513 DC, 14 April 2005, *Loi relative aux aéroports*, JORF, 21 April 2005, p. 6974.

Décision 2005-528 DC, 15 December 2005, JORF, 20 December 2005, RFD Adm 2006 note Schoettl.

Décision 2005-530 DC, 29 December 2005, *Loi de finances pour 2006*, JORF, 31 December 2005, 20705.

Décision 2006-2 LP, 5 April 5 2006, *Loi du pays relative à la représentativité des organisations syndicales de salaries*, JORF, 11 April 2006, p. 5439.

Décision 2006-540 DC, 27 July 2006, *Loi relative au droit d'auteur et aux droits voisins dans la société de l'information*, Rec. 88, JORF, 3 August 2006, p. 11541.

Décision 2006-543 DC, 30 November 2006, *Loi relative au secteur de l'énergie*, Rec. 120, JORF, 8 December 2006, p. 18544.

Décision 2006-543 DC, *Loi relative au secteur de l'énergie*, JORF, 8 December 2006, p. 18544.

Décision 2007-548 DC, *Loi relative aux règles d'urbanisme applicables dans le périmètre de l'opération d'intérêt national de La Défense et portant création d'un établissement public de gestion du quartier d'affaires de La Défense*, JORF, 28 February 2007, p. 3683.

Décision 2008-564 DC, 19 June 2008, *Loi relative aux organismes génétiquement modifiés*, JORF, 26 June 2008, p. 10228.

Administrative courts (Conseil d'État, CAA and TA)

CE, Ass., 30 May 1952, *Dame Kirkwood* Rec. 291.

CE, 15 Mars 1972, *Dame veuve Sadok Ali* Rec. 213.

CE, 8 December 1978, *Groupe d'Intervention et de Soutien des Travailleurs Immigrés et a.* Rec., 493.

CE, 23 October 1987, *Consort Metrat*, AJDA 1987, 758.

CE, Ass. 30 October 1998, *M. Sarran, Levacher et autres* Rec. 369; *RFDA* (1998), 1091.

CE, Ass., 3 February 1989, *Compagnie Alitalia* Rec. 44.

CE, Ass., 20 October 1989, *Nicolo* Rec. 190, conc. Frydman.

CE, 29 June 1990, *GISTI* JCP 1991 II 61.

CE, 24 September 1990, *M. Boisdet* Rec. 251.

CE, Ass., 28 February 1992, *S.A. Rothmans International France et S.A. Philip Morris France* Rec. 81.

CE, 4 January 1995, *Ministere de l'Interieur c/Rossi*, n. 94967.

CE, 25 September 1998, *Association Green Peace France*, n. 194348.

CE, 29 October 1999, *Société Rustica Programme Génétique SA et autres*, n 206687 & 206373.

CAA Marseilles, 13 June 2002, *Association AIPE c/Commune de Cagnes sur Mer*, n. 97MA05052.

CE, 22 August 2002, *SFR c/ Commune de Valauris*, n. 245624.

CE, 22 October 2003, *Association 'SOS-rivières et environnement' et autres*, n. 231953.

TA, Châlons-sur-Marne, 29 April 2005, AJDA 2005, 978.

CE 15 February 2006, *Association Ban Asbestos France et autres*, n. 288801

CE, 29 March 2006, *Haut-commissaire de la République en Polynésie française, M. Fritch*, n. 282335.

CE, 6 April 2006, *Ligue pour la protection des oiseaux* (LPO), n. 283103.

CE, 28 April 2006, *Fédération des Syndicats Agricoles MODEF*, n. 274458.

CE, 19 June 2006, *Association Eau et Rivières de Bretagne*, n. 282456.

CE, 10 July 2006, *Association interdépartementale et intercommunale pour la protection du lac de Ste Croix, des lacs et sites du Verdon et autres*, n. 288108.

Ordonnance du juge des référés du 9 mai 2006, Fédération Transpyrénéenne des Eleveurs de Montagne et autres, n. 292398.

CE, 7 June 2006, *Association Aides et autres*, com. Aubert, AJDA, 22/2006, 1189.

CE, 29 December 2006, *M.A*, unpublished, n. 289548.

CE, 24 January 2007, *Association du Toulois pour la Preservation du Cadre de Vie*, unpublished, n. 287248.

CE, 26 January 2007, *Société Arcelor Atlantique et Lorraine et autres*, n. 287110.

CE, 26 January 2007, *M.X.*, n. 279522.

CE, 2 February 2007, *Association Convention vie et Nature Pour Une Ecologie Radicale, Ligue Pour La Protection des Oiseaux, Ligue pour la Preservation de la Faune Sauvage et la Défense des Non-Chasseurs, Association France Nature Environnement*, unpublished, n. 289758.

CE, 8 February 2007, *Arcelor*, n. 287110.

CE, 22 February 2007, *M. F. et autres Requête* n. 299649.

CE, 7 May 2007, *ANPER-TOS, Association OABA*, n. 286103.

CE 6 June 2007, *Commune de Groslay, Association Ville et Aéroport*, n. 292942.

CE, 6 June 2007, *Association Sortir Du Nucleaire*, n. 292386.

CE, 27 June 2007, *ANPER-TOS*, n. 297531.

CE, *référés*, 10 October 2007, *Association Ornithologique et Mammalogique de Saône et Loire*, unpublished, n. 309286.

CE, 26 October 2007, *ADVOCNAR*, n. 297301.

CE, 26 October 2007, *CIRENA*, unpublished, n. 298490.

CE, 26 October 2007, *M. F, M. E, M. C, M et Mme B., M. et Mme A*, unpublished, n. 299883.

CE, 21 December 2007, *Ministre de l'Economie, Des Finances et de l'Industrie*, n. 300041.

CE, 19 March 2008, *Association General des Producteurs de Mais, SCEA de Malaprade et s., Monsanto et s., Pioneer Genetique et s., SEPROMA, SA Caussade Semences, SA Limagrain Verneuil, SA Maisadour Semences, SA RAGT Semences, SAS Euralise Semences et s.,* unpublished, n. 313547.

CE, 7 May 2008, *Association Ornithologique et Mammalogique de Saône et Loire,* unpublished, n. 309285.

CE, 7 August 2008, *Collectif Inter-Associatif du Refus des Nuisances Dans le Nord-Ouest, M. A, Departement du Val d'Oise, Commune de Groslay, et s., Association de Defense contre les Nuisances Aeriennes et la Commune de Gonesse,* unpublished, n. 306109.

CE, 26 August 2008, *Association SOS Grand Bleu,* unpublished, n. 320025.

Judiciary courts (TGI, Cour d'appel, Cour de cassation)

C. Cass. (Ch. Mixte), 24 May 1975, *Société des Cafés Jacques Vabre, Dalloz* 1975 conc. Touffait.

Cour d'appel de Toulouse, 15 November 2005, n. 004/01065, http://www.legifrance. gouv.fr/WAspad/Visu?cid=11874&indice=1&table=CAPP&ligneDeb=1 (last accessed 20 March 2007).

C.Cass. (crim.), 7 February 2007, *Actes dits de 'fauchage volontaire',* n 06-80.108 Arrêt 220 du 7 février 2007.

Conference papers, press conferences and speeches

'Actes du Colloque', 'Aux Racines du Mal Français', Maison des Polytechniciens 19 et 20 octobre 2005, Table Ronde 1: Le Déficit Démocratique. Online at: http://www.udf.org/participer/colloques/racines/actes_table1.pdf (last accessed 15 August 2007).

Allocution de M. le président de la République, Après le vote de la Loi autorisant la ratification du Traité de Lisbonne, Palais de l'Élysée, 10 February 2008.

J. Chirac:

—— Orléans, 3 May 2001. Online at: http://www.elysee.fr/elysee/francais/interventions/discours_et_declarations/2001/mai/discours_de_m_jacques_chirac_president_de_la_republique_sur_l_environnement-orleans.3005.html (last accessed 20 October 2006).

—— Avranches, 18 March 2002 (*Campagne électorale pour l'élection présidentielle*). Online at: http://www.elysee.fr/elysee/francais/interventions/discours_et_declarations/2002/mars/discours_de_m_jacques_chirac_a_avranches-campagne_electorale_pour_l_election_presidentielle.919.html (last accessed 20 October 2006).

—— Palais de l'Élysée, 1 March 2006 (*premier anniversaire de la promulgation de la charte de l'environnement*). Online at: http://www.elysee.fr/elysee/elysee.fr/francais/interventions/discours_et_declarations/2006/mars/allocution_du_president_de_la_republique_a_l_occasion_du_premier_anniversaire_de_la_promulgation_de_la_charte_de_l_environnement.42132.html (last accessed 20 October 2006).

Conférence de Presse de M. Nicolas Sarkozy président de la République, Sommet Informel des Chefs d'Etat et de Gouvernement de l'Union Européenne, Session de la Conférence Intergouvernementale, Centre International de Lisbonne, 19 October 2007.

Ost, F., 'Les Détours de Babel', paper presented at the Colloque International 'interpréter et traduire', 25–26 November 2005, USTV Toulon, France.

Websites

www.assemblee-nationale.fr
www.charles-de-gaulle.org
www.conseil-constitutionnel.fr
www.courdecassation.fr
www.dglf.culture.gouv.fr
www.elysee.fr
www.interieur.gouv.fr
www.iucn.org
www.ldh-toulon.net
www.legifrance.gouv.fr
www.opsi.gov.uk
www.senat.fr
untreaty.un.org

European legislation and cases (inc. ECtHr)

Committee of the Regions, 10 October 2003, 2003 JO C 244; CDR-02/DEVE; BOCKLET, 26–30.
Council Directive (EC) 2003/86 on the right to family reunification [2003] OJ L 251/12).
Directive 2000/31/CE [2000] OJ L 178, 1–16.
Directive 2000/43/CE *du Conseil du 29 juin 2000 relative à la mise en œuvre du principe de l'égalité de traitement entre les personnes sans distinction de race ou d'origine ethnique.*
Directive 2000/78/CE *du Conseil du 27 novembre 2000 portant création d'un cadre général en faveur de l'égalité de traitement en matière d'emploi et de travail.*
Directive 2002/73/CE *du Parlement européen et du Conseil du 23 septembre 2002 modifiant la directive 76/207/CEE du Conseil relative à la mise en œuvre du principe de l'égalité de traitement entre hommes et femmes en ce qui concerne l'accès à l'emploi, à la formation et à la promotion professionnelles, et les conditions de travail.*
Directive 2004/113/CE *du Conseil du 13 décembre 2004 mettant en œuvre le principe de l'égalité de traitement entre les femmes et les hommes dans l'accès à des biens et services et la fourniture de biens et services.*
Directive 2006/54/CE *du Parlement européen et du Conseil du 5 juillet 2006 relative à la mise en œuvre du principe de l'égalité des chances et de l'égalité de traitement entre hommes et femmes en matière d'emploi et de travail.*
Directive 79-409 79/409/CEE 2 April 1979 modified.
Treaty Establishing the European Community, Consolidated version, Official Journal C 325, 24 December 2002.
Case C-127/08 *Metock and Others* v. *Minister for Justice, Equality and Law Reform* [2008] ECR 00000.
Case 100/77 *Commission* v. *Italy* [1978] EUECJ C-100/77; Rec. 879.
Case 102/79 *Commission of the European Communities* v. *Kingdom of Belgium* [1981] 1 CMLR 282; [1980] EUECJ C-102/79.
Joined Cases C-6/90 & 9/90 *Andrea Francovich and Danila Bonifaci and others* v. *Italian Republic* [1991] ECR I 5357.
Athannossoplan & Others v. *Switzerland*, 6 April 2000, ECHR no. 27644/95.

Chasagnou & Others v. *France* [GC], 29 April 1999, nos. 25088/94, 28331/95 & 28443/95, § 112, ECHR 1999-III.*Fadeïeva* v. *Russia*, 9 June 2005, no. 55723/00, ECHR 2005-IV.

Fredin v. *Sweden (N.1)*, 18 February 1991, § 48, serie A, no. 192.

Giacomelli v. *Italia*, 2 November 2006, no. 59909/00, ECHR 2006-XII.

Guerra & Others v. *Italy*, 19 February 1998, *Reports* 1998-I.

Immobiliare Saffi v. *Italy* [GC], no. 22774/93, ECHR 1999-V.

International Federation of Human Rights Leagues (FIDH) v. *France*, (14/2003), (2005) 40 EHRR SE25.

Köktepe v. *Turkey*, 22 July 2008, no. 35785/03 (in French).

Kyrtatos v. *Greece*, 22 May 2003, no. 41666/98, § 52, ECHR 2003-VI.

Moreno Gómez v. *Spain*, 16 November 2004, no. 4143/02, ECHR 2004-X.

Taşkın and Others v. *Turkey*, 10 November 2004, no. 46117/99, ECHR 2004-X.

X v. *Island*, 18 May 1976, Commission decision no. 6825/74, D.R., vol. 5, p. 87.

Foreign and international legislation

1937 Constitution of Ireland.

Universal Declaration of Human Rights (United Nations, 1948).

G.A. Res. 1514, U.N. GAOR, 15th Sess., Supp. No. 16, U.N. Doc. A/4684 (1960).

International Covenant on Civil and Political Rights, General Assembly resolution 2200A (XXI), 16 December 1966.

Index

a-patride 57
abnormal function: of the Constitution 25, 29, 32, 35
abortion *see* IVG case
absence of accountability: presidential 19
absolute rights: non-nationals 60
acceleration of time: perception of 8–9
accords see Matignon agreement; Nouméa agreement
activists: legal action against 51–3
acts of parliament 16, 19, 38, 73
administrative courts 82–3, *see also Conseil d'État*; *tribunals administratifs*
administrative litigation: use of the Charter in 49–51
administrative organisation 88–9
administrative system: centralised 87
African immigration 59
Agamben, G. 18
Agence nationale de l'accueil des étrangers et des migrations (ANAEM) 64
Aide Médicale de l'État (AME) 69–70
Algeria 5, 18, 27, 28
Alitalia case (1989) 81
Alpes Maritimes 93
alterity: identity v. 128
alternance 8, 31
Althusser, L.P. 110, 111
ambivalence: about organisation of polity 11
amendments (constitutional) *see* modifications
Amsterdam Treaty (1999) 58

ancien régime 3, 11, 93
Anne de Gaulle Foundation for Down's Syndrome 21
anthropocentric Charter 43
anthropocentric humanism 41
arbitre 27, 35
Arcelor case 83, 84
aristocracy 1
Aristotle 1–2
army leadership 19
art: virtue as an 2
Article 1: 1789 Declaration 64, 65, 68; 1958 Constitution 64, 65, 68, 87, 104, 122, 125, 126; Charter for the Environment 45, 46, 50, 53, 54, 55; Law 99-210 95–6; National Convention 3–4
Article 2: 1789 Declaration 126; 1958 Constitution 15, 109, 121, 122, 123, 126; Charter for the Environment 54, 55; ECHR 52; National Convention 4
Article 3: 1958 Constitution 15; Charter for the Environment 44, 55
Article 3-1: *Convention relative aux droits de l'enfant* 70
Article 3.2.1: Nouméa Agreement 106
Article 4: Charter for the Environment 44, 53, 55; Law 99-209 104
Article 5: 1958 Constitution 19; Charter for the Environment 43, 44, 47, 55
Article 6: 1958 Constitution 20; Charter for the Environment 46–7, 48, 55

Article 7: 1958 Constitution 19;
Charter for the Environment 45,
53, 55
Article 8: 1958 Constitution 17, 18,
28; Charter for the Environment 45,
55; of the ECHR 52, 62
Article 9: 1958 constitution 19;
Charter for the Environment 45, 55
Article 10: Charter for the
Environment 45, 55
Article 11: 1789 Declaration 109,
122; 1958 Constitution 18, 27, 28,
85–6
Article 12: 1958 Constitution 17–18
Article 13: 1958 Constitution 28, 31;
European Social Charter 70
Article 15: 1958 Constitution 19, 29;
internal regulation (2006) 120
Article 16: 1958 Constitution 18
Article 17: European Social Charter 70
Article 18: 1958 Constitution 18
Article 19: 1958 Constitution 17,
18–19
Article 20: 1958 Constitution 27
Article 21: 1958 Constitution 27, 29
Article 22: Law 99-209 99
Article 29: 1958 Constitution 16
Article 34: 2000 Statute concerning
overseas territories 119
Article 42: 2008 constitutional
amendment 127
Article 47: 2004 statute 119
Article 52: 1958 Constitution 105
Article 53: 1958 Constitution 90, 105
Article 54: 1958 Constitution 18,
76, 78
Article 55: 1958 Constitution 74, 75,
76, 78, 79, 80, 83, 84
Article 56: 1958 Constitution 18
Article 57: 2004 *loi organique* 120
Article 61: 1958 Constitution 18, 76
Article 68: 1958 Constitution 19
Article 72: 1958 Constitution 89
Article 73: 1958 Constitution 89
Article 74: 1946 Constitution 91;
1958 Constitution 89, 90
Article 75: 1958 Constitution 102, 125
Article 75-1: 1958 Constitution
125, 126

Article 76: 1946 Constitution 91; 1958
Constitution 95
Article 77: 1946 Constitution 91; 1958
Constitution 95, 101
Article 79: 1946 Constitution 91
Article 88-1: 1958 Constitution 77, 79,
82, 83, 84
Article 90: 1946 Constitution 6
Article 95: Treaty of Rome 80
Article 111: Villers-Cotterêts
ordinance 115
Article 115: 1996 statute 119
Article 188: Law 99-209 103–4
Article 217: Law 99-209 101
Article 218: Law 99-209 101
Article 265: Customs Code 80
Article D.161-25-2: Social Security
Code 69
Article L.110-1.1°: Environmental
Code 43
Article L.111-1: Immigration code
(CESEDA) 57
Article L.113-1: Education Code 66
Article L.131-4: Education Code 66
Article L.229-5: Environment
Code 83
Article L.311-1: Immigration code 61
Article L.311-2: Immigration code
61, 65
Article L.311-3: Immigration code 65
Article L.313-7: Immigration code 66
Article L.313-10: Immigration code 65
Article L.411-1: Immigration
code 62–3
Article L.1132-1: Employment Code 64
Article L.5221-5: Employment
Code 64
Article L.O. 121: Electoral Code 32
Article R.5121-11: Employment
Code 65
Articles 7-19: Law 99-209 102
Articles 83-98: L.99-209 97–8
Asians 56, 66
assemblée de province 94, 99
Assemblée nationale 16, 20; account-
ability of Prime Ministers to 21, 23;
blocking of CED treaty 72; New
Caledonian deputies and senators
at 95; Presidents granted a similar

stature to 21; Presidents' majority
in synchronisation with that of 15,
25–9; term of office 29
assemblée territoriale 91, 92
assesseurs coutumiers 103
assises territoriales 40
asylum: right of 58–9, 60
Attali, Jacques 34
Auriol, Vincent 72
authorisation: registration of children
in primary school 66; to enter
French territory 63; to stay on
French territory 61, 65
authoritarian education 42
authoritarian socio-political
organisation 41
autonomy: New Caledonia 92, 93, 94,
100, 124; overseas territories 89, 91,
124; presidential 14–15
Ayrault, Jean-Marc 34

Babel 116, 117
Badiou, Alain 33
'the bad' immigrant: myth of 59
Balladur, Edouard 30, 131
Barre, Raymond 26–7
bears: use of Charter against the
re-introduction of 50
Beck, Ulrich 58, 75, 86, 107, 130, 131
Belfast Agreement (1998) 114
Belgium 115, 118
Bell, John 16
Besson, Eric 34
bicameral parliament 16
bicephalous executive 13, 25, 26, 29
bilateral agreements 106
bilingualism 115, 118, 123
bills: presidential powers 18, 19;
referral to the *Conseil constitutionnel*
38; relating to energy 48, 49
bills of rights 37, 38, 39, 40, 58,
60–1, 71, *see also* Charter for the
Environment; Declaration of the
Rights of Man and of the Citizen
'biocentric deep' ecology 41
bloc de constitutionnalité 38, 59, 130
Boisdet case (1990) 81
Bourg, Dominique 41
Boyron, Sophie 71

Brundtland Report 41, 43
Brunet, Professor Pierre 109

Casanova, Jean-Claude 11
case law 80
Catholic Church 116
Celtic language 115
centralisation 42, 87, 130, *see also*
decentralisation
CESEDA 57, 59, 61, 62–3, 65, 66
Chambord, Comte de 22
Chapsal, Professor Jacques 29
Charter for the Environment 36, 37;
draft proposal 40; elaboration process
39–41; greener constitutional
future 53–4; impacts on French
legal system 44–53; philosophical
substance 41–4
chef du territoire 91, 92
Chirac, Jacques 18, 23, 26, 27, 28,
30–1, 32, 33, 35, 36, 39, 40, 41,
45, 67
Christian Democrat party 5
church: hatred of 3
Cicero 2
CIMADE 68
circulaires: authorisation of non-nationals
(2007) 65; limiting of foreign
students working in France 71;
regularisation of school-age children
(2006) 58, 66, 67, 68
citizenship: and exclusion 56, 57–8;
New Caledonia 103–5
civil courts: impact of Charter on 51–3
civil law(s) 57, 81, 93, 96, 98
civil liability 19
civil liberty(ies) 38, 50, 59, 96
civil rules 102–3
clear legal effects: Charter for the
Environment 46–9
Code Civil 38, 103
Code de la Sécurité Sociale 69
Code de l'action sociale et des familles 70
Code de l'Education 66
*Code de l'entrée et du séjour des étrangers
et du droit d'asile* 57
Code de l'Environnement 43, 83
Code des Douanes 80
Code du Travail 64, 65

cohabitations 8, 22, 23, 25, 29, 30, 31, 32
cohesive national groups 90, 91, 105
collaboration: with European law 77–8; of powers, parliamentary regimes 12, 13
collectivité à status particulier 89
collectivité d'outre mer (COM) 89, 90
colonisation 56, 111, 112, *see also* decolonisation
Commissaire délegué de la République pour la Province des Iles Loyauté 96
Commissaire délegué de la République pour la Province Nord 96
Commissaire délegué de la République pour la Province Sud 96
Committee for Decolonisation of the UN 104
Common European Defence Treaty (CED): blocking of 72, 73
common good 4
common law partners 63
common rules 103
communes 89, 100
'concrete block' metaphor 129–30
conditions of form: 1958 Constitution 6
conditions of substance: 1958 Constitution 6
conflict: between statute law and European treaties 79
Congrès 37, 40
Congrès de la Nouvelle-Calédonie 92, 93, 94; composition 96–7; government elected by 98; inauguration 96; norm-making function 97–8; respect of international agreements 105; transfer of competence 96
Conseil constitutionnel 40; Charter for the Environment as an interpretive tool for 54; collaboration with European law 77–8; constitutional control 38, 45, 46, 47, 74, 76, 130; consultation on electoral matters 32–3; control of conformity of statute to the Constitution 83; discretionary presidential powers 18; European law in relation to statute law 79–80; express uses of the Charter 47–8; (false) harmony with European law 78; and immigration 58, 59, 60; implied uses of the charter 48–9; paradigm of unity 122–3; referral to constitutional values 43; resistance to European law 76, 77; review of norm-making, New Caledonia 97; right to family reunification 62; ruling on *loi Toubon* 109; scrutiny of treaties 76; teaching of the Corsican language 104; transposition of directives 82, 83, 84; unity of language 125
conseil consultatif coutumier 92, 94
conseil de ministres 5, 28, 40, 92
conseil de région 92
Conseil d'État 5; *Congrès de la Nouvelle-Calédonie* as adviser to 98; control of conformity of regulations to statute 83; European law and the administrative courts 82–3; European law in relation to statute law 79, 80–2, 86; and human rights 60, 66, 70; problem of breach of European law 84; regularisation of non-nationals 58; supremacy of the Constitution over other texts 59–60; use of the Charter for the Environment 49, 50–1; on use of French language 120, 124
conseil du government 91, 92
conseil économique et social (CES) 99
conseil exécutif 92, 93
conseil supérieur de l'audiovisuel (CSA) 102
conseiller d'État 102
conseillers de la Nouvelle-Calédonie 96
conseils coutumiers 98, 99, 103
constitution(s): Finnish 14, 15; post-colonial 58–9; post-revolution (1791) 13, 42, 129; recognition of environmental issues in foreign 37–8
Constitution for Europe (European Treaty) 37, 47, 72, 85
Constitution of the First Republic 4, 87
Constitution of the Second Republic 4, 13, 16

Constitution of the Third Republic 1, 16, 132; establishment 4; as a parliamentary regime 12, 13, 16
Constitution of the Fourth Republic 16, 58; establishment 4; international treaties and agreements 73; as a parliamentary regime 12, 16; TOM administration 91, *see also* modifications to the Fourth Constitution; Preamble to the Fourth Constitution
Constitution of the Fifth Republic 7–10; act setting conditions of substance and form 6; administration of New Caledonia under 91–4; Articles *see* Articles; 'concrete block' metaphor 129–30; contextual influences 1; decolonisation 58; draft text 6–7; drafting and implementation 129; dynamics of 1, 132; establishment of 4; European law in relation to 75–9; fiftieth anniversary 1, 7; *gaullienne* reading 21, 22, 24, 31, 34, 85; infra-constitutional and supra-legislative position of international norms 73–4; limitation of sovereignty 131; modifications *see* modifications to the 1958 Constitution; *non-gaullienne reading of* 22; non-synchronisation 22, 24, 25, 29–32; norms *see* constitutional norms; original institutional arrangement and its evolutions 15–24; recognition of linguistic plurality 124–7; rights guaranteed under 61–70; as a semi-presidential regime 11–12, 13–14, 15; synchronisation 15, 18, 23, 24, 25–9; theoretical framework 12–15; v. populations of overseas territories 119–24, *see also* Preamble to the 1958 Constitution
Constitution of the Monarchy 1
constitutional control 16, 38, 60, 76, 130; and the Charter for the Environment 44, 45, 46–7, 48, 49, 50, 53
constitutional court *see Conseil constitutionnel*
constitutional identity 82
constitutional law 129
constitutional norms 38, 43, 47, 58, 59, 60, 73, 76, 130, *see also* hierarchy of norms
constitutional review 53, 76, 97, 127
constitutional rights 38–9, 41, 43, 50, 54, 58, 64, 69
constitutional texts 11
constitutional value: Charter for the Environment 43, 44, 45, 50, 53; and human rights 60; *pacta sunt servanda* 75; transposition of directives 82; treaties' lack of 76, 77
constitutionalisation: of French language 109; protection of human rights 59
constitutionality: priority preliminary ruling on 16
consult: governmental requirement to 6; presidential power to 18
contrat d'accueil et d'intégration 63
Convention relative aux droits de l'enfant 70
Coppens Commission 40
corruption: avoidance through virtue 2
Corsica 89
Corsican language 104, 121, 123–4
cosmopolitan society 72, 79, 86, 106, 131
cosmopolitan state 131
Coty, President René 5
council(s) *see Conseil*
countersigning of acts 19
Cour Administrative d'Appel, de Marseilles 49
Cour d'Appel: de Riom 51; *de Toulouse* 51; *de Versailles* 53
Cour de Cassation: de Versailles 51; European law in relation to statute law 80, 86; supremacy of Constitution over other texts 59–60
courts: impact of Charter on 49–53; traditional separation of 81, *see also* administrative courts; judicial courts
Cousseran, P. 123
Couve de Murville, Maurice 21
Couverture Maladie Universelle (CMU) 69–70

criminal immunity: presidential 19
criminal litigation: impact of Charter
51–3
criminal responsibility 51
cultural belonging: language 110
cultural diversity 121, 128
cultural identity 120, 121, 123, 127
cultural superiority 128
customary civil rules 99, 102–3
customary laws 103
customs: competence of, New
Caledonia 105
Customs Code 80

d'Alembert 3
Dame Kirkwood case 80–1
Dante, Alighieri 111
Danton, Georges 87
days: changes to names of 3
de facto exclusion 56, 58, 60, 61,
62, 64
de jure exclusion 56, 58, 60, 62
De Villepin, Dominique 33
De vulgari eloquentia 111
Debord, Guy 9
Debré, Michel 21, 27, 28–9
decentralisation 7, 87, 89, 93, 97,
118, 126
Decision 93-325 (*Conseil
constitutionnel*) 60
Decision 2006-540 (*Conseil
constitutionnel*) 82
Decision 2006-543 (*Conseil
constitutionnel*) 82
Declaration of the Rights of Man and
of the Citizen (1789) 6, 38, 41, 53,
56, 60; Articles *see* Articles
declarations of rights 38–9
decolonisation 11, 58, 90, 91, 104,
105, 106
*Décret de la Convention nationale,
concernant l'ère des Français* 3–4
deep ecology 41
defence matters 31
Defence Minister 29
'defence of necessity' 51, 52, 53
degenerate regimes 1, 2
Délégation Générale de la Langue Française
(DGLF) 108

*Délégation Générale de la Langue Française
et aux Langues de France* (DGLFLF)
108, 109
déliberations 97, 98, 99, 123
democracy 1, 2, 7, 8, 12, 23,
41, 73
democratic election: parliamentary
12–13
denial of access: to education 66
département d'outre mer (DOM) 89
départements 89, 93
députés 95
deputies' mandate: presidential mandate
aligned to 22–4
derogatory civil rules 102, 103
derogatory framework: Corsica 89
Derrida, Jacques 112, 118, 124–5
despotism 2
d'Estaing, Valéry Giscard 23, 26, 27,
28, 30, 32
devolution 97, 113, 115, 118
dialects: attempt to annihilate 116
Dictionnaire encyclopédique 3
Diderot 3
digital economy: parliamentary bill on
77
diplomatic matters 31
direct effect: doctrine of 74, 75, 86
directives: semi-presidential regimes 14,
see also European directives
discretionary powers: French
administrative 66; presidential
17–19, 28, 31
discrimination: against non-nationals
65; protection against 64, 69
diversity: cultural 121, 128; and
identity 112; linguistic 108
divorce: New Caledonia 103
droit administratif 51
duty of care: against environmental
damage 54
Duverger, Maurice 11, 14, 15, 25, 26

Échec du Roi 11, 14
eco-tax 46
ecological consciousness 39
ecology: biocentric deep 41;
departmental minister of 39;
humanist 41; teaching of 42

education: aim of 129; environmental
    42–3; and French language 42, 117;
    and human rights 65–8; priority
    given to 42
egocentrism 106
elections *see* democratic election;
    general elections; presidential
    elections
Electoral College 25, 26
Electronic Commerce directive (2000)
    77–8
Elgie, Robert 14
emergency powers 18
emergency summary procedures 50
empire 7, *see also* French Empire;
    Second Empire
employment: of non-nationals 64–5
energy sector: bill relating to 48, 49
English language 109, 113, 114, 115
environmental education 42–3
environmental law 38, 51
environmental principles 43, *see also*
    individual principles
environmental projects 46
environmental protection 39, 43, 48,
    49, 50
environmental rights:
    constitutionalisation *see* Charter
    for the Environment
equal access: to education 65; to
    professional and social representative
    organisations 7
equality principle 48, 61, 64, 104
'era of the French' 3–4
État de droit 16, 76
European Charter for Regional or
    Minority Languages (EChRML) 114,
    121, 122–3, 126
European Coal and Steel Community
    (ECSC) 73
European Committee of Social Rights
    (ECSR) 70
European Community (EC) system 73
European Convention on Human
    Rights (ECHR) 52, 62, 76
European directives: 96/61/CE 83;
    2003/87/EC 83; compulsory 81;
    problem of 74–5; transposition of
    77, 82, 83, 84

European immigration 59
European integration 73, 77, 106
European law(s): integration of 73,
    75; in relation to the French
    Constitution 75–9; in relation to
    French statute law 79–82
European Social Charter 70
European Treaty (Constitution for
    Europe) 37, 47, 72, 85
European Union Court of Justice
    (EUCJ) 77
exceptional resident permits 67
exclusion: ambivalent normative
    approach to 56; *de facto* 56, 58, 60,
    61, 62, 64; *de jure* 56, 58, 60, 62;
    and human rights in action 61–70;
    nationality, citizenship and
    immigration 57–8
executive: bicephalous 13, 25, 26, 29;
    parliamentary regimes 13; power
    16–17, 93; presidential regimes 13;
    semi-presidential regimes 13;
    separation from legislative body 15
express presidential discretionary
    powers 17–18
express uses: of the Charter for the
    Environment 47–8
external minorities: reality of pluri-
    linguistic 118–27
external relations: New Caledonia
    105–6

fait majoritaire 22, 25, 26, 28, 29, 33
false harmony: with European law 78–9
family reunification: right to 62–4
fast-track procedure to modify the
    Fourth Constitution 6
father of the French Constitution 11, 27
father of the horde 4, 36
fatherland 57
Faucheurs Volontaires 51
federalism 87, 118
federalists: fight between sovereignists
    and 72
*Fédération internationale des ligues des droit
    de l'Homme* (FIDH) 70
Finland 14, 15
'first-past-the-post' system 13
five-year tenure (*quinquennat*) 23, 24

Force de loi 118
forced synchronisation 23, 32–6
Fourth Republic: decolonisation 91;
    end of 5–7; rejection of a draft bill
    ratifying a treaty establishing the
    CED 72, *see also* Constitution of the
    Fourth Republic
France: love-hate relationship between
    European law and 72–86; as
    model of the unitary state 87, 89;
    monolingualism and construction
    of 113–18; presence in Europe 72;
    pretenders to the throne of 22;
    relationship between New Caledonia
    and 88–90; in a state of grace 8; two
    'violent' moments in 118, *see also*
    the Republic
France métropolitaine 89
François I 115
Francovich case 78
françoys 115
fraternity 56
freedom of expression 122, 126
French Empire 58, 88, 90, 108
French language 7; as an issue of
    sovereignty 127; during sixteenth
    century 115–16; education and 42,
    117; foreigner integration and
    assessment of 64; legal aspects
    109; and myth of the nation 111;
    numbers speaking 108; and the
    paradigm of unity 116, 117;
    position in legal framework 108;
    promotion of 111–12; protection
    against English language 108–9;
    royal ordinance proclaiming
    official status 115; theoretical
    aspects 109–10; use of in public
    and private sphere 122, *see also*
    monolingualism; pluralism,
    linguistic
French Polynesia 89, 90, 119, 120–1,
    123
French Revolution 42, 56, 71, 87, 107,
    116, 117, 118, 129
Freud, S. 4, 72
Front National de Libération (FLN) 5
'full citizenship-New Caledonia
    nationality' 104

full powers 5–6, 18
fundamental freedom(s) 46, 50, 58, 60,
    68–9
Futuna 124

Gaelic Language (Scotland) Act
    (2005) 114
Gaulle, Charles de: 1967 general
    election 29–30; conjectural and
    structural tasks facing government
    5; design of the new constitution 15;
    formation of post-war government 5;
    government's full powers 5–6;
    ideological influence 12, 15;
    influence of Maurras on 11;
    modifications to Constitution
    under 20, 21; period of pure
    synchronisation 26, 27; political
    leadership 36, 76; presentation of
    text for new constitution 7; speech
    on birth of the new republic 132;
    use of Article 11 18, 27
gaullienne reading of the Constitution
    21, 22, 24, 31, 34, 85
gender equality 7
General Assembly of the UN
    Committee on Decolonisation 106
general elections 32, 33, 34; (1967)
    29–30
Genetically Modified Organisms
    (GMOs) 39, 44, 49, 51
Germany 38
Giddens, Anthony 86
Girondins 87, 116
GISTI case (1978) 62
Good Friday Agreement (1998) 114
the good immigrant 59
the good state 1
gouvernement du territoire 92
government: dialectical relationship
    between two poles of 11; French/
    Republican model 4, 7; New
    Caledonia 98; parliamentary scrutiny
    6, 15; on pure and degenerate forms
    1–2; as a representative regime 11;
    requirement to consult 6; towards a
    postmodern 35–6
governmental regulations 5–6, 28
Gramsci, Antonio 111

Greece 38
green tutor: of the legislative
    process 47
Grégoire, Abbot Henri-Baptiste 2,
    116, 117
group language 110
Groupe d'information et de soutien des
    immigrés (GISTI) 70
GSM antennas 49
Guigoux, Elizabeth, Minister for Justice
    23–4

Hans 72
hate 72
hatred: of church and monarchy 3
Haute autorité de lutte contre les
    discriminations (HALDE) 65, 68
heads of state: as above political parties
    15, 27; establishment of institution
    of 16; one-person 4; parliamentary
    regimes 13; personification of
    function 21; physical presence in
    parliament 18; presidential regimes
    13; semi-presidential regimes 14,
    see also presidents
health: and human rights 68–70; use
    of the Charter in public 49
health system 62
Heidegger, Martin 110, 115
hierarchy of environmental
    principles 43
hierarchy of norms 16, 38, 46, 60,
    73–5, 78, 82
high commissioners: New Caledonia
    92, 93, 94, 95–6, 97
Hirsch, Martin 34
Hollande, François 8, 34, 35, 85, 127,
    131
hour: division into ten parts 3
House of Commons 13, 24
human language 110
human rights: in action 61–70;
    constitutionalisation as best
    protection of 59; and immigration
    56; legal framework 59–61, *see also*
    European Convention on Human
    Rights; Universal Declaration of
    Human Rights
human-other species 110
humanisation of rights 60

humanism 41, 42
humanist ecology 41
humanity: *instituteurs* as representatives
    of 42
hussard noir de la République 42, 129
hyper-President 33, 34

ideal city 1–2
ideas and ideals: revolutionary/
    republican 42, 60, 71, 107,
    129, 130
identification 8, 110, 112
identity: constitutional 82; cultural
    120, 121, 123, 127; and diversity
    109, 112, 114; generating a positive
    French 112; Kanak people 98, 99,
    104, 119; and language 110; v.
    alterity 128
ideology: separation of powers
    87; of Third Republic 11, 12,
    15, 118
image: Republic of the 8–9
immigrant(s) 56, 59, 62, 66; myth of
    'the good' and 'bad' 59; resident in
    France (2004) 57
immigration: attempt at rationalisation
    61; constitutional norms 60; and
    exclusion 57; and human rights 56,
    61–7; modern and postmodern 61;
    policy 67, 68; as a problem of the
    past 58
immunity: presidential 19, 21, 24
implied presidential discretionary
    powers 18–19
independence 91; New Caledonia 4, 92,
    93, 96, 100–1
indivisibility of the Republic 7, 87,
    88, 90, 92, 94, 97, 100, 104, 119,
    122, 125
Indo-European society 11, 21
infra-constitutional: international
    norms/treaties as 74, 76
instituteurs 42, 129
institutional balance/equilibrium
    15–16, 20, 30
integration: European 73, 77, 106
inter-subjectivity 110, 112
internal minorities: myth of one
    language unifying 113–18; reality
    of pluri-linguistic 118–27

International Federation of Human Rights Leagues (FIDH) v. *France* (2004) 70
International Labour Organisation Convention 118 (1962) 68
international law(s) 73, 74, 75, 76, 77, 78, 79
international norms 73–4, 75, 79
international relations 31
international treaties/instruments 59, 73, 74, 84, 105, *see also individual treaties*
Ireland *see* Northern Ireland; Republic of Ireland
Irish language 114, 115
Italy 24, 37, 87–8, 111
Ives, Peter 111
IVG case (*interruption volontaire de grossesse*) 76, 79, 80

Jacobinism 117, 125
Jacobins (*Montagnards*) 87, 116
Jones, Stuart 118
Jospin, Lionel 23, 31, 131
Jouhaud, General 5
Jouyet, Jean-Pierre 34
judicial authority 6
judicial courts 82, *see also Cour d'Appel*; *Cour de Cassation*
Juppé, Alain 34
justice 1

Kanak 92, 98, 99, 103, 104, 107, 119
Kelly, Maurice 130
Kelsen's pyramid of norms 74
Kouchner, Bernard 34

La consultation sur l'accession à la pleine souveraineté 101
labour law 64
Lacan, Jacques 110, 112
Lacanian theory 8
land law: customary 103
Lang, Jack 34
language(s): Corsican 104, 121, 123–4; French Polynesian 119, 120–1, 123; Grégoire's report on need to destroy other 116, 117; the unitary state and problem of 113–15; violent imposition of 112, 116, 117, 118, *see also* French language

langues de France 108, 109, 119
Latin 111, 115, 116, 118
Law 99-209 97–8, 99, 101–2, 103–4
Law 99-210 95–6
laws 2
Le Monde 33
Le Pen, Jean-Marie 33
Le Plus Petit Atlas du Monde 88
leadership: of the army 19; language and assertion of 116; presidential 22, 27, 36; strong political 76
left-wing parties 23, 34
left-wing President: facing a right-wing Prime Minister 30
left-wing Prime Minister: facing a right-wing President 30–2
legal aspects: French language 109
legal pluralism 97, 99, 103, 131
legal system: decreasing influence of 89; impact of Charter for the Environment 44–53
legislative assimilation 89
legislative body(ies): parliamentary regimes 13; presidential regimes 13; separation of executive from 15
legislative process: green tutor of 47
legislative subsidiarity 89
legitimacy: presidential 21, 27, 85
Levi-Strauss, Claude 110
lex posterior derogat priori 79
liberal tradition 41
liberté fondamentale 46
liberty 4
Ligue français des droits de l'Homme (LDH) 70
linguistic diversity 108, 109, 114
linguistic terror 117
Lisbon Treaty 82, 84–5
litigation: and the Charter for the Environment 49–53
local languages: war against 116
Loi constitutionelle modifiant la procédure de révision de la Constitution, prévue par l'article 90 de la Constitution de 1946 6, 15, 19
loi du pays 97, 98, 99, 120
loi écran 81, 83
loi organique 7, 32, 95, 96, 103, 120
loi Toubon 109, 119

love 72
Luchaire, Professor François 43

Maastricht I 75, 78
Maastricht II 75, 78
Maastricht III 75
Maastricht Treaty (1992) 78
Mac Mahon, Maréchal de 22
Machiavelli 111
Maghreb 56, 62, 66
Maitrisse de l'immigration 60
majoritarian voting 12–13
mankind: reference to, in the Charter
    for the Environment 41
Marat, Jean-Paul 87
maritime register: bill concerning
    creation of 47–8
marriage 103
Marx, Karl 111
masculinity: primacy of 103
Massot, Jean 23
Massu, General 5
Master-Signifier 112
Matignon agreement (1988) 93, 100
Maurras, Charles 11, 15
medical care 69–70
métropole 89, 100
Migaud, Didier 34
military discourse: and education 42, 43
mirror stage (Lacanian theory) 8
Mitterrand, François 8, 11–12, 17, 23,
    26, 27, 30, 31, 32, 78
mixed government 4
modernisation (constitutional) 1, 131
modernity: first period of 130; second
    phase of 75, 86, 106
modifications to the 1946 Constitution:
    constitutional act 6–7, 15
modifications to the 1958
    Constitution: (1962) 12, 15, 19–20,
    21, 25, 26, 36; (2000) 12, 15, 20,
    22, 23, 25, 32, 33, 34, 36; (2008)
    1, 2, 12, 16, 18, 24, 35, 36, 38,
    125, 127, 130, 131; bill of
    rights (2005) 37; concerning the
    president 15, 18, 19–20, 21, 22–3;
    constitutionalisation of French
    language 109; decentralised
    system of government 89; forced

synchronisation based on 32–6;
    ratification of Maastricht Treaty 78
monarchy 1; abolition of 2, 3;
    dialectic between democracy and 12;
    equilibrium between Republic and
    7–8; hatred of 3; seven-year tenure
    linked to 22; virtual and physical
    elimination of 4, *see also* François I
Monnet, Jean 86
monolingualism: construction of
    France and the Republic 113–18,
    121–2
Monsanto 52
Montagnards (Jacobins) 87, 116
Montesquieu 2
Montessori schools 66
months: changes to names of 3
motto: of the Republic 7
multilateral organisations 105–6
multilateral treaties 75
multilingualism 116, 123
myth(s): of French republicanism
    109, 118; of the 'good and bad'
    immigrant 59; of law as supreme
    expression of the general will 16;
    monolingual 113; of the nation,
    French language and 111; of the
    primal horde 4; of unity 127
mythical army 117
mythical power 72
mythical republics 7, 87, 118, 132

Napoleon I 4
Napoleon III 11, 88
'Napoleonic soldier' metaphor 42
nation state 36, 58, 72, 79, 106,
    130, 131
National Administration School
    (ENA) 82
national anthem 7
National Assembly *see Assemblée nationale*
National Convention: abolition of the
    monarchy and the older order 2, 3;
    and the 'era of the French' 3–4
national health insurance 69
National Institute for Agricultural
    Research (INRA) 52
National Liberation Front (Algeria) 5
national symbol 7

national unity: unified language and
111, *see also* unity of state
nationalism 42, 106
nationality 56, 57, 58, 96, 103,
104, 105
New Caledonia: administration 90;
areas of competence 95, 96, 99,
105; changes in the jurisdiction
of the state 96; citizenship 103–5;
communes 100; *Congrès* 96–8; *Conseil
économique et social* 99; evolution
under the Fifth Republic (1958–99)
91–4; government 98; independence
92, 93, 94, 96, 100–1; Kanak
people 92, 98, 103, 104, 107, 119;
norm-making 92, 97–8, 99, 100;
postwar decolonisation and the
Fourth French Republic (1945–58)
91; provinces 100; regional
cooperation and external relations
105–6; representation of the state at
territory level 95–6; representation
of the territory at state level 95;
self-determination operation
101–2; self-determination versus
indivisibility of the Republic 88;
sénat and *conseils coutumiers* 98–9;
as a *sui generis collectivité d'outre-mer*
94–5
new era 3, 4
new republic *see* Constitution of the
Fifth Republic
Nicolo case 81
non-action approach: to
synchronisation 35
non-discrimination 61
non-gaullienne reading of the
Constitution 22
non-nationals: absolute rights 60;
discrimination against 65; exclusion
of 57, 61; human rights 60, 61–70;
regularisation 58, 66–7, *see also*
undocumented non-nationals
non-state norms 92
non-synchronisation 22, 24, 25, 29–32
norm-making: New Caledonia 92,
97–8, 99, 100
'normal' reading of the Constitution 25,
32, 33

norms *see* constitutional norms;
international norms; non-state
norms; transnational norms
Northern Ireland 114, 123
Norway 111
Nouméa agreement (1998) 94–5, 104,
106, 119
nuclear weapons: discretionary power
to use 19

Oakes, Leigh 111–12
*Office français de l'immigration et de
l'intégration* (OFI) 64
old order: abolition of 3
oligarchy 1, 2
omni-President 33, 34
ordonnances 5, 31
Ost, François 116
other languages 119, 123
other(s)/otherness 58, 68, 110, 112, 113
overseas populations: v. French
Constitution 119–24
overstayers 65

pacta sunt servanda 75
palabre 103
paradigm of unity 109, 110–13, 116,
117, 119, 121, 122–3, 124, 130
Paris 89
Paris, Comte de 22
parliamentarism 29
parliamentary ratification: of treaties 85
parliamentary regimes 11, 12–13
parliamentary representation: New
Caledonia 95
parliamentary system: with presidential
features 16–17
parricide 4
Parti Socialiste (PS) 30, 34
participation principle 50
'passionate-vertical-hierarchical'
natural system: equilibrium between
rational-horizontal-egalitarian
enterprise and 7–8
paternal figure(head) 8, 21
patrie 57
patrimony: environmental 41; linguistic
119, 124, 125, 126
Péguy, Charles 42, 129

people: changing relationship between
    nation and 36; cohesive national
    groups 90, 91, 105; need for
    organisation of relations between
    nation and 6; presidential election
    by 20–2; the Republic as a plurality
    of 105
people-nation 117, 131
période normale 25
permanent *coup d'État* 11
Pétain, Marshall 5
Petit Clamart terrorist attack (1962) 20
Pfimlin, Pierre 5
Plato 1, 2
pluralism: legal 131; linguistic 116,
    118–27, 130
plurality 97, 99, 103, 105
political accountability: parliamentary
    regimes 13; of the President 19–20;
    of the Prime Minister 21, 23;
    semi-presidential regimes 15
political effects: Charter for the
    Environment 45–6
political hegemony 117
political leadership: language and
    assertion of 116
polity: ambivalence about organisation
    of 11
Pompidou, Georges 21, 23, 26
popular government: principle of 73
Popular Republican Movement
    (MRP) 5
popular sovereignty 4
Portugal 37–8
post-Revolution Constitution (1791)
    13, 42, 129
postcolonial constitutions 58–9
postcolonial voices 107
postmodern government 35–6
power(s): against power 31;
    centralisation of 130; collaboration,
    parliamentary regimes 12, 13;
    executive 16–17, 93; mythical
    French 72; sharing, semi-presidential
    regimes 14, *see also* full powers;
    presidential powers; separation of
    powers; symbolic power
practical approach: to classifying
    presidential power 14

Preamble to the 1946 Constitution 6,
    38, 41, 58–9, 62, 63, 64, 65, 68, 73,
    74, 91
Preamble to the 1958 Constitution 37,
    38, 40, 41, 47, 59, 74, 90
Preamble to the Charter for the
    Environment 45
precautionary principle 43–4, 49, 50
préfet de la Marne 50
President(s) 13; as above political
    parties 27; granted a similar stature
    to that of the national assembly 21;
    importance of political accountability
    19–20; New Caledonia 94, 97, 98,
    105; in non-synchronisation
    situations 30–2; pre-eminence
    in international relations 31;
    semi-presidential regimes 14; in
    synchronisation situations 25–9,
    see also individual presidents
President citizen 23
président du congrès 92, 93
président du conseil 5
President monarch 22, 23, 35
président normal 8
presidential elections 19, 20–2, 32, 33,
    34, 39
presidential features: parliamentary
    system with 16–17
presidential leadership 22, 27, 36
presidential legitimacy 21, 27, 85
presidential mandate 9, 22–4
presidential powers: discretionary
    17–19, 28, 31; scale of
    semi-presidential regimes according
    to 14–15
presidential regimes 11, 13
presidentialisation 18
presidentialism 9, 29
pretenders: to the throne of France 22
prevention principle 43, 44
primal horde: myth of 4
Prime Minister(s): parliamentary
    regimes 13; political accountability
    21, 23; presidential appointment 17;
    resignation of 28; semi-presidential
    regimes 14; in situations of
    non-synchronization 29, 30–2,
    see also individual prime ministers

prince President 9
principe générale du droit 62
Principle 1: Rio Declaration 41
Principle 15: Rio Declaration 43
'principle of constitutional value'
    (unique) *see* precautionary principle
private sphere: use of French language
    in 122
pro-active approach: to synchronisation
    35
projet de loi 16
promulgation procedure 97
proportional representation 13, 98
proposition de loi 16
Provence-Alpes-Côte d'Azur 93
provinces 93, 94, 95–6, 100
provincial dialects: attempt to
    annihilate 116
public law 63, 68, 73, 86, 88, 90, 109,
    120, 122
public policies: sustainable development
    in 45, 48
public sphere: use of French language
    in 122
pure synchronisation 25, 26–9, 33

quasi-contract: language as a 110
question prioritaire de constitutionnalité
    (QPC) 53
quinquennat (five year tenure) 23, 24

R/D/C schema 89, 95, 97, 99
Raffarin, Jean-Pierre 33
Rassemblement Pour la République
    (RPR) 26
'rational-horizontal-egalitarian'
    enterprise: equilibrium between
    'passionate-vertical-hierarchical'
    natural system and 7–8
rationality 3
re-education 129
reciprocity: international treaties and
    condition of 73, 74, 75, 84
référé liberté 50
referendum(s): approval of the 1958
    Constitution 6; government advice
    on 28; government by 73; local, on
    independence, New Caledonia (1987)
    93; national, on New Caledonia

(1988) 94; presidential legitimacy
    21, 85; presidential power 18; treaty
    ratification 85–6
reflection in the mirror (Lacanian
    theory) 8
regicide 4
région d'outre mer (ROM) 89
regional cooperation: New Caledonia
    105–6
regional languages 108; recognition
    of 125–6
régions 89, 92, 93
registration: of children in education 66
regularisation: of non-nationals 58,
    66–7
Renucci, Jean François 59
representative regime: governing body
    as 11
Republic of Ireland 24, 72, 114, 115
republican spirit 1, 9
republicanism 4, 42, 88, 109, 118,
    129, 130
The Republic 2
the Republic: attempts to protect itself
    from human rights 68; birthday of
    4; contextual influences on spirit
    of 1; decaying foundations of 88;
    early philosophical links 1–2;
    equilibrium between monarchy and
    7–8; ideas and ideals of 42, 60, 71,
    107, 129, 130; indivisibility of 7,
    87, 88, 90, 92, 94, 97, 100, 104,
    119, 122, 125; monolingualism and
    construction of 113–18; national
    anthem, motto and symbol 7;
    proclamation of the first (1792) 2;
    time before and after 3–4
res publica 2
Réseau éducation sans frontière (RESF) 68
residence: benefits based on condition of
    69, 70; permits 63, 66, 67
resignation: of the president 19; of the
    Prime Minister 28
resistance: to European law 76–7
responsibility: repartition of, New
    Caledonia 95
responsibility principle 44
right of cohesive national groups
    90, 91

right-wing President: facing a left-wing
    Prime Minister 30–2
right-wing Prime Minister: facing a
    left-wing President 30
rights *see* bills of rights; constitutional
    rights; human rights
Rio Declaration 41, 43, 49
riots 93
risk society 86, 130, 131
Risorgimento: Italian 111
Robespierre, Maximilien de 87, 117
Rocard, Michel 32
Rome Treaty (1957) 75, 80, 81
Rothman et Philip Morris case (1992) 81
Rousseau, Jean-Jacques 2, 24
royal ordinance: Viller-Cotterêts 115
rule of law 4, 39, 76

Sacco, Rodolpho 128
Salan, General 5
Sanford, F.A. 123
sans papiers see undocumented
    non-nationals
Sarkozy, Nicolas 1, 8, 33–4, 34–5, 56,
    67, 84–5, 86, 125, 130, 131
Sartori, Giovanni 12, 13, 14, 15, 16
Saussure, Ferdinand de 110, 111,
    115, 116
Schengen Agreement 58
Schengen space 58
school-age children: registration 66;
    regularisation of 58, 66, 67, 68
scientific spirit 3
Scotland 114, 123
'screen law' doctrine 81, 83
Second Empire 11, 22
second modernity thesis 75, 86, 106
Second Republic 9, *see also* Constitution
    of the Second Republic
self-determination: right to 90; versus
    indivisibility of the Republic 88
self-determination operation, New
    Caledonia: campaign 102;
    control 102; document concerning
    possibility of 101; electorate 101–2;
    outcome 101; timescale 101
semi-presidential regime: Fifth
    Republic as 11–12, 13–14, 15
Sénat 16, 20

sénat coutumier 98–9, 103
separation of powers 6, 13, 14, 15,
    81, 87
seven-year tenure (*septennat*) 22, 23,
    24, 26
short-term: Republic of the 8–9
social security 68, 69
Societé Jacques Vabre 80
socio-economic rights 41, 62, 64–5, 68
socio-political organisation 11, 41, 111
sole non-national-specific rights 62–4
sovereignists: fight between federalists
    and 72
sovereignty: French language as
    an issue of 127; language and
    assertion of 116; limitation on
    73, 131; New Caledonia 101;
    parliamentary regimes 12, 13; of
    people-nation 131; period of
    first modernity 130; popular 4;
    postwar waves of accession to 106;
    presidential leadership 31
Spain 37, 87–8, 118
spectacle: the Republic of 8–9
Speech of Bayeux 15
speech circuit 110
stability 8
state of exception 18
State Medical Assistance 69–70
statelessness 56, 57, 60
Status de la Corse 121
statut 89–90, 95
statut Billotte (1969) 92
statut Blanc (1988) 93, 94
statut civil 103
statut civil coutumier 102–3
statut Deferre (1956) 91, 92
statut Jacquinot (1963) 92
statut Lemoine (1984) 92
statut Pisani (1985) 92, 93
statut Pons I (1986) 93
statut Pons II (1988) 93, 94
statut Stirne (1976) 92
statute law(s) 16; in relation to EC/EU
    law 74, 79–82
Strauss-Kahn, Dominique 34
strength (constitutional) 8
structural economic problems 36
structuralism 110

summa divisio 2
summary procedures 50
supra-legislative: international norms as 74
supranational entities 106
supremacy: doctrine of 75
supreme courts *see Conseil constitutionnel*; *Conseil d'État*; *Cour de Cassation*
sustainable development 39, 41, 45, 46–7, 48
Switzerland 111, 115, 118
symbolic power 119
synchronisation 15, 18, 23, 24, 25–9

Tahitian language 120–1, 123
télépresident 8, 34
terre d'accueil 59, 60, 61–2
terres coutumières 103
territoire d'outre-mer (TOM) 91
terrorist attack (1962) 20
theoretical approach: to classifying presidential power 14
'third pillar' of rights 40
Third Republic 5; ideology 11, 12, 15, 118; *instituteurs* in 42; tradition of seven-year tenure 22; unity of language 118, *see also* Constitution of the Third Republic
time: before and after the Republic 3–4; perception of acceleration of 8–9
Titre de la Constitution relatif aux collectivités territoriales 126
Titre VIII De l'Union française 91
Titre XI: Law 99-209 101
Totemism 110
Toubon, Jacques 109
trans-individual bond: language as a 110
transnational institutions 86
transnational law 73, 74, 75, 78, 81, 86
transnational norms 75, 76, 86
transnational society 36, 58, 86
transnationalisation: of French legal order 86
transposition: of legislation/regulations/directives 64, 74, 75, 77, 82, 83, 84
travaux préparatoires 23
Treaty of Amsterdam (1999) 58

Treaty of Lisbon 82, 84–5
Treaty of Maastricht (1992) 78
Treaty of Rome (1957) 75, 80, 81
Treaty on Stability, Coordination and Governance in the Economic and Monetary Union 85
tribunal correctionel: de Clermont-Ferrand 52; de Lille 52; de Riom 51–2; de Toulouse 51; de Versailles 51, 52–3; d'Orléans 51, 52
Tribunal of First Instance 83
tribunals administratifs: de Châlon-en-Champagne 50; New Caledonia 97
tricolour flag 7, 22

Ulster-Scots 114
UN Committee on Decolonisation 106
unclear legal effects: of Charter for the Environment 45–6
undocumented non-nationals (*sans papiers*) 58, 61, 65, 67, 69, 70, 71
unicameral assembly 13
uniformity 3
Union Française 91
Union for a Popular Movement (UMP) 34
unitary state(s): France as a model of 87, 89; movement towards a more flexible 87; problem of language 113–15
United Kingdom: parliamentary regime 12–13; the unitary state and the problem of language 113–15
United States: presidential mandate 24; presidential regime 13
unity of language: structuring (the idea of) France 115–16; structuring (the idea of) the Republic 116–18; unity of state and 110, 111
unity of state: absence of 94; education linked to 42; myth of 127; unity of language and 110, 111, *see also* paradigm of unity
Universal Declaration of Human Rights (1948) 41, 68
universal sickness cover 69–70
universal suffrage 6, 20, 25, 33

validity: of a directive 78, 83; of norms
    38, 74, 75; of a treaty 79
values: republican 43, 64, 71, *see also*
    constitutional value
Vichy regime 12
Villers-Cotterêts royal ordinance 115
violent imposition: of languages 112,
    116, 117, 118
virtue 2, 4
vulgar era 3, 4

Wallis 124
Washington system 13

week: change to a ten day 3
Welsh Language Act (1993) 113–14
Westminster system 12–13, 17
Wilmer, F. 119
World Environment Organisation 39
World Trade Organisation (WTO) 39

years: renumbering of 3

Žižek, Slavoj 112

Lightning Source UK Ltd.
Milton Keynes UK
UKHW020601130519
342540UK00009B/235/P